WEIRD JOHN BROWN

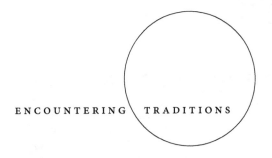

ENCOUNTERING TRADITIONS

Stanley Hauerwas, Peter Ochs, Randi Rashkover, and Maria Dakake
EDITORS

Nicholas Adams, Rumee Ahmed, and Jonathan Tran
SERIES BOARD

WEIRD JOHN BROWN

Divine Violence and the Limits of Ethics

TED A. SMITH

STANFORD UNIVERSITY PRESS
STANFORD, CALIFORNIA

Stanford University Press
Stanford, California

Parts of Chapters 2 and 3 have originally appeared in "Politics in the Wake of Divine Violence," *Studies in Christian Ethics* 25, no. 4 (Fall 2012): 454–472, by Sage Publications, Ltd. All rights reserved.

Printed in the United States of America on acid-free, archival-quality paper

Library of Congress Cataloging-in-Publication Data

Smith, Ted A., author.
  Weird John Brown : divine violence and the limits of ethics / Ted A. Smith.
    pages cm -- (Encountering traditions)
  Includes bibliographical references and index.
  ISBN 978-0-8047-8850-2 (cloth : alk. paper) --
  ISBN 978-0-8047-9330-8 (pbk. : alk. paper)
  1. Brown, John, 1800-1859--Ethics. 2. Political violence--Moral and ethical aspects. 3. Political violence--Religious aspects--Christianity. 4. Slavery--Moral and ethical aspects--United States. 5. Political theology. 6. Ethics, Modern. I. Title. II. Series: Encountering traditions.
  E451.S65 2014
  973.7'116092--dc23
                                        2014025815
  ISBN 978-0-8047-9345-2 (electronic)

Typeset by Bruce Lundquist in 10/14 Minion

For Susan, with thanks

Was John Brown simply an episode, or was he an eternal truth?
And if a truth, how speaks that truth today?

W. E. B. Du Bois

CONTENTS

FIGURES

ACKNOWLEDGMENTS

I am grateful for three long-running conversations with friends who have done much to shape my thinking in this book. John Blake and I have talked so many times about race, religion, and politics that it was inevitable that we would start talking about John Brown. We haven't stopped. Christian Noble understands extremism as well as anyone I know. In more than a decade of conversations since 9/11, he has helped me see both the horror and the allure of John Brown. Mark Jordan and I did not talk about John Brown until fairly recently. But for many years he has been teaching me how to think through my concerns about ethics that expand to absorb every other kind of practical reason. And it was Mark who helped me understand my need to write this book.

The book was written between Vanderbilt and Emory, and I am grateful for guidance and support I received from each school. The Provost's Office at Vanderbilt made a promise of a semester of leave that Candler's Dean Jan Love generously kept after I moved to Emory. Kelly Williams provided early support for my research at Vanderbilt. Stephen Speakman helped in the later stages of this project at Emory.

I was thankful for the chance to develop the chapters of the book through presentations at Wilson College, Santa Clara University, the Danforth Center on Religion and Politics at Washington University, the University of Virginia, Emory University, the Society of Christian Ethics, the Academy of Homiletics, Broad Street Presbyterian Church (Columbus, Ohio), First United Methodist Church (Orlando, Florida), and Westminster Presbyterian Church (Nashville, Tennessee). Across these settings I learned especially from the comments of John Carlson, Mark Douglas, Trent Frank, Marie Griffith, Jon Gunnemann, Hannah Hofheinz, Susan Hylen, Paul Dafydd Jones, John Kiess, Steven Kraftchick, Theresa Ladrigan-Whelpley, Roy Lewicki, Thomas Long, Charles Marsh, Ellen Ott Marshall, Charles Mathewes, Mick McCarthy, John McClure,

Peter Ochs, Christian Scharen, Lee Schmidt, Steven Tipton, David True, Andrea White, Jacob Wright, and Diane Yeager.

The book is much stronger because of the time that colleagues took with drafts of the manuscript. Edward Blum, Brooks Holifield, and Vincent Lloyd each offered extraordinarily helpful comments on the entire book. Angela Cowser, Keri Day, Michael Evans, Mark Jordan, Kyle Lambelet, Asante Todd, and Kirk Wegter-McNelly gave critical guidance for individual chapters. Jon Gunnemann, Karin Gunnemann, and Lorri Mills helped polish the final copy.

The editors and readers at Stanford University Press helped me turn a collection of ideas into a book. I am especially grateful to Emily-Jane Cohen, whose vision for the book drew mine into something more interesting; to Cynthia Lindlof, who trimmed errors and excesses in ways that let the better parts shine; to Randi Rashkover, whose guidance shaped the project at a critical stage; and to William Cavanaugh and Stanley Hauerwas, who helped me see what the book needed to do most.

As these acknowledgments begin to suggest, the book is much better because of the generosity of others. Whatever is worthwhile in it can be traced back to many sources. Errors of every kind—of fact, judgment, style, and more—should be attributed to me alone.

Susan Hylen did not just make the book better; she made it possible. Over many years, and especially the years in which I have written this book, she has shown me a grace that renews the sources of ethics even as it runs past the limits of ethics. Such gifts can and should be reciprocated, but even then they are not repaid. They endure as occasions for gratitude and wonder.

WEIRD JOHN BROWN

FIGURE I.1 Undated photo of John Brown. Boyd B. Stutler Collection, West Virginia State Archives.

INTRODUCTION

Hanging from the beam,
Slowly swaying (such the law),
Gaunt the shadow on your green,
Shenandoah!
The cut is on the crown
(Lo, John Brown),
And the stabs shall heal no more.

Hidden in the cap
Is the anguish none can draw;
So your future veils its face,
Shenandoah!
But the streaming beard is shown
(Weird John Brown),
The meteor of the war.

Herman Melville, "The Portent"[1]

JOHN BROWN, Herman Melville wrote, was *weird*. While Brown struck many people as unusual, even odd, Melville's poem made a stronger claim. It described Brown as weird like the Three Sisters in *Macbeth*, who were "so withered, and so wild in their attire" that they looked "not like th' inhabitants o' the earth, And yet [were] on 't" (1.3.39). Like Shakespeare's weird women, Melville's Brown was in the world but not entirely of it.

Melville's placement of the poem in the collection of his poems about the war further illumined its vision of Brown as one whose significance could not be fully contained in the ordinary flow of history. "The Portent" was the first poem in Melville's *Battle-Pieces and Aspects of the War*. The poems that followed moved mostly chronologically through the Civil War, from accounts of early misgivings all the way to a description of Robert E. Lee's visit to the Capitol after his defeat. That final poem was followed by a closing meditation and then—as if to make sure there would be no heroic ending—a prose supplement. "The Portent" started this long cycle. But in the original edition of 1866 it did not appear in the table of contents. It was an unlisted introduction to a set of historical events of which it was not a member. The poem about John Brown was an exception. It was separated from the poems that followed not only by its omission from the table of contents but also by the ways in which it was printed. Alone among the poems, "The Portent" was set entirely in italics. A blank folio page—the only gap in the book—divided it from what followed. Like the body it described, the poem was suspended between heaven and earth.

The first stanza of the poem depicted the destruction of John Brown's body and the body politic that executed him. "Hanging from the beam," the poem began. But it did not say just what, or who, was hanging. The second line described the body as "slowly swaying," but it still did not resolve the question of the body's identity. Its parenthetical reference ("such the law") could mean both that the body was hanging in accordance with the law and that *this was the manner in which the law itself was hanged.* In this hanging the law was executed in two senses: it was both followed and destroyed. The rest of the stanza only deepened this sense that the hanging executed both Brown and the order that killed him. The hanging body cast a shadow on the whole Shenandoah Valley. "The cut is on the crown," both of Brown's head and of the ruling power. Brown and Virginia were wounded together in this execution. "And the stabs shall heal no more."

The second stanza filled out the poem's vision of the hanging as a sign, even as it insisted that the referent of this sign was not known. Unknown anguish was hidden in the cap the hangman put over Brown's head. With that hangman's cap, Shenandoah's future was placed behind a veil. No mortal hand could move this veil, as no hand could move the veil and live to tell what lay beneath in Friedrich Schiller's poem "The Veiled Statue at Sais."[2] But Melville's veil did not cover everything. Brown's beard streamed out from under the cap like the tails of the meteors that people reported seeing in the sky around the time of his execution.[3] The poem called Brown himself "the meteor of the war." The tail of his beard indicated that some kind of sign in the night sky was under the hood. But the face of the meteor remained hidden. In Melville's telling, the final significance of Brown remained open. He was a sign whose referent was not secured. He was a portent.

The poem depicted Brown's execution as having some meaning beyond ordinary history. The hanging of John Brown destroyed not just the body of one old man but the legitimacy of the sovereign powers that once prevailed in the Shenandoah Valley. The poem described the destructive power of Brown's execution. But because the poem did not know the full significance of Brown—because it could not lift the veil—it could not write Brown's execution into a story with an ending that made sense of the suffering along the way. It could not make Brown's execution into the sacrifice that founded a new social order. The portent of John Brown, in Melville's poem, signaled the destruction of an order committed to slavery without authorizing anything to take its place.

Such weird violence—like what Walter Benjamin called "divine violence"— was both above and below what ethics as it is usually practiced today can consider.[4] When the old standards are destroyed and new ones are not yet established, it is not clear how any kind of ethical evaluation can be offered. Infused with this sensibility, "The Portent" was notable for its lack of moralizing. It was especially notable in contrast to poems written by other Northerners around the time of its composition. They tended to offer confident appraisals both of the meaning of Brown's death and of the morality of the violence done by and to him. Louisa May Alcott's tribute to Brown, for instance, celebrated the ways that "Living, he made life beautiful,— / Dying, made death divine."[5] William Dean Howells sounded a similar theme in his poem "Old Brown":

> Death kills not. In a later time,
> (O, slow, but all-accomplishing!)
> Thy shouted name abroad shall ring,
> Wherever right makes war sublime.[6]

Amid lines like these, Melville's stark images and understated rhymes stood out. They did not elevate Brown's death, his cause, or his violence to sublime heights. But neither did they strip Brown of significance that transcended historical events. Melville's lines insisted on some significance for Brown's death, but they did not present his life as right or wrong. They did not even reduce his violence to an ethical dilemma in which each side had some merit and some fault. Instead, they presented Brown as a portent, a sign whose meaning was not yet known. The tone of Melville's lines was not ethical ambivalence but eschatological fear and trembling.

Perspectives like Melville's have been rare in the more than 150 years that Americans have been remembering John Brown. The ethics of Brown's actions have been endlessly debated, and with strong arguments on every side. Conversations about Brown have tended to proceed as if getting the ethics right would tell us all we needed to know about John Brown—and ourselves. In this book, however, I hope to show the limits of ethics for thinking about the violence done to and by John Brown. I hope to show the costs of forgetting those limits. And I hope to stir theological imaginations that can remember both John Brown and the nation that endlessly tells his story as weird.

⌒

In remembering John Brown as weird, I hope to make connections to three different conversations: one about the limits of ethics for practical reasoning, a second about the relationship between religion and violence, and a third about the significance of race for any truthful story about the United States. These conversations do not always overlap. But they are held together in the body of John Brown.

As Melville saw, close considerations of John Brown's story make visible the limits of ethics. "Ethics" can mean many different things, of course, and I do not mean to lump them all together. Instead, I intend to make a more focused argument against the sufficiency of one particular but pervasive mode of ethics, a mode marked by its granting of a privileged place to universalizable moral obligations that play out within immanent networks of cause and effect. Ethics in this sense might appeal to "secular" motives, "religious" motives, or some combination of the two. What defines this mode is not the source of the motivation but the nature of the obligation.

The obligations that matter most for this mode of ethics share three important features. First, they apply equally to all moral agents in all situations. This emphasis on universalizability has perhaps been developed most explicitly in traditions that run through the categorical imperative of Immanuel Kant and the (U)-Principle of Jürgen Habermas. But the emphasis on universalizability ranges far beyond this set of traditions. It extends to consequentialist ethics that cannot imagine situations in which we should not seek the greatest good. It even shapes those modern accounts of virtue that describe universal obligations to promote human flourishing. Universalization can shape many forms of ethics. What it cannot do is imagine good reasons to make exceptions.

The obligations that define the ethics I mean to describe share a second feature. They have a distinctly *moral* quality that is assumed to give them precedence over obligations related to other kinds of goods, like beauty, piety, or rational inquiry. They make a claim not just about what is pleasurable, for instance, but what is *right*. And they assume that what is right should take priority over what is pleasurable, what is beautiful, what is true, and every other kind of good. Of course, ethics could be, and often has been, expanded to include other kinds of value. But this capacity for expansion only underscores the tendency of ethics to stand in for the whole of practical reasoning. And it does not happen without cost. When this expansion happens within the wider frame of moral obligation, it changes the character of the other goods at stake. Goods like playing with a child, eating delicious food, enjoying pleasurable sex, loving a neighbor, and praying without ceasing all suffer qualitative transformations when they become moral obligations.[7]

A final common feature marks the obligations that feature most prominently in the frameworks I am trying to resist here: these obligations come to life entirely within immanent networks of cause and effect. A mode of ethical reasoning that highlighted such obligations might take into account things like the this-worldly consequences of an action, the empirical features of an action in itself, or the character of the actor. It could evaluate any of these dimensions morally. But it would refuse to take into account any reference to something that exceeded the web of immanent cause and effect. It would refuse, for instance, a vision like the one the narrator ascribes to Joseph at the end of the book of Genesis. Joseph's brothers had betrayed him. They had sold him into slavery. But then Joseph's story takes a turn, and he rises to become a powerful adviser to the pharaoh. When his brothers come before him to beg for food, they do not recognize him. And when he makes himself known to them, they are terrified. But Joseph reassures them, saying, "Do not be afraid! Am I in the place of God? Even though you intended to do harm to me, God intended it for good, in order to preserve a numerous people, as he is doing today" (50:19–20).[8] The mode of ethics I am trying to criticize here would not disagree with Joseph's assessment so much as it would rule it out of order. An ethics of immanent moral obligation can accommodate many kinds of moral reasoning. But it resists any interpretation that suggests that the decisive significance of an act, consequence, or character lies beyond the immanent frame of this-worldly relationships. It resists any sense that the meaning of historical realities—and so our ultimate evaluation of them, and so the actions we should take in relation to them—might be defined by a moment that exceeds the ordinary course of history.[9]

This constellation of universalizable moral obligations within immanent chains of cause and effect does much to define contemporary imaginations of religion and politics. There are significant exceptions and outliers, even in relatively recent times. Thinkers as diverse as W. E. B. Du Bois, Karl Barth, Mary Daly, Oscar Romero, Pope John Paul II, and John Howard Yoder only begin the list of those who have offered visions that exceed this frame. But it continues to exert a strong gravitational pull. That pull can be seen in academic work that translates theological commitments into ethics, political reasoning that turns the rule of law into an ideology, and manifold forms of everyday life that make immanent moral obligation the sole source of meaning.

In arguing against the *sufficiency* of universalizable immanent moral obligations, I do not mean to refuse all of their claims. On the contrary, I will argue that they should play a significant role in any practical reasoning. I only mean to resist the idea that universalizable immanent moral obligations can stand alone to define the whole of practical reasoning. If they are significant, they are not sufficient in themselves.

Considerations of universalizable immanent moral obligations have played an especially significant role in contemporary discussions of violence. Philosophers and theologians often describe love in terms that exceed or defy each of the features I have described for the obligations that constitute this kind of ethics.[10] But the great stronghold—and historically important source—for the social imaginary that privileges this kind of obligation comes in considerations of violence.

If we can imagine exceptions to universal norms in relation to love, we resist exceptions pertaining to violence. Here the universal quality of the norms—whether of just war, pacifism, or some other standard—is taken to be inviolable. Moreover, depictions of violent actions that stress their aesthetic qualities, like the films of Quentin Tarantino, feel transgressive because they grate against deeply shared assumptions that moral categories, not aesthetic ones, provide the resources with which we should think about violence. Just so, religions are sometimes taken to be problematic precisely because they can suggest ways of thinking about violence, like those performed in sacrifice, that cannot be reduced to distinctively moral obligations. If religions sometimes seem to challenge the primacy of moral categories for thinking about violence, they can also seem dangerous because they involve ways of understanding violence that outrun immanent chains of cause and effect. Notions of "divine violence" become especially problematic. Usually exceptional, not necessarily moral, and decidedly not immanent, notions of divine violence cannot be easily assimilated to frameworks that stress the sufficiency of universalizable immanent moral obligations. Modern critics of religion have therefore tended to describe the ways religions pull reasoning about violence beyond the frame of such obligations. At the same time, apologists for religion have tended to renounce or reinterpret any talk of divine violence to make it fit within this frame.

In the chapters that follow I take a different tack. I try to show the interpretive poverty of frameworks that stress the sufficiency of universalizable immanent moral obligation for practical reasoning. And I try to display the steady collusion of these claims to sufficiency with the legitimation and expansion of state violence. These two features become especially clear when thinking about John Brown. Brown's theological visions of the meaning of violence in history were so baldly stated and so bluntly performed that considerations of Brown bring more immanent understandings of violence into the high relief that only contrast can provide. In this book I do not affirm Brown's theological understanding of his violence. But I do try to argue with him on his own terms. I follow the conversation beyond the bounds of immanent moral obligation. I try to show the ways that some notion of "divine violence" can enrich our understanding of the world and our reasoning about how to live together in it. That is, I take up the old genre of John Brown's story with the old intention of doing political theology.

My purpose is not to dig up new facts about Brown's life, not even about the theology he in fact espoused. A raft of excellent biographies of Brown has appeared in recent years, and I depend on them throughout the book.[11] Likewise, my ultimate goal is not to give a history of the interpretation of John Brown in and beyond the United States. Again, a series of recent books has done much to meet this need.[12] My primary purpose is rather to *add to* the history of interpretation with a series of critical, constructive, theological reflections on John Brown. Through those reflections I hope to show the difference that a theological imagination can make for questions of religion and violence.

It is impossible to think about John Brown without thinking about race (though more than one commentator has tried). The violence of John Brown has come to matter in the ways it does because he was a white man who tried to attack a system that enslaved African Americans. The evils of that system and its legacies are so destructive and so pervasive that Brown's violence demands to be taken seriously. The system of slavery enshrined murder, rape, kidnapping, forcible servitude, torture, humiliation, and other evils on a massive scale. It was already, as Brown saw, a state of war. It was also established in law. Thousands of state and local statutes and the Constitution itself secured its place. Deep-seated social customs in every part of the country presumed its existence. It is hard to imagine its disappearance without violent action.[13] One need not engage in the profane parlor game of comparative atrocities to say that if any states of affairs have ever justified violent action outside the law, the system of slavery in the United States was one of them. Perhaps even more strongly, we might say that if there have ever been moments for which talk of "divine violence" would be fitting, the destruction of the system of slavery in the United States defined one of them. If slavery in the United States were not so evil—if race did not matter as much as it did and does—John Brown would not pose difficult questions.

Those questions take on an even sharper edge because Brown was white. If he himself had been an enslaved African American, like Nat Turner, his violence might be wrapped in the familiar paper of self-defense. If he were a free African American advocating armed resistance, like Henry Highland Garnet, he might be framed as a fairly typical revolutionary. But because he was white, and because the structures of American society have worked so hard to separate black and white in both fact and thought, Brown poses a different kind of question. Because commentators have not seen him as fighting for "his own" people, his religious motives come into sharper focus. He looks like more of an extremist. Racism, then, did not just fuel the evil that defined John Brown's times. It also shapes the ways that questions about Brown are asked today—even for those who would reject racism root and branch. Realizing the significance of racism in framing questions about John Brown does not dissolve the questions that he poses. On the contrary, it raises the stakes for thinking about them critically.

Attempts to think about race, religion, and violence rightly lead to considerations of ethics. Any conversation about race in the United States must attend to universalizable immanent moral obligations. But I will argue that coming to terms with the full horrors of the violence of slavery and its legacies will require more from us than such obligations can measure. They cannot supply the whole of our vocabularies for interpreting the world and thinking about how to live in it, especially when the wounds in this world are as deep and enduring as the wounds left by slavery. In each chapter that follows I try to show the ways that an ethics of universalizable immanent moral obligation, when taken to be sufficient in itself, distorts and limits our abilities to understand situations and act in relation to them. I try to show some of the visions that a richer kind of practical reason might make visible and some of the actions that it might make thinkable. I argue that we need to cultivate the ability to reason about situations in ways that leave room for exceptions, that do not reduce all goods to moral obligations, and that cannot fit within an immanent frame. In particular, I argue that we need some notion of divine violence.

❧

This work of thinking beyond the limits of ethics has particular urgency for what is sometimes called "mainline" Protestant Christianity in the United States. Marilynne Robinson gestured toward that need in her Pulitzer Prize–

winning novel, *Gilead*. The novel is, among other things, an eschatological recollection of Christian ministry. It tells the story of three generations of Congregationalist ministers at a time when the next generation is still to be defined. In telling these stories, it gives a theologically inflected history of American Protestantism from the middle of the nineteenth century to the middle of the twentieth. John Brown haunts the book as a powerful presence who stays just outside the narrator's line of sight. Brown is heard more than seen. But he leaves his mark.

The narrator, writing as an old man in the 1950s, remembers that his grandfather had provided a safe house for Brown. The grandfather preached with a pistol in his belt and a bloody shirt on his back, both relics of the guerrilla war Brown helped lead against slavery in Kansas. For the grandfather's generation, Brown was the prophet who made the faith come alive. Brown's violence was a kind of sacrament, making manifest the presence of God in the world. For the next generation, though, Brown was the fanatic who had caused violence on a massive scale. Like many preachers who came of age after the Civil War, the narrator's father became a pacifist on principle. Out of that principle he rejected any talk of divine violence. And when he pulled violence within the frame of universalizable immanent moral obligations, he could find nothing but reasons to reject it.

The third generation in Robinson's novel displays more ambivalence, neither celebrating Brown nor rejecting him but trying to make sense of him. The narrator himself is part of this generation. He refuses both his grandfather's flat identification of Brown's violence with the work of God and his father's refusal to entertain any possibility of divine violence. In thinking through his own times, he recalls a sermon that he wrote when Spanish influenza was raging through his corner of Iowa. It was especially intense at Fort Riley, where the troops were mustering to join the fighting in World War I. The ordinary work of the fort ground to a halt, as barracks were converted to hospital wards. The whole place had to be closed down. "Now," the narrator writes, "if these things were not signs, I don't know what a sign would look like. So I wrote a sermon about it."

> I said, or I meant to say, that these deaths were rescuing foolish young men from the consequences of their own ignorance and courage, that the Lord was gathering them in before they could go off and commit murder against their brothers. And I said that their deaths were a sign and a warning to the rest of us that the desire for war would bring the consequences of war, because there is no ocean

big enough to protect us from the Lord's judgment when we decide to hammer our plowshares into swords and our pruning hooks into spears, in contempt of the will and the grace of God.[14]

The narrator's sermon combined his grandfather's willingness to think about violence outside an immanent frame with his father's pacifist conclusions. "It was," he writes, "quite a sermon . . . the only sermon I wouldn't mind answering for in another world." But he never preached it. He knew that the only people who would be at the worship service would be "a few old women who were already about as sad and apprehensive as they could stand to be and no more approving of the war than I was." He burned the sermon and preached instead on the Parable of the Lost Sheep.[15]

It was his greatest sermon, yet he never preached it. He "meant every word," so he burned the manuscript. Thus, the narrator's sermon, like John Brown himself, haunts *Gilead* without ever quite appearing as an event within the narrative. Talk of divine violence should be undertaken with such hesitation, indirection, and modesty. If in this book I sometimes write in less graceful ways, I do so because the idea of divine violence has been buried so thoroughly that it can be raised only with some strain. In *Gilead*'s chronicle of generations, I would write as the narrator's grandson. Any sense of divine violence has faded, especially in the Protestant tradition Robinson describes and that I call home. Blunt words, perhaps too much in themselves, are necessary to reopen the possibility of the indirection that is more appropriate to the topic.

The generations of "mainline" Protestant Christians in the United States since Robinson's narrator have continued to work to close that possibility down. We have tended to take up violence within the frameworks of universalizable immanent moral obligation just described. What has marked considerations of these immanent phenomena as "theological" has often been the source of the norms used to evaluate them. If those norms come from the Bible, or church teaching, or a sense that God wills justice, then the reasoning is taken to be theological. But something is lost in the reduction of theology to a source of norms for ethical reasoning within an immanent frame.[16]

Wrestling with John Brown's story helps make that loss visible. On his way to the gallows Brown described the violence that he did and the violence done to him as part of a process in which the land was purged of its sins with blood. For Brown, the significance of violence extended beyond any chain of this-worldly cause and effect. It was part of an eschatological history of redemption. Brown's critics have seized upon this remark as a sign of his fanaticism. And Brown's contemporary defenders, whether they have identified as religious or secular, have tended to ignore it or translate it away. They have tended to defend Brown from within an immanent frame that would have been alien to him. That frame has come to seem natural through many social processes, but the Protestant generations *Gilead* describes have played a crucial role in its production. In straining against this immanent frame for thinking about violence, I am trying to criticize one of the great legacies of this tradition even as I work within it.

This book is therefore part of a tradition of Protestant Christian reflection on politics, violence, and the meaning of history. But it does not draw exclusively on sources that might be identified as Protestant, Christian, or even theological. Indeed, the most significant source for these reflections is Walter Benjamin's 1921 essay "Critique of Violence." I read Benjamin as one of the greatest thinkers of messianic hope within the conditions of modernity. The present book aspires to something like that hope. But, again, this is not a book *about* Benjamin. While I have tried to give serious attention to Benjamin's writings and significant commentaries on them, and while I do offer interpretations of "Critique of Violence" and other texts, the primary purpose of this book is not to make a contribution to the secondary literature on Benjamin. It is to do Christian political theology in ways that have learned from Benjamin. There is a risk here of seeming to conscript Benjamin into the service of Christian theology, to baptize him into the church after his death. Nothing could be further from my intentions or, I hope, the effects of these pages. I will leave to Benjamin's biographers the questions of how to describe his complex identity in relation to religion.[17] Whatever it was, though, it was not the kind of thing that involved him in anything that should be described as Christian political theology. The present book does not claim identity with Benjamin. It does not make a claim to the mantle of his authority. It is more like the fruits of interfaith dialogue. One could argue that any number of sources more closely identified with Christian traditions could have done that work. That is surely true, even if layers of commentary can make it difficult to hear people like Julian of Norwich or Augustine of Hippo as anything but right-minded ethicists. As it happened, though, it was not one of these figures who convinced me of these things. It was Benjamin who roused me from my normative slumbers.

❧

A political theology that makes visible the limits of ethics need not spell the end of ethics. It can instead restore an immanent ethics to its rightful place in practical deliberation. Delivered of the pretense of being all-in-all, aware of it-self as a practical reason for the time between the times, an ethics of immanent obligation can return to offer guidance for everyday choices. With the state-ment of this hope another of the book's deepest affinities becomes clear. I am trying to write about Brown in ways inspired by Søren Kierkegaard's *Fear and Trembling*. I want to tell a story in which Harpers Ferry appears as an American Mount Moriah. As Kierkegaard's opening meditations sought to break the hold of immanent moral obligations on the ways his readers imagined Abraham, I mean to critique merely ethical accounts of Brown's violence. And as Kierke-gaard negated ethical understandings to open up the space theology would fill to overflowing, I try to negate ethical interpretations of Brown in order to form desires for a political theology that cannot be reduced to social ethics. Kierke-gaard's "teleological suspension of the ethical" meant not the end of ethics but a renewal of a chastened ethics. Just so, I hope to suggest the possibilities for a political theology that reveals the limits of ethical discourse in ways that renew the critical potential of ethical discourse.[18]

I begin in Chapter 1 by giving a short history of Brown's life and tracing his role as a touchstone that reveals qualities of American national life that are usu-ally hidden from view. Debates about Brown have tended to revolve around the question of whether he was a freedom fighter or a fanatic. Those two options seem to exhaust the field only because the prevailing social imaginary is so deeply structured by the twin assumptions that violence should be considered within the bounds of ethics alone and that the state should have a monopoly on legitimate violence for political ends. The largely unquestioned status of those assumptions comes with a cost. In Chapter 2 I begin to count that cost, espe-cially for the years after 9/11. I describe the ways these assumptions combine to offer mythological justifications for violence and the ways those justifications legitimate escalations of violence by the state. I argue that we need to develop a capacity for reasoning about exceptions—a political theology—to diagnose this dynamic and break this pattern. In Chapter 3 I turn more explicitly to Ben-jamin to develop a political theology that can do that work. In particular, I try to develop a notion of "divine violence" that makes possible eschatological memories of a weird John Brown.

In Chapters 4, 5, and 6 I take up the task of remembering Brown by consid-ering a string of perennial questions about him. I appeal to divine violence in order to blast concepts like the higher law (Chapter 4), pardon (Chapter 5), and sacrifice (Chapter 6) out of discourses defined by assumptions of monopolies of ethics on practical reasoning and of the state on legitimate violence. The chapters try to imagine these concepts in relation not to the sovereignty of the state but to the redeeming sovereignty of God. What would it mean, for instance, to imagine "the higher law" not as a better version of the laws on the books—a code the state might be reformed to follow, a code that might be enforced by violence—but as a divine gift that broke the hold of unjust laws and made possible free response? In these chapters I try to show how insisting on the sovereignty of God changes not just the locus but also the *qualities* of sovereignty.

Sovereignty is a risky concept to invoke for political reasoning. It has often been used to reinforce the racist structures I hope to subvert and suppress the democratic energies I hope to encourage.[19] But appealing to the sovereignty of God need not commit a political theology to any kind of fundamentalism. That is, it need not lead to declarations of *identity* between the will of God and particular actions or entities. On the contrary, I try throughout this book to describe the sovereignty of God as manifest, in this age, in a divine violence that negates any claims—including those of lawful states, religious organizations, fugitive movements, and ethically minded NGOs—to sovereign violence.

These claims to identity with some sovereign power could be criticized in other ways. One could, for instance, deny the epistemic possibility or political relevance of anything beyond a code of universalizable immanent moral obligations. But this kind of denial is not the same as the negation performed by divine violence. Negation defines a *saeculum* that is a moment in a larger history of redemption, not a secularized universe of causes and effects that is taken to constitute all that is relevant for practical reasoning. Negation reveals the ideological qualities of these attempts to eliminate ideology. Thus, divine violence opens up alternatives to both "religious" and "secular" fundamentalisms that function as if the politics of this age were complete in themselves.

The divine violence described in this book does not directly generate a particular kind of politics. "The guiding principle," as Walter Benjamin wrote, is that "authentic divine power can manifest itself *other than destructively* only in the world to come (the world of fulfillment)."[20] Divine violence does not found a political order. But it does break the grip of dominant orders to open up a space for genuinely free response, a space in which practical reasoning about public goods can be developed and refined in conversation. Divine violence therefore produces neither theocracy nor a political sphere that has been purged of every trace of theology but a negative presence, a present negation, that makes politics possible.

1 THE TOUCHSTONE

A man there came, whence none could tell,
Bearing a touchstone in his hand,
And tested all things in the land,
By its unerring spell.

William Allingham, "The Touchstone"[1]

JOHN BROWN TESTED AMERICA. As the Irish poet William Allingham saw, Brown was like a touchstone: a quartz-hard surface against which the metal of the nation could be rubbed to reveal its true composition. Like a touchstone, Brown could assay the qualities of others while remaining opaque himself. Brown both baffled and fascinated the people who met him. He spoke as plainly as a person could speak, but just this plainness made him an enigma even to his allies. Brown's impenetrability elicited argument, conviction, even theology. Thus the touchstone did its work. Rubbed against the hard opacity of John Brown, individuals and institutions showed themselves for what they were.[2]

Brown's powers to assay have been renewed in every age since his death. Again and again thinkers have pressed the questions of the day against the hard memory of John Brown. Brown's execution sparked a spiral of reactions and reactions to reactions that polarized North and South and helped push the nation into war. After the war Frederick Douglass hailed Reconstruction as a project that would finish the work Brown started. When Reconstruction was undermined by desires for reconciliation between Northern and Southern whites, entrepreneurs repackaged Brown as a sensational event that could be shared in a renewed national memory. They transported the blockhouse in which he made his last stand to the 1893 Columbian Exposition in Chicago and sold souvenirs engraved with his last words, which described the blood that would be required for redemption of the nation (see Figure 1.1).[3]

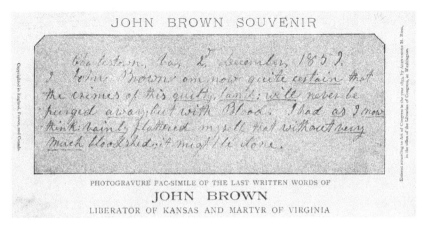

FIGURE 1.1 "John Brown Souvenir" from the World's Columbian Exposition in Chicago, 1893. Boyd B. Stutler Collection, West Virginia State Archives.

Not everyone at the turn of the century accepted this transformation of Brown into a fairground attraction. Insisting on the unfinished quality of any redemption, W. E. B. Du Bois led a group in the first decade of the twentieth century in founding the Niagara Movement at the site of Brown's raid on the federal arsenal at Harpers Ferry. In that same decade socialist leader Eugene V. Debs decried the oppression of workers and called for a "John Brown of wage slavery." A few years later Social Gospel preacher Charles Sheldon celebrated Brown's muscular Christianity in contrast to "those soft youth this nation rears." In the 1930s Countee Cullen and Langston Hughes reclaimed Brown for a new generation's judgment of the segregation that still prevailed. In these same decades most white American views were turning sharply against Brown. Those currents found vivid expression in *The Santa Fe Trail*, a 1940 film that projected a crazed, homicidal Brown on movie screens across the country. A similar image, muted by the genre of the academic essay, stood behind C. Vann Woodward's use of Brown to condemn Cold War fanatics on every side.[4]

As the movement for civil rights gained strength in the second half of the twentieth century, more positive images of Brown returned to national prominence. Both Lerone Bennett Jr. and Malcolm X recalled Brown's example in criticism of more tepid white liberals. More sympathetic novels and biographies by white authors also began to appear again. But attention to civil rights waned at the turn of millennium and then, after September 11, 2001, was largely overwhelmed by national preoccupations with terrorism. Readings of Brown registered the shift. They came to be dominated by questions about religion, extremism, and violence. In the years since 9/11 Christopher Hitchens, Barbara Ehrenreich, and a host of others have invoked Brown in the course of arguments about terrorism. Museums have told Brown's story in order to ask if Brown was "so different from today's bombers from Oklahoma City to Iraq." Timothy McVeigh, who blew up the Murrah Federal Building in Oklahoma City, had his own answer to that question. He explicitly appealed to Brown as a precedent. In the most recent years, as concerns have arisen not only about terrorism but also about the state's response to fear of terrorism, Brown has been invoked again. Cornel West recently tweeted that "Brother Edward Snowden is the John Brown of the National Security State." As these examples show, the touchstone of John Brown is not only revelatory but also mutable—and combustible. This touchstone is not kept safely under glass in a museum.[5]

Brown has been such a significant touchstone for American political imaginations in part because of his ability to figure sovereignty.[6] In speaking of "sovereignty," I mean to describe a kind of authority that goes beyond the law, a righteous power that can ground, legitimate, limit, exceed, and even overturn the law. Because Brown claimed that kind of authority for his work, Brown's story has the power to make the questions of sovereignty concrete. The story of John Brown asks whether such a notion of sovereignty should play any role at all in our political reasoning. It presses the question of whether there is a "higher law" that can legitimate actions that defy the laws of the state. It asks where such sovereign authority might reside, how it might be known, and how it might relate to individuals, states, and movements in this age. It asks about the possibility of a sovereign pardon that would run beyond and even against anything ethics might require. It asks whether it makes sense to speak of any sovereign power at work in history and what role sovereign violence might play in the unfolding of history. John Brown's story asks if the state should have a monopoly on the means of legitimate violence. It asks what, if anything, God might make of violence. John Brown's story makes visible some of the most basic questions of political theology. Indeed, talk about Brown has served as one of the most important genres in which Americans have done political theology over the last 150 years.

To make sovereignty visible for America is no small feat, for Americans cast off the most established ways of figuring sovereignty when they cast off monarchy. As Ernst Kantorowicz argued, European nations came to understand the sovereign as having two bodies, one "natural" and the other "politic." The king's natural body might be subject to disability, moral failing, and even mortality, but the body politic represented, "like the angels, the Immutable within Time." Sharing in God's own rule, the body politic secured the legitimacy of the rule exerted by the king's natural body. The king's natural body was "backed" and "underwritten," in Eric Santner's words, by the sacred flesh of the body politic. And the body politic was in turn realized in the king's natural body. The king's complex body was sovereign power made flesh.[7]

America's rejection of a king disrupted these conventions by which sovereignty could appear. In one strand of republican political theory, the people moved into the role of the sovereign. If the locus of the sovereign's natural body changed, the logic of sovereignty did not.[8] But "the people" has always been a plural and dispersed reality. It is difficult for something like the natural body of a sovereign people to appear, and even more difficult for it to act in decisive ways. Moreover, the transfer of sovereignty to the people created a need for some new narrative that could give ultimate legitimation to the political body of the sovereign people and then tie that political body to a natural counterpart.

Stories of American exceptionalism have helped fill this need. They have linked the American people to the redeeming work of God in the world and so underwritten the sovereignty of the people. But even these stories need focal points. They depend on individuals and events that represent the people as a whole. John Brown has often been pressed into this role. Variously cast as Puritan, frontiersman, heir to the Revolution, Yankee, transcendentalist, and more, Brown has served as a figure of the American people. As Henry David Thoreau said in an 1859 address, "No man in America has ever stood up so persistently and effectively for the dignity of human nature, knowing himself for a man, and the equal of any and all governments. In that sense he was the most American of us all."[9] Even those who have loathed Brown have tended to assign him some representative role. The "most American of us all" has been a site for making the people visible to itself, for arguing about the virtues and vices of the people, and for asking whether the body politic of the people is connected to God in ways that underwrite its authority in relation to law. When the people are taken to be sovereign, and John Brown is taken to stand for the people exactly at their point of connection—or lack of connection—to an authority beyond themselves, arguments about the character of John Brown can become arguments about sovereignty.

Arguments that have used Brown to figure sovereignty have often wrenched him out of the wide network of relationships in which he actually lived and acted. The Brown of political memory typically stands apart from important relationships with family members, business partners, fellow raiders, wealthy backers who supplied money and weapons, and many others, both black and white. At times in this book I engage Brown's story on those terms, for they are the terms that order political memories, and one of my hopes is to intervene in those memories. The body politic matters. At other times—as when considering pardon or the temptation to narratives of blood sacrifice—I try to stress the political significance of remembering Brown in the dense network of relationships in which he actually lived. Whether Brown's relationships are in the foreground or the background of my depictions of him, they are always there. The natural body must not be ignored.

John Brown's body has helped figure sovereignty for a polity in which sovereignty is often invisible. Part of this invisibility comes from the ideal of a sovereign people. But another strand of republican political theory has made sovereignty even more difficult to discuss directly. This strand would reject any reference to authority outside or beyond the law. Hannah Arendt articulated this view when she argued, "The great, and in the long run, perhaps the greatest American innovation in politics as such was the consistent abolition of sovereignty within the body politic of the republic, the insight that in the realm of human affairs sovereignty and tyranny are the same."[10] Such an ideal would bury questions of sovereignty, not so much answering them as smothering them. When the rule of law is taken to exclude reference to any power beyond the law, discussions of sovereignty have to happen with borrowed resources and in fugitive forms.

These fugitive deliberations have happened in different sites in different eras. Talal Asad has argued that the figure of the suicide bomber has served as one such site in the years since September 11, 2001. In Asad's view, the suicide bomber is a figure through which liberal democracies work out the repressed knowledge of the lawless violence at work in their own founding and ongoing existence—the sovereignty that dare not speak its name. As a figure for the return of the repressed, the suicide bomber both fascinates and repels. As a figure freighted with significance for its interpreters, the suicide bomber elicits not just ordinary police action but endless discourses of interpretation. These attempts to explain suicide bombing, Asad wrote, "tell us more about liberal assumptions of religious subjectivities and political violence than they do about what is ostensibly being explained."[11] Because these explanatory discourses reveal assumptions of political theology that often remain unarticulated, they can become a site for critical conversation.

John Brown has played a role like the one Asad describes for suicide bombers for almost two centuries.[12] Brown holds a special place in American political imaginations because of the wide sympathy for the ends he sought. For most Americans, the 9/11 hijackers can be condemned on the basis of their cause alone. And if their end was not good, their use of violent means beyond the law never becomes a serious question. Questions of sovereignty can be evaded. But Brown cannot be dismissed so easily. As Du Bois wrote, Brown poses the "riddle of the Sphinx" because he was right about so much.[13] Brown was right that slavery was an abomination. And he was right that legal means were not going to break the system of slavery anytime soon. Enslaved people had been emancipated in fits and starts in Northern states in the years after the Revolution, but by the 1850s the formal political processes that might have produced complete emancipation had ground to a standstill. Moral suasion might have moved some hearts, but it was no serious threat to entrenched slavery in the South. In the end it was bloodshed, and bloodshed that the law had to scramble to accommodate, that ended slavery in the United States. If it could have happened another way, it did not. Widespread acceptance of Brown's ends puts the question of his means in terms that are difficult to evade. Because those means included violence beyond the law, Brown raises questions of sovereignty in direct and vivid forms.

Like a European monarch, John Brown has two bodies. What Kantorowicz would have called Brown's natural body lies a mouldering in the grave, just as the song says, but Brown's soul, his body politic, marches on as a figure for sovereignty in a nation with deep suspicions of sovereignty. Kantorowicz described the medieval king's body politic as providing a kind of stability and security for the realm. The ability of later rulers to share in this body guaranteed a continuity of legitimate power. The living body of John Brown offers no such assurances. It is not immutable but different in every age. It appears again and again, but not as a steady statement that can undergird ongoing claims to sovereignty. The living body of John Brown appears instead as an interruption, a question posed to successive moments in national history. It does not so much secure existing powers as reveal them for what they are. The hard rock of John Brown is not a foundation but a touchstone.

The Natural Body of John Brown

This book focuses especially on the body politic of John Brown. But the best reflections on Brown's political body will not float free from empirical histories of his natural body. They will instead cling closely to this body, seeking new angles of vision from a spot close to the ground.

Born in Torrington, Connecticut, in 1800, Brown grew up in a family with deep roots in Puritan New England and a strong commitment to the abolition of slavery.[14] The family moved to the Western Reserve in 1805, part of a wave of migration from New England. Brown would suffer a lifetime of losses, and they started early. His mother, Ruth Mills Brown, died in 1808.

After a brief flirtation with theological studies, Brown followed his father into the tanning business. He married Dianthe Lusk in 1820, and they had seven children together. In 1826 they moved to New Richmond, Pennsylvania, where the family enjoyed one of its most stable and conventional periods. Brown's tannery thrived, and he helped start both a Congregationalist church and a school. But the losses continued. A son, Frederick, died in 1831. Dianthe died in 1832. After a relatively brief time as a widower, Brown married the teen-aged Mary Day in 1833. They would have thirteen children together, but only six would live into full adulthood. When Brown's tannery started to struggle, the family moved back to Ohio. Brown, like many others, began to speculate in land. But the Panic of 1837 wiped out the credit markets on which Brown and other speculators depended, and he never fully recovered. He declared bankruptcy in 1842 and then, in the terrible year of 1843, buried four more children.

If Brown's life was marked by loss, it was defined by his commitment to ending slavery. As the story goes, Brown was in the middle of a worship service in Hudson, Ohio, in 1837—the year when the financial panic hit its peak—when he heard about the murder of Elijah Lovejoy, a Presbyterian minister who ran an abolitionist press in Alton, Illinois. Lovejoy died defending the press from a proslavery mob that was trying to destroy it. When Brown heard the news, he rose and committed his life that day to the abolition of slavery.

Brown's abolitionist commitments deepened when he and his family moved to Springfield, Massachusetts, in 1846. Brown joined with a partner from Akron to set up a company that would trade in wool. While in Springfield, Brown attended the Sanford Street Church, a congregation led by African American abolitionists and widely known as the Free Church. Through this congregation Brown met speakers like Frederick Douglass and Sojourner Truth. He developed a circle of white and black abolitionist connections that included Gerrit Smith and James McCune Smith. Meanwhile, the wool business was changing rapidly. The Walker Tariff lowered the duty paid on imported wool. And the end of the Mexican War opened up significant new sources for imports. Prices spiraled downward, and Brown did not adapt. The collapse of his wool business led to another bankruptcy. It also provided the occasion for Brown to live into his antislavery commitments more deeply. In 1849 he and his family moved to join a small community of mostly African American families in North Elba, New York.

While Mary and the children settled in North Elba, John Brown traveled more and more for antislavery causes. He first came to national attention for his involvement in the violent struggles between free-state and proslavery forces unleashed by the Kansas-Nebraska Act of 1854. The act dissolved the uneasy truce of the Missouri Compromise of 1820 and reopened the possibility of slavery in the northern part of the Louisiana Purchase. It provided for "popular sovereignty" to decide whether a state would be slave or free, and so touched off a bloody scramble to establish that sovereignty. Brown collected money and arms at a meeting of the Radical Abolitionist Party in Syracuse in 1855 on his way to join some of his sons in Kansas. When he arrived in Kansas later that year, he assumed the role of captain of the Pottawatomie Rifles in the Liberty Guard, a free-state militia. Violence was a constant fact of life in "bleeding Kansas." It came to a head on May 21, 1856, when proslavery forces sacked and burned Lawrence, the free-state capital. The next day Charles Sumner, an antislavery Republican senator from Massachusetts, railed against the violence on the floor of the Senate. Representative Preston Brooks of South Carolina responded by beating Sumner into unconsciousness with a metal-tipped cane. The chance for a political solution to the problem of slavery seemed to be slipping away. Two days after the caning of Sumner, John Brown directed the midnight massacre of five proslavery settlers. Brown's crew pulled the men from their homes and hacked them to pieces with broadswords.

If Brown's role in the murders was well known in Kansas, it did not stop him from traveling in the North. In 1857 and 1858 he made repeated trips to abolitionist hubs like Rochester, Boston, Concord, and Chatham, Canada. He met with some of the most prominent antislavery leaders in the country, including Frederick Douglass, Charles Sumner, Henry David Thoreau, Ralph Waldo Emerson, James McCune Smith, and Theodore Parker. Far more than most white abolitionists, Brown stayed as a guest of African American households when he traveled. He was a houseguest not only of Douglass but also of James Newton Gloucester in Brooklyn, Isaac Holden in Chatham, and Stephen Smith in Philadelphia.[15] His travels took him back to Kansas at the end of 1858. In a daring raid that added to his mystique, he led a group that freed eleven enslaved people from a plantation in Missouri and then escorted them all the way to freedom in Canada.

In the course of these years Brown began to think more and more about taking his fight to the heart of the South. While his plans were often cryptic and always shifting, he seems to have envisioned an ongoing guerrilla war based in the Appalachian Mountains. A raid on the federal arsenal at Harpers Ferry, itself hard by the mountains, was the first step. Brown had a cache of pikes and rifles supplied in part by the so-called Secret Six, a network of wealthy and prominent Northern abolitionists. Brown planned to seize more weapons from the arsenal at Harpers Ferry, encourage enslaved men and women to run away to join him, and then retreat into the mountains. He and his allies would move through the mountains and use the rough terrain as a staging ground for raids throughout the South, growing stronger through the addition of escaped slaves and smuggled weapons. Brown had studied the successful slave revolt in Haiti, which he thought had worked something like this. And he had sought the advice of Harriet Tubman, who knew better than anyone else how to make use of the mountains.

On the night of October 16, 1859, Brown led a band of twenty-one raiders in seizing the federal arsenal at Harpers Ferry. The group included five African American men and three of Brown's sons. Brown and the main party quickly took the rifle works, the armory, and the arsenal. They cut the telegraph wires. A second group moved through the countryside freeing slaves and collecting slaveholders as hostages. When a train to Baltimore arrived in the middle of the night, a watchman who had escaped the raiders enlisted a hotel clerk to help him flag it down. The conductor and a few others went ahead of the train to check the tracks for sabotage. They met some of Brown's men in a covered bridge that enclosed a portion of the tracks. Shots were fired, and Brown's raiders killed a free black baggage handler named Heyward Shepherd. Despite the gunfire, the train rolled on—and quickly spread news of the raid.

By the morning of October 17 local militias had begun to muster and march on Harpers Ferry. President Buchanan ordered federal troops to join them. Brown tarried through a long day, perhaps waiting for slaves to escape and join him, and perhaps despairing of this possibility and giving up the plan for guerrilla war in favor of a martyr's death. As the day went on, the townspeople armed and organized themselves to fight back. More and more companies of militia began to arrive. Brown and the raiders suffered rising casualties. When local forces finally cut off every possible escape route, Brown's band retreated into a blockhouse with the hostages. The small group of men held off hundreds of people from this "fort." That night a company of federal marines led by Colonel Robert E. Lee and Lieutenant J. E. B Stuart arrived. The next day the marines stormed the blockhouse with bayonets, capturing or killing all the remaining raiders. Townspeople, militiamen, and marines killed ten members of the original raiding party, including two of Brown's sons. At least two escaped slaves also died. The raiders killed four people and wounded at least nine more. None of the white hostages were killed.

The raid ended quickly and with little immediate military effect. But Brown's story took on a new level of significance when he began to explain himself in letters, interviews, and speeches in the courtroom. His words divided the country, inspiring some and repulsing others. He fused heroic action and warm sentimentality in ways that appealed to Yankee sensibilities. He called upon the history, traditions, and ideals of the nation. Above all, he appealed to the Bible, speaking in phrases and cadences that recalled those of preachers in both the South and the North.

Brown's rhetoric charged debates about slavery with fresh theological urgency for both sides. More than eight hundred people tried to visit Brown in prison.[16] A group of black women in New York promised Mary they would pray for her and take up a collection to support her. "Tell your dear husband," they wrote, "that henceforth you shall be our own."[17] Appeals for clemency poured in. The appeals only moved Virginia Governor Henry A. Wise to convene a more massive display of military power for Brown's execution on December 2, 1859.

The story of John Brown's natural body did not end with its death. The mobs and medical students who desecrated the bodies of John Copeland and Shields Green, two of the black raiders, were denied access to Brown's body. P. T. Barnum's offer of one hundred dollars for Brown's clothing and a pike was refused. Instead, J. M. Hopper, the undertaker hired to care for Brown's body, received forty-five dollars for a walnut coffin and for services that included washing the body, keeping it on ice, and fitting it with a cravat collar that would cover the scars where the rope had cut into Brown's neck.[18] Mary Brown accompanied the body through cheering crowds and winter slush to its final resting place in North Elba. The white abolitionist Wendell Phillips preached. Lyman Epps, a free black neighbor, sang "Blow Ye the Trumpet, Blow." And John Brown's body was buried in the ground.

Freedom Fighter or Fanatic?

Even before Brown's natural body was buried, debates about the meaning of his political body began. Early on, two main options emerged: Brown was either a "freedom fighter" or a "fanatic." This way of framing the questions posed by

Brown continues to dominate discussions both in the academy and in wider publics. In the introduction to a book on the legacy of Brown, Paul Finkelman frames the question of the book by asking, "Was he a murderer or a madman, a monster or a humanitarian? Was he a liberator of slaves or a terrorist murdering innocent civilians?"[19] A 2008 lecture on Brown by the Yale historian David Blight reiterated this frame, asking if "John Brown's Holy War" made him a "Terrorist or Heroic Revolutionary?"[20] And a flyer prepared by the Franklin County (Pennsylvania) Historical Society offered an alliterative version of the same question: "Freedom Fighter or Fanatic?"[21] Interpreters of Brown disagree deeply about the answer to this question. But they have tended to accept its structure. And, I will argue, that structure reveals much about our shared imagination of religion and violence.

White Northern Republicans initially sought to define a category that escaped the bipolar frame of freedom fighter or fanatic. In the days immediately following the raid on Harpers Ferry, they overwhelmingly described Brown as a madman who lacked the political significance of a true fanatic. Some— including his lawyers—sought to save his life by appealing to the relatively new M'Naghten rules, which allowed a person to be declared not guilty by reason of insanity. And almost all sought to distance Brown from Republican politics by declaring him to be a solitary madman with no connections to wider political movements. The *Independent*, a New York newspaper edited by Theodore Tilton, got out in front of the story, labeling Brown as "mad" as early as October 20. Henry Ward Beecher, the most prominent preacher in the country—and a member of the Secret Six who had sent arms and money to Brown—called Brown's actions "mad and feeble" just ten days later. He attributed Brown's madness to the loss of his son Frederick in Kansas. "The shot that struck the child's heart crazed the father's brain," Beecher said. Horace Greeley made clear the implications of Brown's madness, referring to him as "this private man."[22] White Northern Republicans initially pressed for this clinical and apolitical description of Brown as mad. But the sense that Brown was abnormal was soon absorbed into a category that could accommodate wide varieties of clinical conditions even as it insisted upon political significance: the fanatic.

Governor Henry Wise of Virginia considered the possibility that Brown was insane, even writing a letter asking the state asylum to evaluate him. But Wise never sent the letter.[23] A verdict of insanity would have played well with some of the Northern Democrats Wise hoped would support his bid to become the Democrats' nominee for president in 1860. It would have been disastrous, though, for Wise's fortunes in the South. Not only could it have saved Brown from hanging but it also could have suggested that a mentally incompetent Yankee could keep hundreds of Virginians at bay until federal troops arrived to save the day. Wise needed Brown to be sane, formidable, and wrong in ways that went beyond the lawbreaking of a common criminal.[24] And he seems to have found Brown to possess just that combination. The language of "fanaticism," suggesting extremism but not necessarily insanity, described the man Wise met and gave him what he needed politically. Wise insisted, "They are themselves mistaken who take him to be a madman." Brown was "a bundle of the best nerves I ever saw, cut and thrust and bleeding in bonds. He is a man of clear head, of courage, fortitude, and simple ingenuousness. He is cool, collected, and indomitable . . . fanatic, vain, and garrulous, but firm, truthful, and intelligent."[25] Wise went on to describe Brown as no more crazy than the next New Englander. This just was what transcendentalism looked like. Appeals to the "higher law" would end in religiously motivated violence—violence without state sanction—which Wise lifted up as the defining mark of fanaticism.

Brown appealed to a higher law to challenge the state's monopoly on violence. Wise answered with a liturgy of sovereignty that defended, displayed, and produced the state's right to legitimate violence. Wise worked hard to make sure that the Commonwealth of Virginia was at the center of this liturgy. Jurisdiction over Brown's case was not initially clear. Much of Harpers Ferry, including the arsenal and armory, was on federal land. And federal troops had been the ones to capture Brown. But the sovereignty of states was one of the pressing issues of the day, and Wise moved quickly, and without any real opposition from the federal government, to assert Virginia's rightful jurisdiction in this case. He also took pains to protect Brown from the vigilantes who wanted to lynch him. Neither the mob nor the United States would usurp Virginia's role.

Wise declared a kind of martial law, ordering the military to take over the Winchester and Potomac railroads, restrict civilian traffic, and detain strangers. He reasserted the boundaries of the state, posting militia along the borders and warning the governors of Pennsylvania, Maryland, and Ohio that Virginians would repel invaders and drive them back across state lines. Wise planned an even more dramatic display of Virginia's sovereignty at the execution. He had the scaffold for Brown built in an empty field that allowed clear views of any force attempting a rescue—and, not coincidentally, of the artillery, cavalry, and fifteen hundred infantrymen assembled in formation around the scaffold. Viewers got the message. David Hunter Strother, the Virginia-born illustrator who published under the name Porte Crayon, commented, "No man capable of reflection could have witnessed that scene without being deeply impressed with the truth that then and there was exhibited, not the vengeance of an outraged people, but the awful majesty of the law."[26] Brown was not killed as a criminal or an enemy soldier. He was executed as a fanatic (see Figure 1.2).

Wise's depiction of Brown offered an early example of what became a venerable tradition of interpreting Brown as a fanatic. At the time Wise offered it, the diagnosis of "fanatic" was shared widely across the South and among proslavery sympathizers in the North. Moderate Republicans like Tilton and Greeley initially endorsed a variation of this view that stressed Brown's mental illness. As war came, though, and as sectional tensions hardened, more and more Northerners came to remember Brown as a martyr for freedom. This view dominated the North for more than a decade, but it began to slip with the end of Reconstruction and the steady elaboration of Jim Crow segregation. Change accelerated in the last years of the nineteenth century, as white leaders in both the North and the South became more interested in building national unity than promoting racial equality. Even white leaders of the Social

FIGURE 1.2 Execution of John Brown, from the *New York Illustrated News*, December 10, 1859. Periodicals Collection, West Virginia State Archives.

Gospel Movement had little to say about the old man. Social Gospel preachers like Washington Gladden and Walter Rauschenbusch were in many ways the heirs of Northern white liberal Protestant ministers like Theodore Parker and Thomas Wentworth Higginson—the people who had done so much to establish Brown as a martyr. But Gladden and Rauschenbusch did not continue this part of the liberal Protestant tradition. They scarcely mentioned Brown at all, and when they did, they treated him with great ambivalence. In his *Recollections*, for instance, Gladden made clear that Brown had been working for the right cause—but that he had used "fanatical" means.[27] By this Gladden did not mean simply that Brown had used violence. While Gladden described himself as a "pacifist," he was clear that he did not seek "peace at any price."[28] Violent means *were* an option for Gladden. What made Brown a fanatic was his use of violence outside the rule of law. As the twentieth century began, even white liberals who opposed slavery could label Brown a fanatic.

Historian Sean Wilentz displayed the enduring power of this line of interpretation almost one hundred years after Gladden. In his 2005 review of David Reynolds's biography of Brown, Wilentz rejects talk of Brown as freedom fighter and argues instead that Brown must be remembered as a fanatic. Wilentz shows no sympathy with slaveholders. On the contrary, in this review and in a distinguished scholarly career, Wilentz has repeatedly set forth a vision of a deeply democratic society. But this democratic vision has no place for Old John Brown. In his review essay Wilentz reminds readers that Brown was cited as an inspiration by the Unabomber, Timothy McVeigh, and many other domestic terrorists. Wilentz does not hesitate to extend that label to Brown, calling him an example of a long line of "righteous American terrorists." The contrast, Wilentz writes, is not between moderate and radical. "The contrast posed by Brown is between a savage, heedless politics of purity and a politics of the possible." Brown was a fanatic. And the mark of his fanaticism was his religiously motivated violence.[29]

The view of Brown as a fanatic has come to subsume more clinical debates about his mental state. Republicans of Brown's era had hoped that a diagnosis of mental illness might point to a possibility in which Brown was labeled neither as freedom fighter nor fanatic but as politically irrelevant madman. Debates about Brown's mental state continue, sometimes in absurd forms, but they no longer hold out the possibility of a diagnosis that would deny his political significance. And that political significance makes even a mentally ill Brown into a fanatic. Clinical psychologist Kenneth R. Carroll, for instance, asked three experts on Brown to take the Minnesota Multiphasic Personality Inventory (MMPI-2) as if they were Brown. The results, Carroll argues in a 2005 essay, suggest that Brown should be evaluated for bipolar affective disorder (with some possibility that he might be diagnosed as having schizophrenia, paranoid type). But this diagnosis does not render Brown a "private man," as Greeley had hoped 150 years before. On the contrary, Carroll concludes that Brown "tumbled headlong into the vortex. And, for good or ill, pulled the world in after him."[30] The clinical diagnosis of mental illness has become entirely compatible with the more overtly political label of fanatic. The framing question of contemporary historians James West Davidson and Mark Hamilton Lytle makes this shift clear: "Was Brown a heroic martyr—a white man in a racist society with the courage to lay down his life on behalf of his black brothers and the principles of the Declaration of Independence? Or was he an emotionally unbalanced fanatic whose taste for wanton violence propelled the nation toward avoidable tragedy?"[31] The possibility that Brown was "emotionally unbalanced" does not open up a third dimension to the frame. Mental illness is entirely compatible with the religiously motivated violence that has come to define the category of fanatic.

A parallel tradition naming Brown as "freedom fighter" runs this same 150-year course. It began with Brown himself. Brown adamantly rejected any suggestion that he was insane. He resisted his lawyers' attempts to introduce the issue at trial. And when a bystander to an interview said that he thought Brown was "fanatical," Brown snapped back, "And I think you are fanatical. 'Whom the gods would destroy they first make mad,' and you are mad."[32] Brown cast himself not as a fanatic but as the sane heir to the American Revolution. This argument involved a willful forgetting of the facts that it was the British who gave weapons to enslaved people during the war and the revolutionaries who established slavery even more firmly in its aftermath. Brown overwhelmed these facts with countless appeals to the Declaration of Independence as a precedent for his politics. He even composed a "Declaration of Liberty" that borrowed liberally from the 1776 document in both form and content. Brown also sent raiders to the home of Lewis Washington, great-grandnephew of George Washington, in part so that they could capture a sword that Frederick the Great had supposedly given to the first president. Brown carried Washington's sword throughout the fighting on October 17 and 18. Prior to the raid, Brown had made arrangements for the gravestone of his grandfather, Captain John Brown, to be brought to North Elba so that he could be buried under it. The older

Captain Brown had died in the Revolution, and his stone told that tale, complete with a death date of 1776. His abolitionist grandson asked to be buried under that same stone, with his own name and dates carved upon it. Brown was seeking to be inscribed into the legacy of revolutionary violence that had founded the country (see Figure 1.3).

FIGURE 1.3 Tombstone inscribed with the names of Captain John Brown (d. 1776); his grandson, John Brown (d. 1859); and his great-grandson, Owen Brown (d. 1859). Photo © Joyce M. Ranieri, Northern New York Tombstone Transcription Project.

Brown's strongest supporters sought to do this same work of transcription in their speeches. Frederick Douglass, likely nearly every African American, rejected the idea that Brown was mad. In an 1859 essay he argued that Brown's civilized treatment of his captives showed a humane man in his right mind. "It is an appalling fact in the history of the American people," Douglass continued, "that they have so far forgotten their own heroic age, as readily to accept the charge of insanity against a man who has imitated the heroes of Lexington, Concord and Bunker Hill." Brown was not mad; he was a patriot.[33] Thoreau, too, made Brown the heir of revolutionary violence, saying that Brown "was like the best of those who stood at Concord Bridge once, on Lexington Common, and on Bunker Hill, only he was firmer and higher principled than any that I have chanced to hear of as there."[34] Even a Quaker supporter, while ambivalent about Brown's use of carnal weapons, praised him as better than George Washington. Washington had resisted a mere tax for seven bloody years. Brown, in comparison, had killed far fewer people in the name of a much higher cause. He was not just a freedom fighter in the American tradition. He was even better than his revolutionary forebears.[35]

If people like Douglass and Thoreau connected Brown to the nation's past, the "John Brown Song" connected him to the nation's present and future. The song's origins are obscure, but it was likely sung first in 1861 by troops at Fort Warren. Soon soldiers throughout the Union army sang variations on the song:

John Brown's body lies a mouldering in the grave,
John Brown's body lies a mouldering in the grave,
John Brown's body lies a mouldering in the grave.
His soul's marching on!

CHORUS.
Glory Hally, Hallelujah! Glory Hally, Hallelujah!
Glory Hally, Hallelujah!
His soul's marching on!

He's gone to be a soldier in the army of our Lord, (3×)
His soul's marching on!

Chorus: Glory Hally, Hallelujah! Glory Hally, Hallelujah!
Glory Hally, Hallelujah!
His soul's marching on!

John Brown's knapsack is strapped upon his back, (3×)
His soul's marching on!

Chorus: Glory Hally, Hallelujah! Glory Hally, Hallelujah!
Glory Hally, Hallelujah!
His soul's marching on!

His pet lamps [lambs] will meet him on the way, - (3×)
They go marching on!

Chorus: Glory Hally, Hallelujah! Glory Hally, Hallelujah!
Glory Hally, Hallelujah!
They go marching on!

They will hang Jeff Davis to a tree! (3×)
As they march along!

Chorus: Glory Hally, Hallelujah! Glory Hally, Hallelujah!
Glory Hally, Hallelujah!
As they march along!

Now, three rousing cheers for the Union! (3×)
As we are marching on!

Chorus: Glory Hally, Hallelujah! Glory Hally, Hallelujah!
Glory Hally, Hallelujah!
Hip, hip, hip, hip Hurrah![36]

In the song Brown was not just a martyr but the risen Christ. "Glory Hally, Hallelujah" offered up an Easter shout. Brown's body may have been a mouldering in the grave, but, the soldiers sang, his soul was raised to new life in and as the Union army. He strapped a knapsack upon his back. Like a good shepherd, he freed enslaved people that the soldiers described as his "pet lambs." Together they would kill Jeff Davis. Brown's own description of violence as part of a divine purgation was nowhere to be found. It was displaced by language that justified violence by locating it in relation to a just cause. John Brown's body was not left in the ground as a blood atonement for sin but raised to new life in the freedom fighters of the Union army. It served as both the "seed" from which that army grew, in Thoreau's words,[37] and a model that taught soldiers how to make sense of their own suffering bodies and the suffering and dying bodies of the men beside them. The song connected soldiers not only to a good cause but also to a social entity—what Kantorowicz called a political body—that would live beyond their death. Singing "John Brown's Body," soldiers not only remembered Brown as a freedom fighter but claimed that label for themselves. As freedom fighters, they could kill and die as part of a resurrected body that lived for a righteous cause.[38]

The great African American Social Gospel leader Reverdy Ransom continued this line of interpretation decades after Brown's death. In the same years that Gladden and Rauschenbusch were silent or ambivalent about Brown, African American leaders kept his cult very much alive. In 1904 W. E. B. Du Bois led a group in founding the Niagara Movement at Harpers Ferry. At the second annual meeting of that group, held again at Harpers Ferry, Ransom preached a sermon on "The Spirit of John Brown."[39] Ransom compared Harpers Ferry to other "historic and sacred" sites like Mount Sinai, Calvary, the Jordan River, Thermopylae, Waterloo, Gettysburg, and—in a striking contemporary reference—Manila Bay (92). "Men like John Brown," Ransom said, "appear only once or twice in a thousand years." He compared Brown to Moses, "the prophets of ancient Israel," Cromwell, and Touissant L'Ouverture (93). Brown was given a "God-appointed task," Ransom said. "He could not choose his course; the hand of the Almighty was upon him" (95, 93). He was sent for the sake of the nation (94). And he armed the "slaves to rise and strike for their freedom" (95). "John Brown's body lies moldering in the tomb," Ransom said, "and his soul goes marching on" (96).

> The dreams of this dreamer at last found fulfillment as his soul went marching on in the Proclamation of Emancipation, in the Thirteenth Amendment to the Constitution, abolishing slavery, the Fourteenth Amendment, bestowing citizenship, and the Fifteenth Amendment, giving the elective franchise to the Negro to protect and defend his citizenship and rights under the Constitution and laws. (96–97)

If those reforms have fallen on hard times in recent years, Ransom said, the "soul of John Brown" lived on in the African Americans "who are aggressively fighting for their rights" (100).

> The gage of battle has been thrown down. The lines are clearly drawn; the supremacy of the Constitution has been challenged. In fighting for his rights the Negro defends the nation. His weapons are more powerful than pikes and Sharp's rifles which John Brown sought to place in his hands at Harpers Ferry. He has the Constitution, the courts, the ballot, the power to organize, to protest, to resist. (100)

Brown lived on, Ransom said, in the freedom fighters who would use the full moral and coercive powers of the law to win the rights of a people and save the soul of a nation.

A string of contemporary historians have given fresh emphasis to an understanding of John Brown as freedom fighter. Authors like Louis DeCaro and David Reynolds have located Brown in a long line of people who have fought for full equality for people of every race.[40] Like the soldiers who sang of Brown as they marched, these historians have named a fundamental continuity between Brown's raid and the prosecution of the war by federal troops. They extend that continuity to include leaders like Du Bois and Ransom, who fought against Jim Crow, and the civil rights leaders and national guardsmen who helped end legal segregation in the 1950s, 1960s, and 1970s. Seen as part of this line, they argue, Brown's violence was not fanatical. It was even more than a means that was justified by the goodness of its end. Because it was continuous with violent means used by the state to seek the same end, the violence of John Brown—like the violence of soldiers in the Revolution—can be grafted in to the legitimacy that supports state violence. Thus, Reynolds argues in an essay published in the *New York Times* on the 150th anniversary of Brown's hanging, Brown was not a fanatical enemy of the state. He should instead be regarded as one of "our national heroes."[41] As a freedom fighter, he is not just a hero of a social movement, or a particular religious community, or a race. He is a hero of the *nation*.

An 1889 debate between Frederick Douglass Jr. and T. Thomas Fortune made clear the degree to which Brown, as freedom fighter, had already been assimilated into the history of the state. Douglass proposed that African American people should raise money to build a monument to Brown. Fortune, the editor of the *New York Age*, one of the nation's most influential black newspapers, disagreed. He argued that African Americans should instead raise money for a monument to Nat Turner. While Brown was worthy, Fortune wrote, Turner was more likely to be forgotten. The memory of John Brown was less precarious because "his memory is part of the history of the government."[42] Any visit today to Harpers Ferry, North Elba, or Osawatomie—all marked by state-sponsored monuments—gives evidence for Fortune's point. In a nation dedicated to freedom, a freedom fighter can be incorporated into the political body. This incorporation, more than any ethical calculations of means and ends, connects the violence of the freedom fighter with the deepest sources of legitimacy behind and within the state.

Critique of Violence

For more than 150 years people have argued whether John Brown should be understood as freedom fighter or fanatic. My purpose in this book is not to decide that debate but to venture a critique of it. This critique begins immanently, in what Theodor Adorno called "felt contact" with its object. It seeks to describe the often-invisible structures of the ways we think about Brown's violence, to account for those structures, and to trace their unacknowledged consequences. Such critique brings taken-for-granted categories—like freedom fighter and fanatic—into view as objects of thought. To bring something into view is not necessarily to dissolve it. But it is to name it as made, not given. Such critique means, in Giorgio Agamben's phrase, "to return appearance itself to appearance, to cause appearance itself to appear."[43]

"Freedom fighter" and "fanatic" can seem to exhaust the field of options for interpreting Brown. They seem to create a wide field, presenting themselves as very different and even mutually exclusive. But this focus on the differences between them misses two much deeper features they have in common.

First, both categories assume that violence can be justified only through appeal to moral obligations defined in relation to this-worldly human flourishing. Both assume a kind of *disenchantment* of violence such that moral reasoning about violence must take place within what Charles Taylor has called an "immanent frame." An immanent frame is elastic enough to expand to include consequentialist, deontological, or virtue-centered forms of moral reasoning. What matters is not the form of moral reasoning but the focus on goods, goals, and virtues that fit with intramundane accounts of the good. An immanent frame can even accommodate theological reasoning that gives warrants or motives for particular commitments. What defines the relevant kind of immanence is not the *source* of the commitment but the this-worldly nature of the *content* of the commitment. What an immanent frame cannot contain is reasoning about violence that cannot be translated into concern for some sort of this-worldly flourishing—especially if that reasoning leads to conclusions that run counter to existing accounts of what it means to flourish in this world. An immanent frame can make room for a defense of human rights rooted in a belief that every human being is created in the image of God. It can make room for just war traditions that include roots in religion, realpolitik, or both. It can even make sense of a prudential pacifism grounded in a belief that violence leads only to more violence. But it cannot comprehend commitments to nonviolence that make no earthly sense. It is appalled by biblical narratives of holy war. An immanent frame cannot make room for rituals that impose hardships designed to share in an atonement God has made if those hardships do not promise to "improve" the self or its this-worldly relationships in this age. An immanent frame cannot accommodate the shedding of blood to purge a nation of its sins.

Both those who have called Brown a freedom fighter and those who have called him a fanatic in recent years have tended to work within this immanent frame. They have shared a sense of the disenchantment of violence. Those who have called Brown a freedom fighter have often appealed to a kind of consequentialism in their arguments. They have said he was right that slavery was a terrible wrong, that the violence he used was justified by the lack of other options, that his violence was proportionate to the wrong he resisted, and that his plan had a reasonable chance of some kind of success. Those who have called Brown a fanatic have tended to pay more attention to deontological constraints, insisting on the need for rightful authority, the rule of law, or even a complete ban on what Brown's Quaker correspondent called "carnal weapons." But both sides have engaged in moral reasoning that is intelligible within an immanent frame. This is true even when they have cited theological reasons for their ethical commitments, as Reverdy Ransom and Washington Gladden did on opposite sides of the question. Both sides have shared a sense that violence has to be justified within the language of immanent moral obligation. It is just that one side has believed that they could offer that kind of justification for Brown, and the other has not.

A second shared conviction is perhaps even more striking. Both sides have assumed the state's monopoly on legitimate violence. This is obvious in the case of those who have labeled Brown a fanatic. Wise executed Brown in a ritual performance designed to reproduce state sovereignty. Gladden and Wilentz believed in Brown's cause, but the fact that he took up arms without the sanction of the state, and for reasons that exceeded any immanent frame, pushed him beyond the pale for them.

Brown's defenders might have disagreed with the verdicts of Wise, Gladden, and Wilentz, but they have tended to share their opponents' assumption that the state is the seat of legitimacy for violence. Thoreau and Douglass justified Brown's violence by writing him into the national narrative. The "John Brown Song" described Brown's body as raised to new life in federal troops. Reverdy Ransom preached about the spirit of John Brown rolling on through the army and then the Constitution. David Reynolds extended this history, adding more laws, and more federal troops, to the line that flows from Brown.

Legitimation flows in two directions in these stories of Brown as freedom fighter. It is because the state eventually took up his cause that Brown is justified. And it is because of Brown's martyrdom that the state's cause has a sacred quality that can demand further sacrifice from citizens now. Again, the disagreement between those who have seen Brown as a freedom fighter and those who have seen him as a fanatic is not about whether the state is the center of legitimate violence. It is about whether Brown can be assimilated to this center.

The ironies of the advocacy offered by Brown's defenders should not be missed. Brown sometimes spoke in the language of this-worldly moral obligation. But that language, for Brown, was never separated from language that burst the bounds of any immanent frame. When Brown founded the League of Gileadites, he did not mean to recall a biblical story that proved the strategic value of a small, disciplined army. He meant to create a living antitype of a band whose poverty and purity would allow it to show forth the power of God. And when he spoke of the blood needed to purge the land, he was not making a claim about the means necessary to accomplish some this-worldly project. He was working instead within an irreducibly theological language of purgation, satisfaction, and atonement. Brown's defenders have tended to skip over this language or translate it into the dialect of immanent ethics.

In a related fashion, those who have defended Brown have seemed to forget that he raided a federal arsenal in order to steal weapons to give to people who were forbidden by law to possess any kind of weapon. As both strategic and symbolic action, the Harpers Ferry raid was a direct assault on the state's monopoly on violence. But Brown's chief defenders have almost always cast him as a freedom fighter whose violence was legitimate because of its continuity with the violence that had established the state and with violence the state would pursue in the Civil War and beyond. Swaddled in the Revolution before and the Civil War after, Brown's violence becomes legitimate in a story about the state's founding, redemption, and ongoing sanctification. This process has not been named so much as performed. Thus Brown's defenders have tended to mystify and endorse the state's monopoly on legitimate violence—and so sacralize the very account of legitimacy that Brown resisted.

That two sides could hold such significant commitments in common without being aware of what they share begins to suggest the power of these ideas. These two convictions—that violence should be evaluated within the bounds of immanent ethics alone, and that the state should hold a monopoly on violence—are all the more powerful because they rarely become explicit topics of debate. Instead, they set the boundaries of debate. Often invisible, at least for all practical purposes, they come together in a powerful constellation in the modern social imaginary. While the two display elective affinities, and while they arose together historically, they do not logically entail one another. They are two distinct concepts. The connections between them are contingent and historical. The story of what John Brown's critics and defenders have made of him shows some of the ways those connections have been made in time. But the historicity and contingency of the connections between the two concepts do not make them any less powerful. The constellation of ethical violence and the state's monopoly on violence has a strong hold on our collective imagination, strong enough to bend even our memories of John Brown into its orbit.

Performing a critique of the power of this constellation—making its appearance appear—reveals the question that is most deeply at issue in these debates about Brown. Both sides share a commitment to the state's monopoly on violence that is legitimated by reasons that work within the bounds of immanent ethics alone. But of course the United States, the bearer of this legitimacy, was itself founded by an act of extralegal violence in the American Revolution. The logic of both those who see Brown as freedom fighter and those who see him as fanatic make room for this revolutionary founding as an *exception*, a singular event. The question, then, is whether John Brown can participate in that exception, whether the mantle of Bunker Hill can be stretched to cover Harpers Ferry. This question cannot be answered within the frame of an immanent ethics. Its structure mirrors that of old questions in Christian theology. Can a later event share in the exception made for the founding? Is the age of miracles over? Is the canon of prophecy closed? What does it mean to participate in the risen body of Christ? One need not have a stake in such questions—one need not even think that they have meaningful content—in order to acknowledge that their structure gives the deep structure of the prevailing debates about John Brown. Critique of ethical arguments about John Brown, then, opens into political theology.

The Touchstone in the Fire

In naming the need for a political theology of John Brown, I do not mean to call for a better account of the significance of religion for politics, as if what we needed was a prescription for the right relation of spheres of society. Nor do I mean to call for some "religious perspective" on particular moral, political, or policy positions. I seek instead to tease out the dimensions of political life that already, on their own terms, exceed any kind of immanent ethics. I mean, like Ernst Kantorowicz describing the king's two bodies, to name some places where concepts most thoroughly elaborated in theological discourse are already at work in political discourse. And I mean to show that attending to the theological nature of these concepts can enable clearer insight into contemporary social formations.[44]

In this book I seek not only to describe the political theologies at work in the world but also to offer the beginnings of a political theology of my own. That offering depends on a small but significant shift in the political theology that is latent in the debate about whether Brown is a freedom fighter or a fanatic. Instead of taking the state's sovereignty for granted, I assume the sovereignty of God. And instead of asking whether Brown can be inscribed into a narrative of state violence, I ask what it would mean for Brown—and for the America he has so often been taken to represent—to be part of the story of God's redeeming work in the world.

John Brown revealed the deep contradiction in the heart of a nation whose founding documents committed it to the idea that all people are created equal and to a system of race-based chattel slavery. If that contradiction came into existence before Brown was born, and if others had named it with courage and clarity before Brown ever addressed the public, Brown's testimony in and after the raid on Harpers Ferry made it plain as never before. "If John Brown did not end the war that ended slavery," Frederick Douglass said, "he did at least begin the war that ended slavery. . . . When John Brown stretched forth his arm the sky was cleared. The time for compromises was gone—the armed hosts of freedom stood face to face over the chasm of a broken Union—and the clash of arms was at hand."[45] Brown made the founding fissure unbearable. His life and death precipitated a storm of violence that would consume more than six hundred thousand lives. William Allingham's poem about Brown as "the Touchstone" concluded with a vision of this power.

> But though they slew him with their swords,
> And in the fire the Touchstone burned,
> Its doings could not be overturned,
> Its undoings restored.

What the Touchstone revealed could not be hidden again. What it undid could not be restored. But one could hope that it might be redeemed. This book is an exercise in such hope.

2 THE FATE OF LAW

ON THE DAY OF HIS EXECUTION John Brown handed a piece of paper to his guards that read, "I John Brown am now quite *certain* that the crimes of this *guilty, land: will* never be purged away; but with Blood. I had *as I now think: vainly* flattered myself that without *verry much* bloodshed; it might be done."[1] Brown's note was soaked through with the language of sacrifice, atonement, and ritual purification—the language of divine violence. Brown spoke and wrote like this throughout his life. He interpreted both the violence he performed and the violence performed on him in theological ways. He offered no systematic theology of violence. His thoughts on violence were vague, shifting, and allusive. But he always thought about violence in relation to something more than immanent chains of cause and effect. And he always thought about violence in ways that exceeded ethical obligations to promote the flourishing of people in this world.

Talk of divine violence grates hard against the sensibilities of modern political formations. These formations have taken so many shapes and accommodated such a wide range of histories, ideologies, economic systems, and styles of governance that it can be misleading to speak of them as sharing any kind of essence. But one can speak of a family resemblance marked especially by three features: some kind of differentiation between political and religious institutions, a monopoly for the state on the legitimate use of violence, and the subordination of violence to the rule of law. These three features have evolved to complement one another.[2] And when John Brown attacked Harpers Ferry in obedience to a higher law, he attacked all three of them.

Brown did not set out to oppose the political formations that were taking shape in the United States in the years before the Civil War. He sought to destroy slavery. But the institutions and ideas of slavery were so deeply entwined with the political formations that opposing slavery meant opposing those formations.

Brown defied each of the three key traits that mark the family resemblance I have just named. In the course of resisting slavery, Brown called upon English and American Puritan traditions to reject the differentiation of religious and political spheres. He did so with a fury that reminded his contemporaries of Oliver Cromwell, whom they took for an icon of the fusion of theology and politics. The abolitionist Wendell Phillips called Brown "a regular Cromwellian, dug up from two centuries." James Hanway, who followed Brown in Kansas, made the identification even stronger, calling Brown "the Oliver Cromwell of America."[3] Brown did not reject the comparison. He wanted his fighting bands to combine military and religious discipline in ways that recalled Cromwell's New Model Army. He wrote a provisional constitution for the United States that promised to bring the laws of the nation in line with God's law.[4] Brown defied not only the differentiation of religious and political institutions but also the state's monopoly on violence. He raided Harpers Ferry, a federal arsenal, to steal rifles to give to enslaved people who were forbidden by the state to carry weapons at all. It is hard to imagine a more direct assault—both materially and symbolically—on the state's monopoly on the legitimate means of violence. Brown rejected the rule of law with similar intensity. He did not just defy the rule of the particular laws that happened to be on the books in Virginia in 1859. In appealing to a "higher law" to justify his actions, he held open the perennial possibility of a binding law beyond the law of any state.

Because Brown opposed deep and defining features of the political order, he was not imprisoned as if he were an ordinary criminal or even an enemy combatant. He was executed as a threat to the foundations of society. His talk of divine violence only confirmed the need for his execution, for divine violence is the necessarily excluded category against which modern political formations have implicitly defined themselves.

In this chapter I argue that modern states, in the process of excluding any talk of divine violence, have tended to occlude their own mythologies and so legitimate their own brands of sacred violence. I argue that a discourse of political theology with reasoning about divine violence at its center can help break this spell. In the next chapter I try to refine a critical concept of divine violence that can do that work. In arguing for this understanding of divine violence, I do not mean to call for a better myth, as some theological critics of modernity have. I argue instead for "a dialectical disenchanting of disenchantment,"[5] a critique of the political by the light of a redemption that is not yet fully realized. I argue that we need a kind of political theology to keep secular politics secular.

The Violence of the Great Separation

The secular state's monopoly on the legitimate means of violence receives one of its most sophisticated recent defenses in Mark Lilla's book *The Stillborn God* (2007). Lilla sees political theology—and the bloodshed he argues it brings with it—as the great and perennial threat to peaceful social orders. Lilla begins his argument with an etiology that attributes the terrible violence in the last six centuries of European history to Christianity's ambiguity about the relation between religious and secular powers. A religion like Islam, Lilla writes, is very clear: the political order is subordinate to religious authority. But Christianity's emphasis on the age to come has made it less clear about the politics of this present age. This ambiguity touched off a spiral of violence in Europe:

> Christian fanaticism and intolerance incited violence; violence set secular and religious leaders against one another; and the more violent and fearful political life became, the more fanatical and intolerant Christians became. Christendom had found itself in a vicious theological-political cycle unknown to any previous civilization.[6]

Christianity's ambiguity opened the door to conflict. And its sense that eternal life was at stake in the actions of this world, Lilla writes, accelerated the conflict. "The reason human beings in war commit acts no animal would is, paradoxically, because they believe in God" (84). Religion, especially Christianity, drives violence beyond the bounds of decency—and law.

In Lilla's account, it was the genius of Thomas Hobbes to discern this dynamic and undo it by developing "habits of thinking and talking about politics exclusively in human terms, without appeal to divine revelation or cosmological speculation" (5). Hobbes found ways to "change the subject" of political thought from "God and his nature" to "man and his religious nature" (78). This shift marked what Lilla calls the "Great Separation" of political and theological thought. It is a separation, he writes, that defines the exceptional nature of the modern West. And its emblem, its crown jewel, is the juridical ordering of violence that divides religion from the state and then consolidates violence under the rule of law within the state. This Great Separation is fragile and contingent, Lilla writes, always vulnerable to a theological impulse that seems to be an enduring part of human life. Thus, if the state's juridical ordering of violence is coming undone—and it is currently under enormous pressure—Lilla's story knows in advance the source of the problem and the nature of the solution.[7] The erosion of this order must be due to a crossing of the theological impulse back into political life. And the best response must be to hew again the cleft between theological and political thought.

Lilla rightly sees that challenges to the state's monopoly on the legitimate use of violence often proceed by drawing on reasons or institutions associated with religious traditions like Christianity, Islam, or Judaism. But he writes as if all the threats to the present constellation of state, violence, and law come from outside that constellation—and especially from religious actors who take up violence in the names of their gods. Lilla misses challengers to the modern state that are not especially "theological" in their motivation or operation. More subtly, he misses the ways that the state itself has contributed to the erosion of political formations in which a secular state holds a monopoly on violence within the rule of law.

Some challenges to the state's monopoly on legitimate violence *have* come from outside the state. Terrorist networks may be the most visible form of these challenges, but they are not alone. From pirates in Somalia to drug cartels in Mexico to warlords in Afghanistan, nonstate actors around the world possess capacities to resist, elude, corrupt, and defeat state forces. Even when armed groups pose no significant military threat, their mere existence can amount to a challenge to the legitimacy of the state's monopoly on violence. In some cases the violence of nonstate actors enjoys a kind of local legitimacy, especially in the zones where they have the greatest capacity for violence. But not all of these challengers to the secular state's monopoly on legitimate violence within the rule of law are "religious" in the sense that worries Lilla. And simply enforcing a differentiation of theology and politics, as Lilla proposes, would not begin to address all the problems they create.

Lilla's proposal would also fail to address significant challenges to the state's monopoly on the legitimate use of violence within the rule of law that have originated *within* the state. That monopoly has eroded as states have tolerated or supported violence by nonstate actors. The government of Iran, for instance, has long depended on the Basij militia for violent action against protesters. The most radical Israeli settlers and Hamas militia members have ambivalent relationships to official state powers. The United States has outsourced state violence to private contractors for prisons, security details, and a widening array of military services. "Stand your ground" laws in the United States devolve legitimate violence even further, to individual gun owners. I do not mean to suggest a moral equivalence between any of these phenomena. I only mean to say that they demonstrate a broad, varied pattern in which states have participated in blurring the lines that would mark their monopolies on the legitimate means of violence.

Modern political formations are unraveling not only at the edges of the state's monopoly on violence but also—and perhaps most significantly—at the edges of the rule of law. States' exercise of violence beyond the ordinary confines of law has been most obvious when a government has turned violence on its own citizens, as in Syrian security forces' devastation of the city and people of Homs. State violence beyond law can also be seen in the active sponsorship of terrorism by some states, as in the case of the former Libyan regime's support for the attack that downed Pan Am flight 103.

The United States has also contributed to the unbundling of state violence and the rule of law. In reacting to the terrorist attacks of September 11, 2001, the administration of George W. Bush repeatedly used the state's coercive powers in ways that pressed or crossed legal boundaries. The administration claimed the right to imprison US citizens without observing the Constitution's full range of provisions against wrongful detention. Its National Security Agency violated the Foreign Intelligence Surveillance Act by monitoring phone calls and e-mail messages without obtaining the proper warrants (a practice the Obama administration sought to continue). Its Justice Department authored a series of memos that tried to justify practices of detention and interrogation that violated national and international laws against torture. Other internal memos even made a case for using the military within the United States against US citizens. With such moves the state itself threatens the hold of law on violence.[8]

It can be tempting to tie these threats to "religion" in some way. George W. Bush did sometimes speak about the war on terror as a kind of cosmic struggle between good and evil. He displayed a personal religiosity that irritated many commentators. He welcomed the influence of evangelical, fundamentalist, and Pentecostal Christian leaders on both his policies and his party. And a series of policies—from support for so-called faith-based initiatives to an annual celebration of a National Day of Prayer at the White House—rightly aroused concerns about violations of the First Amendment's provision against the establishment of religion. Lilla's book emerged in the context of these concerns, and it shares their temperament.[9]

There are good reasons to worry about the role of bad theology in American political life. And there are certainly reasons to worry about state violence that exceeds the boundaries set by law. But it is not clear that purifying politics of all theological reasoning, as Lilla proposes, would reduce incidents of state violence beyond the rule of law. At a minimum, such a purge would leave intact the concerns for national security that have played such a significant role in recent actions that have gone beyond or even against the law.

Moreover, the ideal of separating religion and politics can generate its own reasons for violence. If, as Lilla argues, religion escalates violence into spirals that can destroy an entire culture, and if the separation of theology and politics is the defining achievement of Western civilization, and if that separation is at risk, then the United States and other countries would have reasons to engage in violence to sustain that civilization. The West would have reasons to cast people who refuse to separate theology and politics in roles that label them as both different and deficient. Such people would, almost by definition, be understood as unreasonable, impractical, fanatic. They would become the kind of people who "only understand force."[10] What William Cavanaugh calls the "myth of religious violence"

> serves to cast nonsecular social orders, especially Muslim societies, in the role of villain. *They* have not yet learned to remove the dangerous influence of religion from political life. *Their* violence is therefore irrational and fanatical. *Our* violence, being secular, is rational, peace making, and sometimes regrettably necessary to contain their violence. We find ourselves obliged to bomb them into liberal democracy.[11]

Strictly separating politics from theology does not just fail to solve the problem of extralegal violence. It can serve to underwrite new violence, especially violence to protect politics from religion and religion from politics. Bush himself invoked a version of this reasoning when he appealed to "religious freedom" as one of the justifications for the wars in Iraq and Afghanistan.[12] Enforcing the Great Separation can require extreme measures. It might even move a president to break the law.

The Limits of Law

Barack Obama campaigned as the opposite of any kind of holy warrior. In both rhetoric and policy, Obama has steadily narrowed the scope of a "global war on terror" to "war against Al-Qaeda and its allies." He has also abandoned talk of war in the name of freedom or democracy, grounding his policies in a "realism" that he associates with Reinhold Niebuhr.[13] Such realism fits well with the Great Separation Lilla describes. It separates theology and politics in ways that underscore the secular state's monopoly on the legitimate means of violence. But exactly that realism has led the Obama administration to continue to prosecute violence through means that strain the bounds of law. The Obama administration has pursued covert wars in Yemen and Somalia that do not fall under the ordinary legal procedures and reviews for armed conflict. While it has significantly reduced the number of "extraordinary renditions" of suspected terrorists to sites where US laws do not clearly apply, the Obama administration has continued to execute the renditions and so exercise force beyond law.[14] It has also broken significant legal precedents in killing at least three US citizens without trial. A pair of drone strikes in Yemen in 2011 killed radical Muslim cleric Anwar al-Awlaki; his associate, Samir Khan; and his son, Abdulrahman al-Awlaki.[15] Drone strikes against citizens of other countries have risen dramatically. While the practice is subject to review within the executive branch, it is not subject to the full range of authorizations and oversight that normally attend combat operations. All of these operations have continued without any talk of holy war. Realpolitik has led the Obama administration into violence at and beyond the frayed edges of law.[16]

At the same time, the Obama administration has articulated a strong and steady public commitment to the rule of law. In 2011, John O. Brennan, then assistant to the president for Homeland Security and Counterterrorism and director of the Central Intelligence Agency, concluded a speech on the administration's position with a strong statement of this position: "As a people, as a nation, we cannot—and we must not—succumb to the temptation to set aside our laws and our values when we face threats to our security, including and especially from groups as depraved as al-Qa'ida. We're better than that. We're better than them. We're Americans."[17] In Brennan's reasoning, commitment to the rule of law becomes the cornerstone not only of the administration's policy but also of national identity. It becomes what separates us from them.

The Obama administration has strained to reconcile this commitment to the rule of law with its extension of Bush-era policies that often moved beyond the law. In some significant cases the Obama administration has curtailed the practice in question to come more clearly within the bounds of law. Most notably, it has withdrawn the overwhelming majority of US troops from Iraq. It has also banned "enhanced interrogation techniques" that tortured detainees.

More commonly, though, the Obama administration has not curtailed practice so much as extended law and policy to include a limited version of the practice in question. It has stressed that such practices are not undertaken by executive fiat but according to clearly defined policies that have expanded the rule of law to cover new modes of violence. This commitment to eliminating violent exceptions to the rule of law has become the signature of the Obama administration's response to the ongoing possibility of terrorism. Articulated in both rhetoric and policy, this commitment has been presented as the defining distinction between the Obama administration and its predecessor. Emphasis on that distinction has been especially important when actions on the ground have not changed very much, as in the ongoing detentions at Guantánamo Bay. Even (or especially) when the practices have not changed, there is at least a drive to wrap them in law.

One might object to the content of the Obama administration's policies. Its policies directing the use of drones, for instance, have been criticized on both moral and strategic grounds. One might also object to the incompleteness of the administration's project, as practices beyond the rule of law continue. And one might object to what can look like the cynicism of the project, as the administration writes policies that move the frontier of law out to include practices that were once beyond it. I share many of these concerns, but I want to question the administration's vision on a more basic level. I want to question the drive to eliminate exceptions to the rule of law. As a rule of thumb, defined loosely and held pragmatically, a commitment to the rule of law can do much to prevent abuses. But there are good reasons—reasons a person committed to the long-term health of a liberal polity might hold—to resist the rule of law as an absolute principle that functions as a marker of identity.

The years since 9/11 have seen a dramatic expansion of laws and policies of every sort. The emergency created by the attacks has not been marked by the silence of law, as theorists indebted to Carl Schmitt might have imagined. These years have also not seen the emergence of a special set of laws designed to be turned on for a season and then turned off, as political theorists like Bruce Ackerman would suggest.[18] In a 2006 paper, Kim Lane Scheppele names this dynamic clearly. Scheppele argues that times of emergency are "times in which a great deal of new law is created, law that was not anticipated in advance of the emergency." Emergencies are, Scheppele says, "jurisgenerative." One need not expand this into a universal claim in order to say that it offers a good empirical description of processes within societies that value at least the appearance of the rule of law. It certainly describes the United States in the years since the 9/11 attacks. Scheppele explains the proliferation of laws with reference to the deliberative function of lawmaking. Law, she writes, is not just a set of policies to accomplish particular projects. It is more even than an existing moral order. Law is *the way the state talks to itself,* the means and medium by which the state reasons about its most basic questions.[19] Emergencies create particularly acute needs for that kind of deliberation. The events of 9/11 created just such a need, and both the Bush and Obama administrations have tried to meet that need with laws, policies, and guidelines of many kinds.

Law is a risky medium for deliberation, though, as it can be hard to take back a statutory statement once it has been uttered. In times of emergency, laws tend to expand state power—especially executive power—more than those powers will contract when the emergency has passed. Laws can function like a ratchet, moving more easily to increase executive power than to lower it to former levels. And laws can create precedents for actions that cannot be foreseen, let alone intended.

Concerns about this dynamic led early liberal theorists like John Locke, Alexander Hamilton, and William Blackstone to propose concepts of executive prerogative as mechanisms for responding to emergencies. In Locke's *Second Treatise on Government*, for example, he defines prerogative as the "power to act according to discretion, for the public good, without the prescription of the law, and sometimes even against it." Prerogative is necessary in some cases because lawmaking bodies might not be able to act quickly enough to respond to a situation appropriately. Even with ample time, lawmakers cannot foresee every relevant circumstance, so it is impossible "to make such laws as will do no harm, if they are executed with an inflexible rigour, on all occasions, and upon all persons that may come in their way."[20] Any system of laws enforced with perfect rigidity can become tyrannical, Locke writes, and executive prerogative is the best way to provide for exceptions.

Even with this pedigree, frank declarations of prerogative have not played a large role in the practice of the United States. Prerogative squares uneasily with commitments to the rule of law. Worse still for an American political conscience, it calls up echoes of monarchy. The United States has therefore tended to avoid stark forms of executive prerogative, preferring instead statutory delegations of power like the Emergency Act of 1795, passed in response to the Whiskey Rebellion, and the Alien and Sedition Acts of 1798, passed in fear of a revolution like the one in France. In the twentieth century, the Emergency

Banking Act (1933), the National Security Act (1947), the Defense Production Act (1950), and the National Emergencies Act (1976) all shared this basic form. The problem, as Clement Fatovic argues, is that such laws "tend to use the term *emergency* so loosely that they often end up expanding the conditions that might justify the use of enhanced government powers even when they aim to constrain executive power."[21] Seeking to contain prerogative within the rule of law, statutory delegations have, ironically, created precedents that have enhanced executive power. Portions of the Alien and Sedition Acts, for instance, are still on the books.

Justice Robert H. Jackson offered a powerful analysis of this danger in his dissent from the majority in *Korematsu v. United States*, the 1944 decision that upheld the wartime detention of US citizens of Japanese descent. For purposes of the decision, Jackson declared an agnosticism about the military necessity of Executive Order 9066, which commanded the internment. He focused his attention on the move to make the order compatible with law:

> A military order, however unconstitutional, is not apt to last longer than the military emergency. Even during that period, a succeeding commander may revoke it all. But once a judicial opinion rationalizes such an order to show that it conforms to the Constitution, or rather rationalizes the Constitution to show that the Constitution sanctions such an order, the Court for all time has validated the principle of racial discrimination in criminal procedure and of transplanting American citizens. The principle then lies about like a loaded weapon, ready for the hand of any authority that can bring forward a plausible claim of an urgent need. Every repetition imbeds that principle more deeply in our law and thinking and expands it to new purposes.[22]

With this dissent, Jackson traced the twists and turns in one of the tightest knots in the lived fabric of a liberal society. Commitment to the rule of law leads to a desire to eliminate exceptions. But situations arise in which actions that are not clearly legal by current standards come to seem necessary for the survival of the nation. It can be tempting to reconcile those two desires by expanding the law to cover the actions that seem necessary, as the Obama administration has done. But this can leave the new laws waiting "like a loaded weapon" for uses that cannot be imagined at the time. Ironically, a liberal society's desire to maintain the purity of its commitment to the rule of law can lure it into frameworks of law that undermine its core values. It might be better, Jackson suggested, to leave emergency actions outside the law.

Criticism of the internment of Japanese Americans can and should be mounted on other grounds. The policy was racist, as Justice Frank Murphy wrote in his dissent. And it was not necessary for national security. Acknowledging these facts does not invalidate Jackson's reasoning, however, if one can imagine the possibility of threats to the ongoing existence of a society that cannot be answered within its existing legal frameworks. Both the Bush administration and the Obama administration—and a broad, enduring majority of the American public—have seen terrorism as just such a threat. And the last decade has seen just such a statutory expansion of executive power.

As Jackson predicted, the expansion has come through unintended and ironic consequences. Civil liberties activists with the Center for Constitutional Rights won a significant case in 2004 with the Supreme Court's ruling in *Rasul v. Bush*, which established the jurisdiction of the US court system over the detention of foreign nationals at Guantánamo. This decision accelerated the state's conversation with itself through law. In response to the decision, Congress passed a series of laws in 2005 and 2006 that tried to replace ordinary habeas corpus rights for detainees with a system of military and judicial review. The Supreme Court struck down that system in *Boumediene v. Bush* (2008), insisting on the habeas corpus rights of foreign nationals in US custody. The Obama administration filed new briefs in the wake of *Boumediene*, resulting in a series of cases that have established a clear legal basis for detaining people associated with Al-Qaeda and the Taliban "until hostilities cease"—providing that certain burdens of evidence and procedure can be met. The more stringent standards have led to the release of some prisoners, but the deepest effect of this long conversation in law has been to secure the legal basis for indefinite detention at GTMO and other sites in the present and in the future. What once was an emergency measure without clear legal warrant is now established within the law.[23]

The outcome of challenges to indefinite detention can serve as synecdoche for the broader drift of aims and policies during the Obama administration. Concern for national security leads the administration to continue practices that had disputed legal status during the Bush administration. Concern for the rule of law leads the administration to expand policy and contract practice to make the two fit together. If the worst excesses are given up, the main policy is more firmly established not only as a measure for the present but also as a precedent for the future. This pattern has already, in Justice Jackson's words, left a lot of loaded weapons lying about.

Reason Not the Need

The drive to publish policies that will govern every aspect of practice not only sets dangerous precedents but also risks slipping into deeper forms of ideology. This desire to eliminate exceptions grows out of what Charles Taylor has called the "code fetishism" that is itself a product of the spirit of reform that developed especially in Western forms of Christianity.[24] Taylor describes the ways in which Protestant and Catholic Reformers, motivated by a desire to raise the standard of conduct by believers, wrenched norms out of complex forms of life and established them as codes for behavior. Sharing in this ethos, the Obama administration has moved to codify the practices of the war on terror. Both the making of exceptions to law and then the extensions of law that legitimate those exceptions have relied especially on the language of "necessity." And it is just this language that enables and obscures the ways these codes function and the assumptions that lie behind them.

Language of necessity has been at the center of codes crafted in response to 9/11 from the very beginning. The Authorization for Use of Military Force (AUMF) swept through Congress almost unanimously in the days following the 9/11 attacks. The resolution authorizes the president to

> use all necessary and appropriate force against those nations, organizations, or persons he determines planned, authorized, committed, or aided the terrorist attacks that occurred on September 11, 2011, or harbored such organizations or persons, in order to prevent any future acts of international terrorism against the United States by such nations, organizations, or persons.[25]

Talk of necessity might seem to limit the scope of action, allowing only what is necessary to accomplish a particular goal. But when the goal is as broad as preventing "any future acts of international terrorism against the United States" by the "nations, organizations, or persons" that the president determines were involved in the 9/11 attacks, the language of necessity becomes not a fence but a launching pad. And that is exactly how it has functioned. A codified logic of necessity allowed the Bush administration to go beyond the law in the name of the law.

The AUMF's legitimation of "all necessary and appropriate force" opened up a wide field of discretion for the Bush administration. The Obama administration has faced that same field and has not backed away from the logic of necessity. An unsigned, undated Department of Justice memo leaked through NBC News in February 2013 proposes to establish a "legal framework" for drone strikes against US citizens in countries with which the United States is not at war. It acknowledges that such strikes risk violating international laws governing armed conflict as well as constitutional divisions of power between branches of government and protections of due process for individuals. It then defends the legality of the strikes by appealing to multiple precedents, including, crucially, the AUMF of 2001. The Department of Justice memo cites the AUMF as if it were a precedent that restrained the power of the executive. But it uses the AUMF as the Bush administration did, as a law that invokes necessity to authorize the president to go beyond or even against existing law.[26]

The Department of Justice memo relies again on the logic of necessity in its invocation of General Order No. 100, which Abraham Lincoln's administration issued in 1863 as part of the escalation of conflict in the Civil War. The order, which enshrines a set of standards commonly known as the Lieber Code, defines a doctrine of "military necessity" as consisting "in the necessity of those measures which are indispensable for securing the ends of the war, and which are lawful according to the modern law and usages of war" (Art. 14). In the clause cited by the 2013 Department of Justice memo, the Lieber Code says that "military necessity admits of all direct destruction of life or limb of armed enemies" (Art. 15). Again, a precedent cited as a way of keeping actions within the rule of law opens the possibility of going beyond or against the law in the name of necessity-made-law.[27]

When laws are built with the trapdoor of necessity, staying within the box of law can become a trick that fools even the magician. The rapid expansion of laws can obscure but not change this reality. The proliferation of laws can also obscure the role of individual judgment in enacting the law. The drive to eliminate exceptions is driven in part by a republican suspicion of executive prerogative. The expansion of laws, and the insistence that even the president operate within them, promises to reduce the scope of individual judgment. The language of necessity might seem to restrict that scope still further. After all, if something is necessary, it is not chosen so much as imposed. But the AUMF uses language of necessity in ways that do not prescribe actions so much as pose questions. What is necessary to resist and punish those who had planned the attacks? Who is responsible for the attacks? What is necessary to prevent future attacks? The AUMF leaves each of these crucial practical questions to the president's discretion. The Bush administration answered these questions by launching wars in Iraq and Afghanistan, using "black sites" to interrogate suspected terrorists, and establishing the detention camp at Guantánamo Bay.

Seeing the presence of these decisions underscores the gap that is always present between law and action. That the Obama administration made different
decisions does not mean that it simply followed the law, for the most important law authorizing actions against terrorists does not give enough direction
to be "followed." It instead authorizes and demands judgment. Some degree of
decision is always involved, even when policies expand to close the gap, and
especially when those policies authorize the executive to do what is necessary.
Rhetoric focused on the rule of law can shelter these decisions from public
scrutiny and impede practices of democratic accountability.

Talk of necessity therefore can authorize the expansion of violence even
when it promises to limit violence. It can expand the scope of executive discretion even as it promises to set boundaries around it. But it truly slips into ideology, into jargon, when it starts to float free from the ground of explicit answers
to the question it contains within itself: necessary *for what*?

The 2013 Department of Justice memo avoids that question by citing precedents that use language of necessity without letting the language of necessity
creep into its own text. It draws on the authorizing power of necessity without
naming that power directly and so without opening the question of its ground.
The memo's sources are clearer. The AUMF authorizes whatever force is necessary to "prevent any future acts of international terrorism against the United
States" by the "nations, organizations, or persons" who played a role in the 9/11
attacks. The Lieber Code is even more direct: "To save the country is paramount to all other considerations" (Art. 5). As the Lieber Code makes clear,
the language of necessity makes the existence of the state itself an imperative
beyond law.

In a 1921 essay, "Critique of Violence," Walter Benjamin names the way that
such reasoning depends ultimately on a kind of fate (*Schicksal*). When a Great
Separation denies any higher purpose to the state, the state is just the order that
happens to prevail. It is the congealed spoils of past violence. Then, Benjamin
writes, "violence, violence crowned by fate, is the origin of law." And the law is
endlessly involved in "the representation of an order imposed by fate."[28] If the
state is just the accumulated results of past conflicts, and if preservation of the
state becomes the end that grounds necessity, then the fact of violence becomes
a kind of law, and the law, grounded in the need to preserve what fate has established, blurs into the fact of organized violence.

This blurring of the boundaries between law and violence undermines the
significance of keeping violence within the rule of law. That ideal depends on a

meaningful distinction between law and violence. For the rule of law to be able to contribute to the legitimacy of a political order, the law must be something other than the rules made by the people who happen to have the greatest capacity for violence when the laws were made. In order to legitimate violence, law must be something other than sedimented and mystified violence. But language of necessity imagines moments when the facts on the ground become the source and content of norms. Necessity smelts fact and norm into a single complex imperative. It therefore threatens the distinction between violence and law on which the legitimacy of the rule of law depends.[29]

Thus, dynamics *within* the modern state—reasons and institutions on what Mark Lilla identifies as the secular, political side of the Great Separation—have eroded the juridical ordering of violence just as surely as incursions from religious powers outside the state. Lilla's analysis obscures these dynamics. And his proposed remedy would not address them. If some of the dynamics that lead to violence beyond law are indigenous to the state, native to it exactly in its secularity, then purifying the state of religion will not prevent those dynamics from unfolding. On the contrary, insulation of the state from forms of reasoning rendered alien to it—including religious reasoning—can allow the state's logic of necessity to develop into a logic in which the state's own existence comes to be seen as the good that must be realized, the good that contains its own imperative. Such necessity underwrites the zones where fact and law dissolve into one another.

The potentially mythical nature of disenchanted political thought can be clarified through an analogy to Theodor Adorno's critique of positivism. Positivist social science holds out the promise of an objectivity free from the distortions of ideology. Like Lilla's purified political science, it refuses talk of any reality beyond the facts on the ground. It dissolves ideologies into strictly human phenomena. "Yet demythologization devours itself," Adorno writes, "as the mythical gods liked to devour their children. Leaving behind nothing but what merely is, demythologization recoils into the mythus; for the mythus is nothing else than the closed system of immanence, of that which is."[30] Premodern myths fused heaven and earth by seeing the things of this world as direct manifestations of otherworldly goods and gods. They collapsed earth up into heaven. Projects of demythologization proceed in the opposite direction. Casting anything that appears to be beyond the empirical order as nothing more than projections from the empirical order, demythologization pulls heaven down to earth. If the directions of these moves are different, the results are worlds that share a similar one-dimensional nature. This one-dimensional nature, this equation of is and ought, fact and norm, force and law, is what Adorno calls "mythological." Just so, the Great Separation that promises to de-mythologize the political order, to cleanse it of every trace of theology, ends up denying the reality of anything but the existing political order. It elevates "what is" to the status of "all there is." Its flattening of fact and norm opens the way to the discourse of necessity. It allows and even underwrites the mythologization of the state and the global political order in which it is at home.

Political Theology as Exceptional Reasoning

An insistence on the rule of law as an absolute principle enables the state to become an end in itself without having to declare itself as such. And a Great Separation between "politics" and "theology" in the sense Lilla uses those terms forsakes the resources required for critique of this process. Arguments that simply insist that violence must be hemmed within the rule of law will deepen rather than break the hold of this mythologized power. More promising open-ings to critique will come in the form of gaps, fissures, and outliers. They will come in the form of exceptions. We should not seek to eliminate exceptions to the rule, then, but to cultivate forms of life that can engage in reasoned dis-course about exceptions.

In the long run, as Locke, Hamilton, and Blackstone saw, a liberal society is better served by developing an uneasy tolerance for some kind of executive prerogative to make exceptions to the law. The power to make exceptions is neither absolute nor inherent. Prerogative should be guided, Locke writes, by "this fundamental law of nature and government, viz. That as much as may be, all the members of the society are to be preserved" (§ 159).[31] Prerogative seeks some higher end, and that end is not simply the preservation of the system of laws or the state that embodies that system. The obligation to seek that end is grounded, Locke writes, in a "fundamental law of nature" that exceeds the laws of any particular state. Prerogative involves reasoning beyond the law for ends higher than the preservation of the law. Moreover, prerogative power is not inherent in the executive but delegated by the sovereign people (§ 164). And, Locke asks, "who shall judge when this power is made right use of?" Here the people have no "appeal on earth." They can, however, "appeal to heaven: for the rulers, in such attempts, exercising a power the people never put into their hands, (who can never be supposed to consent that any body should rule over them for their harm) do that which they have not a right to do" (§ 168). Locke famously does not specify just what this "appeal to heaven" involves—revolution? prayer? eschatological patience that includes piecemeal resistance and reform?—but he clearly points to forms of reason and practice that go beyond even perfected versions of positive law.

Locke describes a prerogative that is distinct from the power of the "unitary executive" advocated by the Bush administration. It is more temporary, more clearly derivative. It relates to law not as the penthouse at the top of an edifice but as an exception, a hole in the wall. These temporary and exceptional qualities also distinguish Locke's account of prerogative from the Obama administration's drive to expand policy to cover every emergency. But the deepest difference arises in Locke's acknowledgment of some good beyond even the preservation of a system of laws, some heaven to which appeal might be made.

Like the wild margin at the edge of a plowed field or a *pharmakon* that sustains the health of a body in small doses, exceptions to the law can, on rare occasions and in trace amounts, contribute to the wider project of a liberal society. A tolerance for such exceptions must be uneasy. It should have little patience with repetition or duration. And it should be undertaken with as much transparency as possible, replacing formal accountability to law with a democratic accountability to the electorate. Leaving room for executive prerogative creates a need for virtuous executives. "The ultimate paradox," as Clement Fatovic argues, "may be that only virtue can make up for the failures of institutions that have been specifically designed to compensate for the fallibility of virtue."[32]

The most important virtue required by prerogative is the ability to reason about exception without slipping into the jargon of necessity. It is just this capacity that defines what I mean by "political theology." Political theology exercises prerogative, even when it lacks the power to implement its decisions. It reasons about singularities that cannot be made to fit existing structures of law. It can imagine violence in ways that do not reduce to (even a theologically motivated) ethics of the immanent frame. It can think the exception. It can, in Locke's words, make appeals to heaven.

For such political theology to avoid slipping into the worst forms of decisionism, it needs to involve a deliberative kind of rationality. That is, it needs to be capable of giving, receiving, and evaluating reasons for its decisions. The next chapter aims to develop some central concepts for this kind of reasoning. And Chapters 4, 5, and 6 aim to display such reasoning in a series of meditations on the abolitionist John Brown and the raid he led on Harpers Ferry. I try to imagine the raid as a singularity, a sign that has significance that can be captured

neither by deontological ethics, as if it were already complete in itself, having fulfilled or broken some law, nor by consequentialist ethics, as if its meaning could
become complete in a narrative of cause and effect that finds its ending in this
age. I try instead to understand the raid as a sign that depends for its intelligibil-
ity on its quotation into messianic history, a history that in this world reveals
only the destructive power of cross or gallows. I try to imagine the raid—and
the America formed in part by memories of it—as part of a history that requires
divine completion.

3 DIVINE VIOLENCE
AS THE RELIEF OF LAW

JOHN BROWN SPOKE like a nineteenth-century American edition of the
Geneva Bible, complete with Calvinist and Puritan annotations that earned
charges of sedition. In Brown's styling of himself, he was Moses, leading people
from slavery, giving the law of God, and slaughtering those who bowed to the
Golden Calf. He was Gideon, leading a band whose small size and great purity
made clear that its victory came not by its own swords but by the sword of the
Lord. He was Samson, making a fatal mistake that, by the wily providence of
God, allowed him to stand in the very temple of the Philistines—and pull it
down on their heads as well as his own. He was the Suffering Servant by whose
stripes the nation would be healed.

Brown's typological understandings of himself and his world do not translate well into contemporary idioms. It is not just that the stories to which
Brown refers are often unknown, and even more often regarded with a reasonable suspicion. And it is not just that typology of any kind strains modern
imaginations. Even if the stories were known, and trusted, and able to function
as types, our imaginations would tend to remain centered in a frame that evalu-
ates whatever it considers through the categories of an immanent ethics. Stories
of Moses, Gideon, Samson, and the Servant might provide some resistance to
such an imagination, but more than a century of commentary has given a mul-
titude of ways to pull them safely within its fold. Within that space, Brown
appears only as freedom fighter, fanatic, or some combination of those two. If
we are to understand John Brown in richer terms, terms that have the power

to critique the formations that dominate contemporary politics and society, we cannot turn directly to the language that he used about himself. We first need an exercise that can open the registers of political theology.

A Prince of This World

German jurist Carl Schmitt (1888–1985) put political theology back on the table by saying that it had never really left. In a series of writings that span much of the twentieth century, Schmitt argues against the modern state's conception of itself by identifying a set of scarcely secularized theological concepts that give order to its form. Chief among these is the concept of sovereignty. Parliaments might pass bills, but they cannot, by themselves, make those bills function as *laws*. Making law, Schmitt argues in *Political Theology* (1922), requires some kind of sovereign power that exceeds the limits of what the parliamentary state could be or even acknowledge. Schmitt's sense of the limits of a secular state governed by the rule of law contributed to his decision to join Adolf Hitler's National Socialist German Workers Party in 1933. The connections between his ideas and this decision are not incidental. Without radically altering the trajectory of thought he established in the Weimar years, Schmitt was able to write works that provided theoretical support for the role of the Führer and the politics of anti-Semitism. He insists on the need for both some sovereign power beyond the system of law *and* some clear earthly identity for that power. In naming the dependence of a legal system on a sovereignty that exceeds that system, Schmitt opens a theological dimension that can interrupt the mythologization of the state. A legal order dependent on a power beyond itself cannot be all-in-all. It cannot even be necessary in a final way. Schmitt sees the need for a theological account of sovereignty, but in insisting that the sovereign be identical to some this-worldly power, Schmitt provides an ideology that can (and did) legitimate catastrophic violence by idolatrous powers.

In *Political Theology* Schmitt performs what he calls a "sociology of the concept" that traces the structural analogies between the political and theological imaginations of a given era. "The metaphysical image that a definite epoch forges of the world," Schmitt writes, "has the same structure as what the world immediately understands to be appropriate as a form of its political organization."[1] Because theology distills a particular society's view of the world, it makes clear the basic structure of the form of political life that will feel most natural and obvious to that society. Schmitt's sociology of the concept teases out the theological analogues to what can seem like secular political formations.

Schmitt uses the sociology of the concept to describe a process of flattening at work in both theological and political imaginations. That process has steadily eliminated any notion of a sovereign power above or beyond the law. European Christian theologies of the seventeenth and eighteenth centuries, Schmitt argues, were dominated by the idea of a transcendent God who served as the architect for a system of laws that proceeded in regular fashion. Just so, the political imagination of Europe was dominated by the idea of a single sovereign who established a rule of law that could then be relied upon to function in regular ways. René Descartes made the analogy explicit in a letter to Marin Mersenne: "It is God who established these laws in nature just as a king establishes laws in his kingdom" (51–52/47). Over time, Schmitt writes, the scientific worldview that relied on a closed, unchanging system of natural laws came to exert greater and greater influence over political thought. By Schmitt's own time, "the sovereign, who in the deistic view of the world, had remained the engineer of the great machine, has been radically pushed aside. The machine now runs itself" (52/48). Traces of sovereignty survived longer in the United States by migrating to the people (53/49). But on both sides of the Atlantic (and now increasingly around the globe), the rule of law as a comprehensive and self-generating artifact—law without exception—has become the ideal. And that ideal has no place for any sort of sovereign power beyond the law.

Schmitt resists this modern ideal of a system of laws without exception, arguing that it cannot account for the fundamental nature of political life. It cannot account, he says, for the shared, social experience of obligation to the law, the community, and one another. That is, it cannot account for *the political.* A legal system might assume an intricate form that displays remarkable coherence and consistency. But that form does not make it *law*, for the form, in itself, cannot account for a people's sense of obligation to it and connection to one another. The juridical order is incomplete, Schmitt writes, neither because of a gap in some particular law nor because of a gap in the aggregation of every individual law but because of a gap in "law as a whole, which can in no way be filled by juristic conceptual operations" (20–21/15).[2] Giorgio Agamben describes this gap by making an analogy between Schmitt's understanding of law and Ferdinand de Saussure's distinction between *langue* and *parole. Langue,* for Saussure, means a system of signs that does not necessarily denote anything beyond itself. To become the meaningful speech of *parole,* the system of signs requires not additional vocabulary or grammatical rules that extend the system from within—for it could develop in infinitely intricate ways without ever touching reality—but a practical action that is of another order.[3] Schmitt sees the same need for a system of laws. He names the need for a *decision* that will turn a legal system into law that has binding power. The need for decision introduces an aporia into the otherwise closed system of laws. For a decision to close the gap between a juridical order and a social world, Schmitt says, it must not be contained within the juridical order. It cannot be a mere application of the law. The kind of decision necessary for the creation of political life demands the possibility of what Schmitt calls an *exception*.

"The exception," Schmitt writes, "is more interesting than the rule. The rule proves nothing; the exception proves everything: it confirms not only the rule but also its existence, which derives only from the exception" (21/15). The exception, as an exception, confirms the rule. If it did not confirm the rule, it would not be an exception but an anomaly that demanded revision or rejection of the rule. As an exception, though, it confirms the content of the rule that it defies. It also confirms what Schmitt calls the "existence" of the rule. In this second sense the exception confirms the rule *as law*, that is, as something to which people are obliged in a distinctly political way. The exception closes the gap between sign and signified, law and politics.

The exception closes this gap from a position outside the system of laws. It does not close the gap by announcing a new law, for no simple addition to a body of laws could give that body a binding quality. Passing a law that says "all these laws have authority" is like writing a sentence that says "all the words in this language match up to extralinguistic realities." Something of another order is required, Schmitt argues. Because it operates at another level, the exception does not function like a law. It sets no precedents of its own. It contains no "should" that can be generalized.[4] It is in itself particular to a concrete situation. But it establishes the existence of the order to which it is an exception, for it declares—indirectly—the binding applicability of that system in every case except this one. Schmitt's exception, then, occupies a curious space: it is both beyond the juridical order and necessary for its existence as a juridical order.

The opening lines of *Political Theology* name that curious space—and its occupant. "Sovereign is he who decides on the exception" (13/5). Sovereignty, Schmitt writes, is a "borderline concept" (*Grenzbegriff*). This does not mean that it is "vague." And it does not mean that it appears only in select and extreme situations. Schmitt argues instead that "the exception is to be understood to refer to a general concept in the theory of the state, and not merely to a construct applied to any emergency decree or state of siege" (ibid.). The state of exception, in itself, may be an isolated event. But the sovereignty that names it as such permeates the whole of a polity's life. The border (*die Grenze*) is within, for it gives the space whatever shape it has. The exception is always present, for it establishes the rule as a rule. And the sovereign, Schmitt writes, both "stands outside of" and "belongs to" the "normally valid juridical order" (14/7).

Schmitt's notion of sovereignty shatters the flat immanence of the legal systems he sees taking hold in the nineteenth and twentieth centuries. It has a power to critique a disenchanted system of law that pretends to comprehensiveness, denies the possibility of exceptions, and refuses to acknowledge any authority outside itself. Schmitt not only names the possibility of an exception but shows the dependence of the system of law upon an exception. Schmitt therefore prevents the kind of closure that makes a legal system appear to be (at least potentially) complete and comprehensive. In naming this opening to authority beyond the law that is necessary for the law, Schmitt makes possible a kind of critique that is blocked by total separations of theology and politics, like the one Mark Lilla calls for in his description of a Great Separation. Schmitt provides ways of seeing the political order that can interrupt the recoil of disenchantment into new mythology.

In particular, Schmitt helps illumine the dynamics at work in the decisions to use state power in ways that move to or beyond the edge of law (as described in Chapter 2). The ideal of a juridical order that is complete in itself rejects the whole category of sovereignty, whether defined in relation to "the people" or some other entity. With no value outside the juridical order itself, exceptions to such an order have to be justified in the name of that order's survival—just as they are in the Department of Justice memo of 2013, the AUMF of 2001, and the Lieber Code of 1863. Schmitt makes clear the ideological nature of such justifications. They are not a rejection of sovereignty in the name of a juridical order that has left sovereignty behind, as they present themselves, but the elevation of the juridical order itself to the role of sovereign. "The existence of the state is undoubted proof of its superiority over the validity of the legal norm," Schmitt writes. "The decision frees itself from all normative ties and becomes in the true sense absolute. The state suspends the law in the exception on the basis of its right of self-preservation, as one says" (18–19/12). Thus, rejection of the category of sovereignty, and of any authority beyond the immanent order of law, does not eliminate sovereignty but allows the state to assume the role of sovereign, in all its theological significance, and in ways that are covered by a fig leaf of proceduralism.

When a juridical order understands itself as comprehensive, any exceptions can have only a temporary existence. Even exceptions undertaken in the name of necessity need to come under the rule of law. The juridical order would have to expand and the law would have to catch up, just as it has in the Obama administration's legalized extensions of the war on terror. But the creation of new policies does not eliminate the exception. Nor does it eliminate every trace of the sovereign violence involved in declaring the exception. The new policies, forged in the name of necessity, introduce "a zone of anomie" into the heart of law.[5] In declaring the political order sufficient and comprehensive, the separation of theology and politics does not eliminate violence beyond the law. Rather, it obscures the process by which extralegal violence enters into the legal order itself.[6]

Schmitt's analysis makes these dynamics visible with fresh clarity through what he calls "political theology." Schmitt's work supplies two different kinds of content to define this phrase. First, like Ernst Kantorowicz in *The King's Two Bodies*, Schmitt discerns the deep analogies between political and theological worldviews. These analogies help clarify both politics and theology. Schmitt's sociology of the concept sees not only the analogies but the causal links that create them. Given the strength of both the analogies and the causation, banishing attention to theology from political life only obscures the historical sources and inner logics of contemporary political formations. But recognizing the importance of theology for understanding politics does not necessarily imply that one should *do* theology. It simply underscores the historical importance of theological worldviews, thus making a relatively uncontroversial point.

Schmitt performs "political theology" in a second and more controversial sense when he argues that the phenomenology of legal obligation reveals the existence of some kind of sovereign power at work in any legal system—even a system that claims to be complete and without the kind of exception that sovereignty creates and requires. Schmitt names that transcending, sovereign element as "theological," even if it involves no references to any kind of divinity. With or without reference to God, this kind of argument goes beyond the bounds of purely immanent accounts of obligation. It insists on the presence of a sovereignty that is both other than networks of immanent obligation and constitutive of them. It thus offers more direct resistance to the self-understanding of modern political formations. It invites more contentious rebuke.

It is this second sense of political theology that enables Schmitt's critique. Because he recognizes the role of an authority beyond law, Schmitt offers resources for critique of the ways that modern political formations tend to mythologize themselves. He is right to name the enduring presence of some notion of sovereignty. He is right to open up a space for deliberating about sovereignty. But his own candidate for filling that space can only be described as idolatrous. Schmitt's sovereign may be "beyond" the particular order it secures through decision in the state of exception. But Schmitt's sovereign is still very much within the world of human beings and their creations:

> Whether God alone [*nur Gott*] is sovereign, that is, *the one who acts as his acknowledged representative on earth*, or the emperor, or prince, or the people, meaning those who identify themselves directly with the people, the question is always aimed at the subject of sovereignty, at the application of the concept to a concrete situation. (16/10, emphasis mine)

Schmitt considers the possibility of "God alone" as sovereign but quickly defines the phrase to mean "the one who acts as his acknowledged representative on earth." There is no politically meaningful distinction, no gap even of representation, between the two. For the purposes of Schmitt's political theology, God *just is* the one who acts as God's acknowledged representative on earth, whether prophet, pope, prince, or the people as a whole. Schmitt describes a sovereign who is beyond the order of law that sovereign creates and sustains. But he cannot imagine a sovereign who is beyond the sum total of human relations. Thus, the analogy that Schmitt initially draws between politics and theology collapses into a single term. As Samuel Weber writes, Schmitt "construes the analogy between [politics and theology] above all in terms of identity, rather than in terms of transformation or alteration."[7]

In using the structure of theological thought to open up a space outside the rule of law, but then losing any politically relevant sense in which theology can be outside or other to the order of human history, Schmitt opens the door to political theologies that would put humans, individually and collectively, in the role theologies have traditionally set aside for God. Schmitt breaks the mythology of a self-sufficient juridical order. But he does so by shifting the site of mythologization—the place where heaven and earth are fused together—from the juridical order to a sovereign who is very much of this world. So he ends up writing briefs on the limits of parliamentary democracy in the name of the Führer.

The Politics of Pure Means

Walter Benjamin saw the catastrophic failure of Carl Schmitt's political theology, even as he understood its significance. Critical dialogue with Schmitt clearly contributed to the development of Benjamin's thinking about politics. While there is some dispute about who wrote the first work to which the other responded, the record of correspondence and footnotes over many years shows that the two were aware of each other's work.[8] Consciousness of this connection has been especially high since Jacques Derrida made use of it in his 1989 lecture "Force of Law."[9] The tradition of interpreting the two together has been extended by such influential readers as Samuel Weber and Giorgio Agamben. Pairing Schmitt and Benjamin can do much to illumine the work of each. But the *historical* significance of their exchange should not be overstated. Schmitt was only one of many conversation partners for Benjamin, and not the most significant. Benjamin's "Critique of Violence" (1921), the pivotal surviving essay of his politics, was developed in more overt dialogue with Georges Sorel, Erich Unger, and Hermann Cohen. While some English translations suggest an overlap with Schmitt's distinctive vocabulary of *Ausnahme* (exception), the term does not appear in Benjamin's essay.[10] Benjamin's vocabulary owes less to Carl Schmitt than to Immanuel Kant. "Critique of Violence" was written at a time when Benjamin was exploring the possibilities of writing his *Habilitationsschrift* on a topic related to Kant's work, and the essay not only uses a Kantian vocabulary of *Kritik* but also makes explicit reference to a formulation of Kant's categorical imperative.[11] Still other names rise to the fore in Benjamin's sketch of a plan for his writings on politics. That plan features longer works on Ernst Bloch's *Spirit of Utopia*, Paul Scheerbart's novel *Lesabéndio*, and the thought of Max Weber and Werner Sombart.[12] Long-running conversations with Gershom Scholem and Florens Christian Rang ran far deeper than Benjamin's exchanges with Schmitt.[13] I want to acknowledge the great historical significance of these and other conversation partners even as I continue the more recent tradition of interpreting Benjamin in contrast to Schmitt. I pair the two not to make a historical claim about the significance of their influence on one another but to clarify the theory and practice of contemporary politics through the power of this pairing.

   Benjamin and Schmitt both describe the ways that theological concepts give rise to political concepts. But they describe this process of translation in very different ways. Schmitt describes a complete sublation, a perfected *Aufhebung*, in which theology empties its form, content, and even its numinous qualities into political concepts.[14] The authority of theological concepts empties into political concepts and charges them with power. The sovereignty of God, for instance, becomes the sovereignty of the ruler, and without remainder. As in

the political theory of Thomas Hobbes—a favorite of both Lilla and Schmitt—
there is no way to appeal to any power, value, or divinity above the sovereign.
Theology, especially, no longer has resources for this kind of critique, for it
has emptied itself into the political. Schmitt not only describes this process
but also urges it along. While he calls for a "political theology" that can trace
the process of this translation and so name elements that transcend the immanence of a legal positivism, he assigns that transcendence entirely to the
political sovereign. He leaves no room for any kind of "theological" criticism
from whatever is left of the religious sphere. Quoting the Italian jurist Alberico
Gentili, Schmitt admonishes, "Silete theologi in munero alieno!" (Theologian,
be silent on matters that do not concern you!).[15] After Schmitt's sublation of
theology in politics, the region from which theologians should absent themselves becomes wide indeed, expanding to include all of the political.

Like Schmitt, Benjamin describes the ways that theological beliefs and
practices give rise to political counterparts. But Benjamin stresses the *incomplete* quality of this translation. Something of value is lost or left behind. Thus,
Benjamin thinks of this translation as a kind of fall. As Adam and Eve are expelled from the Garden in the book of Genesis, human societies have been
expelled from theological formations into political ones. But even this expulsion does not bring a complete loss of the theological. The people might be
expelled from Eden, but something of Eden lives on in the lives of people who
cannot find their way back to it. In the language of the Christian theology that
runs so closely parallel to Benjamin at this point, the image of God endures,
however disfigured and hidden, in every fallen person. What is lost does not
completely disappear, even if the "theological" form of life that gives rise to it
disappears and the new "political" or "secular" form does not preserve it in a
pure and simple form. Theology has an afterlife, like the hunchbacked dwarf
who moves the hands of the chess-playing automaton in Benjamin's famous
parable from "On the Concept of History." Like theology, the dwarf has to keep
out of sight in the present age. But he gives the secular robot whatever life it
has, and it is only because of the dwarf hidden within that the robot can win
the game.[16] As in this parable, Benjamin describes a theology that has been
poured into the forms of this world, but not without remainder. Something
distinctly theological endures, even if only as an empty vessel.

Benjamin traces this incomplete dialectic of secularization across numerous
phenomena, describing a fall of the name into words, semblance into images,
ritual into art, and, crucially for his politics, the fall from a paradisiacal state he

called justice (*Gerechtigkeit*) into law (*Recht*).[17] The latter concepts in each of these pairs are the concepts of a fallen history. They order the world in which people live now. But the older, more explicitly theological concepts have not dissolved completely into the new, Benjamin writes. They have an afterlife in what Benjamin will later describe as the "wishes" or "dreams" of the fallen concepts. Seeing the fallen concept together with the dream that haunts it produces what Benjamin calls a "wish-image" (*Wunschbild*) or "dialectical image" (*dialektisches Bild*).[18] Benjamin sees wish-images everywhere in a seemingly secular society. They live in world's fairs, iron architecture, gambling, fashion, and more. Even bomber planes, Benjamin writes, quoting Pierre-Maxim Schuhl, "remind us of what Leonardo da Vinci expected of man in flight: that he was to ascend to the skies 'in order to seek snow on the mountaintops and bring it back to the city to spread on the sweltering streets in summer.'"[19] Dreams of paradise—*theological* dreams—live on in forms as fallen as a bomber plane. The bomber does not relate to paradise directly. It cannot fulfill its deepest wish by flying a little farther in the same direction or dropping its bombs with a little more accuracy. But the dream of carrying snow to sweltering streets is not completely alien to it. The paradisiacal promise lives in the bomber, even in its present state, like the image of God in a fallen human being.

The enduring, inverted presence of a theological remainder enables Benjamin to perform a kind of critique that Schmitt's completed sublation tries to make impossible. Because the theological wish Benjamin describes is not just present in the phenomenon but constituent of it, even in its fallen state, his mode of critique can be thoroughly immanent. At the same time, the otherness of the wish to the fallen phenomenon lets the critique call on an ideal that transcends the mere extension of values already explicit in the phenomenon. This combination of immanence and transcendence distinguishes Benjamin's critical perspective from a positivism that can see the phenomenon only on its own terms. If the bomber is just a bomber, or if politics is nothing more than a struggle for the power to dominate others, on what grounds can they be criticized? They are what they are. At the same time, Benjamin's combination of immanence and transcendence distinguishes his perspective from any kind of magical thinking that asserts a simple identity between earthly phenomena—ecclesial, political, aesthetic, or otherwise—and theological ideals. Neither bomber planes nor congregations nor declarations of human rights realize the utopian states of which they dream, even if they are extended infinitely in the right direction. In the language of Christian theology:

the *imago Dei* is restored not by the perfection of health in immortality but by death and resurrection.

Neither positivist nor magical, Benjamin's critique works by tracing the fissures between phenomena and the wishes left over from their theological origins. Benjamin's "Critique of Violence," for example, depends on the gap between the laws of this world and the divine justice of which they dream. The essay does not offer "ethics" in the sense that has come to dominate discussions of violence. Rather, it offers a Kant-inflected *Kritik* of precisely this phenomenon of thinking ethically about violence. Benjamin's essay does not give criteria for saying which kinds of acts can be justified. It starts with the fact that we think about violence in the language of ethics. We make a "fundamental distinction," Benjamin writes, between "so-called sanctioned force and unsanctioned force." Instead of working within that frame, Benjamin queries it, asking, "What light is thrown on the nature of violence by the fact that such criterion or distinction can be applied at all?"[20] With this question, Benjamin opens the way to a *critique* of violence.

Benjamin pursues this critique through what he calls "a philosophico-historical view of law" (182/238). This "philosophico-historical view" gives not just the empirical history of laws but the ur-history of law, a history that includes memories of life before the fall of justice into the present state of law. Such an angle of vision can see laws as dialectical images. It can trace the process by which divine justice is translated into earthly law, and it can register the incompleteness of that translation. It can discern the longing for divine justice that lives on in earthly laws, and it can use that longing as a resource for critique. Thus, Benjamin writes in the first lines of the essay, "The task of a critique of violence can be summarized as that of expounding its relation to law and justice. For a cause, however effective, becomes violent, in the precise sense of the word, only when it enters into moral relations" (179/236). Violence and morality are linked in our minds, Benjamin writes. The task of a critique of violence is not to perfect that link with new and improved criteria for justified violence but to account for that link in ways that help us imagine a justice that goes beyond it.

Benjamin uses the gap between justice and law to shed new light on debates that try to identify which violent acts are justified. Benjamin identifies the primary schools working within the frame of ethical thinking about violence as emphasizing "natural law" or "positive law." With the name of "natural law," Benjamin smears all the fine distinctions between thinkers that might or might not accept this label. He intends only to name those theorists who begin the work of justifying violence with an appeal to ends that are in some sense given apart from the political process. He uses "positive law" to gather up all those who would justify violence by appealing to norms that govern the violent acts as means to other ends. In Benjamin's conception of these two schools, thick conceptions of the good orient natural law to the justice of ends, while thinner, more procedural commitments orient positive law to the legality of means. Despite this "antithesis," Benjamin writes, both schools share a "basic dogma" that just ends can be reconciled with legal means. "Natural law attempts, by the justness of the ends, to 'justify' [*rechtfertigen*] the means, positive law to 'guarantee' [*garantieren*] the justness of the ends through the justification of the means" (180/237). The two schools start at different points, but they move around the same circle of justification.

The circle that justifies both means and ends gives rise to the state's monopoly on legitimate violence. As just ends charge legal means with a moral authority that goes beyond the mere fact of law, legal means reach up to wrap just ends in law. The completed circle displays the "fall" of justice into law, the loss of a conception of justice that can transcend not just this or that law but the form of law itself. Because this fallen circle is complete, it is also *closed*. The desire to reconcile just ends with legal means, Benjamin writes, displaces "natural" ends that can be pursued by natural means with a system of legal ends that can be pursued by legal means. It forecloses the possibility of acting for ends above the law or using means outside the law. Violence outside the law poses a particular threat. It challenges not just some particular statute or social good but the circle of justification itself. What Benjamin calls "the law's interest in a monopoly of violence" arises not from the rational self-interest described in Hobbes's story of the social contract but from law's interest in preserving itself *as law*. It arises from recognition that "violence, when not in the hands of the law, threatens it not by the ends that it may pursue but by its mere existence outside the law" (183/239). The circle of justified law cannot live with such a threat. For law to be what we mean by law, violence outside the law has to be destroyed, denied, or absorbed into justified law.

Benjamin calls the force exerted by this system of justified law "mythic violence" (*mythische Gewalt*). Myth "bastardizes" what Benjamin calls justice with what he calls law (203/252). He calls the resulting combination "mythic" because it retains justice's sense of binding obligation even as it slips into the arbitrariness of a system of positive law that arises through contingent power relations. It therefore assigns an ultimate significance to "the representation and preservation of an order imposed by fate [*Schicksal*]" (187/241). Benjamin describes mythic violence as functioning in two related modes: lawmaking violence (*rechtsetzende Gewalt*) and law-preserving violence (*rechtserhaltende Gewalt*). The two modes are often inseparable, as in police power that fills in the content of law as it enforces law. And both modes perpetuate the order imposed by fate. While mythic violence might present itself as seeking some goal, Benjamin wrote, it is not really a means to ends that are beyond the violence itself. Because the ends it seeks are not outside the circle of justified law, violence for the sake of those ends is not instrumental so much as *expressive*. "Mythic violence in its archetypal form is a mere manifestation of the gods," Benjamin wrote. "Not a means to their ends, scarcely a manifestation of their will, but primarily a manifestation of their existence" (197/248). Whatever justifications it offers for itself, mythic violence is undertaken not as a means to some extrinsic purpose but as an expression of an order imposed by fate. In this mixing of obligation and fate, Benjamin writes, "something rotten [*etwas Morsches*] in the law is revealed, above all to a finer sensibility, because the latter knows itself to be infinitely remote from conditions in which fate might imperiously have shown itself in such a sentence" (188/242). Like Schmitt, Benjamin sees the way that a theological concept (justice) is translated into a political one (law). Unlike Schmitt, Benjamin pronounces the translation rotten.

The circular patterns of reinforcement between just ends and legal means are difficult to break open, Benjamin writes. Schools of positive law and natural law argue over the starting points without critiquing the circle that produces mythic violence. And arguing against any kind of coercion at all ends in what Benjamin calls a "childish anarchism" that can say little more than "what pleases is permitted." Such a move robs action of meaning. And because it blocks reflections on the "philosophico-historical" dimensions of the question, it blocks critique (187/241). Even appeals to some kind of categorical imperative are inadequate to the task. A formulation like Kant's—"act in such a way that at all times you use humanity both in your person and in the person of all others as an end, and never as a means"—can easily be co-opted by mythic violence. "For positive law," Benjamin writes, "if conscious of its roots, will certainly claim to acknowledge and promote the interest of mankind in the person of each individual. It sees this interest in the representation and preservation of an order imposed by fate" (ibid.). It will take something stronger than the categorical imperative to break the hold of myth. More specifically, it will take something that cannot be formulated as an imperative.

Interrupting the cycles of mythic violence will require appeal to the traces of the state of divine justice that are not fully translated into law. But how can one appeal to those traces without turning them into law and so reclosing the circle as an appeal to natural law or a categorical imperative might do? Schmitt falls into a version of this trap. He rejects the law's claims to immanent completeness, identifying a transcendent dimension he calls "theological." But then he describes a "God" who is in practical terms identical to the body or bodies accepted as God's representatives on earth. He therefore legitimates a secularized theocracy, charging the fallen law with fresh theological power and giving new legitimacy to mythic violence.

Benjamin wants to appeal to the theological without pulling it down into the work of justifying morality and so into the circle of mythic violence. At its root, he writes elsewhere, this is a question of "manifestation."[21] That is, politics depends on the way that the state of divine justice manifests itself in the world. He perhaps has the Catholic Schmitt in mind when he writes,

> The problem of Catholicism is that of the (false, secular) theocracy. The guiding principle here is: authentic divine power can manifest itself *other than destructively* only in the world to come (the world of fulfillment). But where divine power enters the secular world, it breathes destruction. That is why in this world nothing constant and no organization can be based on divine power, let alone domination as its supreme principle.[22]

The contrast between Schmitt and Benjamin should not be reduced to a contrast between Catholicism and Judaism, as some commentators have tried to do, for both traditions display a pluralism that defies such flat contrast. But the question between them *is* theological. It concerns the way in which "divine power enters the secular world." The contrast between Schmitt and Benjamin is best articulated in terms closer to the principals. For Schmitt, the sovereign performs a sacred violence in the state of exception, and that sacred violence grounds or renews a social order. For Benjamin, divine justice might describe an ideal state before the fall or after the redemption of the cosmos. But in the meantime, divine justice manifests itself only in destruction. Benjamin calls that destruction "divine violence" (*göttliche Gewalt*). Divine violence is the way that justice manifests itself in this world.

The divine violence Benjamin describes cannot be captured within the justificatory circles of mythic violence. "Just as in all spheres God opposes myth," Benjamin writes, "mythic violence is confronted by the divine" (199/249).

Mythic violence produces and reproduces a fated social order. Divine violence, on the other hand, produces nothing. It is instead a politics of pure means (*reine Mittel*). Benjamin unpacks the distinction in a catalog of contrasts:

> If mythic violence is lawmaking, divine violence is law-destroying; if the former sets boundaries, the latter boundlessly destroys them; if mythic violence brings at once guilt and expiation, divine power only expiates; if the former threatens, the latter strikes; if the former is bloody, the latter is lethal without spilling blood. (199/249)

Each contrast invites commentary. Mythic violence does not just make particular laws but creates the category of justified law as binding obligation. Divine violence, on the other hand, unmasks the collusion of fate and violence within the law, thus undoing the binding power of the law. Mythic violence initiates and depends upon an economy of sacrifice that marks the boundaries of a community. Divine violence shatters the economy of sacrifice and so unmakes the boundaries it creates. Mythic violence creates a system of law by which some violent acts are justified while others are not. It brings "both guilt and expiation," in Benjamin's language. But divine violence only destroys systems of obligation. It therefore brings only expiation. Divine violence does not create or renew a system of obligations, as mythic violence—and Schmitt's decision—does. It instead invites a free response. And it does not just threaten, as mythic violence does, that if this or that act of violence is not done, the whole fabric of society could be torn apart. Divine violence goes ahead and rends the fabric from top to bottom.

In offering this concept of divine violence, Benjamin echoes Schmitt's critique of the self-conception of the modern, parliamentary state as a source of laws that are distinct from (and therefore capable of restraining) violence. He shares with Schmitt a sense of the significance of extralegal violence for founding and sustaining any system of laws. Benjamin does not reject Schmitt's analysis so much as reframe it within a wider angle of vision. In this wider angle, Schmitt's "sovereign" violence appears as what Benjamin calls mythic violence. Such bloody violence does indeed create and sustain social orders, just as Schmitt says. But Benjamin refuses Schmitt's equation of true sovereignty with the authors of these cycles of violence. He holds out a place for a divine violence that is outside—and therefore capable of interrupting—the cycles of mythic violence that Schmitt describes as ultimate. Benjamin describes a sovereignty that exceeds, relativizes, and deposes the earthly powers Schmitt identifies. He holds out hope for a theology that has not been fully sublated in the political. That hope is manifest in this age as divine violence.

The Limits of Ethics

Talk of divine violence rightly makes contemporary readers uneasy. Just as Benjamin wrote in 1921, talk of divine violence can "provoke, particularly today, the most violent reactions" (199/250). The irony of these violent reactions is sharp. But the worries about divine violence are legitimate, for talk of divine violence can be heard as suggesting that people have some kind of holy sanction for killing one another. Indeed, this is the form talk about divine violence usually takes in the present age, when it is hard to imagine a role for theology beyond the legitimation of ethics. But Benjamin intends something very different.

Divine violence, Benjamin writes, is "lethal without spilling blood." Mythic violence, on the other hand, depends on bloodshed. A juridical order arises and sustains itself through the very real sacrifice of bodies. Those bodies become the pledge of the reality of the order, like the gold that once backed currency in another confidence game. But divine violence comes "not by miracles directly performed by God, but by the expiating moment in them that strikes without bloodshed" (199/250). Divine violence expiates; it releases from guilt. It operates not by the destruction of bodies but by the destruction of the systems of law or ethics that declare an action to be right or wrong. It works at the level of what Benjamin calls "systems of relations" (ibid.), the level a social theorist might call "structures of legitimation," the level the Apostle Paul calls "principalities and powers." Divine violence destroys these systems, not the flesh-and-blood bodies that create and inhabit them.

Divine violence, as Benjamin conceives it, might be directed against systems of relations rather than bodies. But because these systems provide so much structure for our world, there is risk that the destruction of them will involve or unleash forces that do violence to bodies. Bloody, bodily violence might play some part in the historical process by which these powers are broken. And it will almost surely follow their destruction. The divine violence of the civil rights movement, for instance, broke the system of relations that sustained one pernicious kind of segregation in the United States. The breaking of that system brought a moral revolution that was in itself bloodless. But it was accompanied by the blood of four little girls in the bombed basement of a Birmingham church in 1963, the blood that flowed from the bodies of those who marched across the Edmund Pettus Bridge in 1965, the blood that ran in the streets of

Newark in 1967, and more. We might offer different moral evaluations of these events, but none of them is identical with divine violence. Divine violence is, however, thickly intertwined with all of these events. For all of them arose in the shattering of a system of relations.

Benjamin can seem to miss the significance of this blood. He pins his hopes on the idea that divine violence annihilates systems of relations "relatively . . . with regard to goods, right, life and suchlike, but never absolutely, with regard to the soul of the living" (200/250). This claim rests on a strong distinction between "goods, right, life and suchlike," on the one hand, and "the soul of the living," on the other. As Judith Butler has argued, there is the potential for a dangerous dualism in this distinction.[23] It misses the deep connections between body and soul. And arguing that divine violence does not harm the soul can imply a blithe disregard for bodily life.

The best appropriations of Benjamin's understanding of violence will insist on the significance of bodily life. They will acknowledge that Benjamin argues against systems of relations that make "mere life" (*bloßes Leben*) into an absolute value. Such systems not only miss the full meaning of human living, he writes, but also underwrite deeper forms of violence (201–202/250–251). The power of this insight has become plain in Agamben's wide-ranging critique of contemporary societies that elevate mere life above all other values—and so reduce the individual to the status of merely living even as they expand state violence to maintain mere life.[24] But one can criticize the mythic violence of a regime of mere life without slipping into disregard for the importance of bodily existence. Indeed, concern for body and soul, in the fullest sense, is what gives this critique the power that it has.

The best appropriations of Benjamin will recall that while he resists the moves that make mere life an absolute value, he does not describe a divine violence that would legitimate killing. His notion of divine violence does not give a new law that can justify actions once forbidden. On the contrary, Benjamin insists that "the question 'May I kill?'" continues to meet "its irreducible answer in the commandment 'Thou shalt not kill.'" The commandment always comes before the action, as if God were restraining the action. But the commandment becomes "inapplicable, incommensurable, once the deed is accomplished. No judgment of the deed can be derived from the commandment" (200/250). *This* is the work Benjamin describes for divine violence: not to press theology into service as a justification for action but to open a gap of incommensurability between the law that would justify or condemn an action and the action itself.

Divine violence does not revoke the commandment, and it does not issue a new commandment. It simply holds open a space for deliberation between the commandment and action. In the wake of divine violence, Benjamin writes, the commandment "exists not as a criterion of judgment, but as a guideline for the actions of persons or communities who have to wrestle with it in solitude and, in monstrous cases [*in ungeheuren Fällen*], to take on themselves the responsibility [*Verantwortung*] to abstain from it [*von ihm abzusehen*]" (201/250).[25] Divine violence offers not legitimation but renewed occasions for responsibility. It breaks the binding obligations of an order that lets a person evade responsibility by saying, "I am just following the law"—whether that law is rooted in the legal means of positive law or the just ends of natural law. Divine violence forces free action. It demands responsibility.

The *form* of Benjamin's divine violence therefore resists fundamentalist interpretations that would frame divine violence as some kind of sacred legitimation of violent human actions. Here he differs not only from those who would claim an external divine warrant for violent action but also from Schmitt, who collapses all authority on heaven and on earth into the sovereign. The sovereign's decision in the state of exception is not legitimated by some standard extrinsic to it but by its own existence. It is self-legitimating. Benjamin, on the other hand, describes a divine violence that does not enable but interrupts the process of legitimation. As the manifestation of a theological remainder that cannot be translated into law, divine violence does not legitimate new laws. It does not even legitimate new ethics that could, in the Kantian ideal, *become* laws. Rather, it insists on the limits of law. It reveals again the limits of ethics.

Practical Reason after the Relief of Law

The very different notions of divine manifestation at work in Schmitt and Benjamin produce differences not only in their accounts of the relationship between law and violence but also in their accounts of practical and political reasoning. Schmitt describes the sovereign's decision as a kind of creation ex nihilo:

> Therefore the sovereign decision [*Entscheidung*] can be explained juridically neither from a norm nor from a concrete order. Neither can it be integrated into the framework of a concrete order. On the contrary, for the decisionist [*Dezisionist*], the decision first grounds both the norm and the order. The sovereign decision is the absolute beginning [*Anfang*], and the beginning (in the

sense of an ἀρχή) is nothing else than a sovereign decision. It springs out of a normative nothingness [*Nichts*] and from a concrete disorder.[26]

In Schmitt's account the sovereign decision does not make use of reason; the sovereign instead creates what will count as reason. Schmitt's brand of decisionism therefore establishes political reason on arbitrary grounds, grounds decided by accumulations of power or, in Benjamin's language, *fate*. In fusing this arbitrary founding with the binding quality of the reason built on top of it, Schmitt again slips into mythic violence.

Like Schmitt's sovereign decision, Benjamin's divine violence does not conform to preexisting rational criteria. He describes the ways divine violence works but hesitates to identify particular moments or movements as divine violence. It is essential to insist on the *possibility* of "the highest manifestation of unalloyed violence," Benjamin writes. "Less possible and also less urgent for mankind, however, is to decide when unalloyed violence has been realized in particular cases" (202/252). Mythic violence can be recognized with certainty, but divine violence cannot, "because the expiatory power of violence is invisible to men" (202–203/252). Benjamin can give no criteria, no guidelines, that might help identify a particular moment as a moment of divine violence, for then the criteria would become a kind of mythic violence, a law before the god who gives the law. Divine violence, by its very nature, is inscrutable. It comes without precedent, apart from any category or criteria, ex nihilo.

The language of creation ex nihilo can make Benjamin sound like Schmitt. In one of the most important criticisms of Benjamin, Gillian Rose makes the case for their similarity. If there are no resources for discerning a moment of divine violence, Rose writes, then there are no ways "to distinguish law-abolishing violence from law-instating violence that *decides* in the state of emergency to usurp divinity, because there is no recognizable rule of law and no benign or wise judgment, no *phronesis*."[27] In Rose's reading, Benjamin gives no resources for reasoning that can distinguish what he calls divine violence from what he calls mythic violence. Benjamin's divine violence thus becomes, in practice, indistinguishable from Schmitt's description of decision in the state of exception. The world becomes one gray wash of violence. The mere possibility of divine violence, the mere promise of the category as empty placeholder, will not shine the light that can illumine the differences between the shades of gray. If divine violence cannot be known for what it is, then it does not enhance our capacity to critique mythic violence as merely mythic, for there is no contrast case in this world. On the contrary, Rose argues, a notion of the divine as inscrutable will only stir up the purposeless longing of melancholy and the random lunges toward this or that candidate for divine violence that it breeds.

In place of this tragedy in which no moment ever can be named as identical with divine violence, Rose proposes a comedy in which we risk naming a moment as one of identity with the divine and then, as that claim of identification plays out, realize the ways in which we were mistaken. She describes a reason that is "adventurous and corrigible,"[28] a fallible Hegelianism written from the midst of history—not the end—in which Spirit just is "the drama of misrecognition which ensues at every stage and transition of the work—a ceaseless comedy, according to which our aims and outcomes constantly mismatch each other, and provoke yet another revised aim, action and discordant outcome."[29] In the constant work of risking and revising, history does not necessarily make progress. It drives not toward the realization of the concept but toward its actuality.

Rose's proposal is, as Rowan Williams sees, "a repristination of the Hegelian project in something like its full ambition."[30] She would knit immanence and transcendence back together in a more modest way that stresses human effort—work—in the long, difficult learning and unlearning of history. But in giving up Benjamin's insistence on the solely destructive quality of divine violence, Rose ends up "staking," as she comes to say, in however tentative and humble a form, a series of claims to identity between transcendent ideals and immanent historical realities. That is, she stakes claims to direct manifestations of divinity. Rose would stake a series of claims that, for now, promise to hold heaven and earth together. The self-conscious corrigibility of this staking does not change the fundamental quality of what it asserts: an identity between divine justice and earthly law. At issue here, still, is the question of manifestation. If Rose stresses fallibilism more than Schmitt, she does not break from Schmitt's sense of how divine justice manifests itself directly in this world. Thus Rose ends up making a case for a fallibilist mythic violence, a kind of trial-and-error theocracy.

But to name a problem with Rose's proposal does not refute her critique of Benjamin. There are readings of Benjamin's sprawling corpus that seem to fit Rose's description of his work. He does sometimes write as if any kind of goodness or truth lies entirely beyond the course of human history and the reach of human knowledge. But there are other readings that can avoid the neo-Kantianism against which Rose has honed her critique.[31] Rose pushes us to develop a reading of this better Benjamin.

Benjamin seems to fit Rose's critique of neo-Kantianism in a short unpublished piece collected under the title "Theologico-Political Fragment":

> Only the Messiah himself contemplates all history, in the sense that he alone redeems, completes, creates its relation to the messianic. For this reason, nothing that is historical can relate itself, *from its own ground* [*von sich aus sich*], to anything messianic. Therefore, the Kingdom of God is not the telos of the historical dynamic; it cannot be established as a goal. From the standpoint of history, it is not the goal but the terminus [*Ende*].[32]

Benjamin's declaration that "nothing that is historical can relate itself . . . to anything messianic" gets quoted in arguments that suppose the absolute separation of history and redemption that Rose names as the source of the problem. But Benjamin does not offer the line without qualification. Nothing historical can relate itself to the messianic, Benjamin writes, "from its own ground," or by its own power. This leaves open the possibility that history might be related to the messianic by a power beyond itself. But what kind of power—what kind of relation—could that be? It is, again, a question of manifestation.

That manifestation is not direct. "The secular order should be erected on the idea of happiness," Benjamin writes. Practical and political reasoning should seek something like the *eudaimonia* described by Aristotle as their rightful end. But this should not be mistaken for a realizing of, or even a working toward, anything like the fullness of redemption. As Benjamin writes, "The quest of free humanity for happiness runs counter to the messianic direction" (203/305). Exactly as it moves against the coming of the Reign of God, though, history plays its part in the arrival of that Reign:

> But just as a force, by virtue of the path it is moving along, can augment another force on the opposite path, so the secular order—because of its nature as secular—promotes the coming of the Messianic Kingdom. The secular, therefore, though not itself a category of the Kingdom, is a decisive category of its most unobtrusive approach. (204/305)

Benjamin's position in this passage does not fit the neo-Kantian mold that Rose criticizes so sharply. He does not describe history as striving toward redemption, failing to reach its goal, and so bereft of any sort of divine presence and dependent on an absolutely alien grace. He describes instead history that is passing away and, in passing away, participating in the arrival of the messianic age. The messianic age relates to history as the sovereign relates to the political order: it is outside and other than history, but its otherness defines and so permeates history. There is a kind of presence without identity.[33]

In this fragment Benjamin does not describe the Godforsaken world that Rose attributes to him. He sounds less like a neo-Kantian and more, as Jacob Taubes has argued, like the Apostle Paul. Benjamin "has a Pauline notion of creation," Taubes writes. He "sees the labor pains of creation, the futility of all creation."[34] Creation groans in Benjamin as it does in the eighth chapter of Paul's letter to the Romans. It groans in the realization that it is not complete. It groans in its distance from the messianic age. And exactly in that groaning, in that desperate futility, it finds itself joined by the Spirit in cries too deep for words. It participates in the work of the Spirit not through its achievements but through its passing away.[35]

The nature of practical reasoning in Benjamin's thought—and the contrast with Schmitt—becomes clearer through a consideration of the ways the two men think of the *Entsetzung* of law. Schmitt uses the term to describe the "suspension" of law by the sovereign in the state of exception. The sovereign, Schmitt writes, has the power to suspend existing law, rule by decrees, and eventually establish a new rule of law. For Schmitt, *Entsetzung* names that moment between the end of one system of law-sustaining violence and before the moment of lawmaking violence that then gives rise to a new system of law-sustaining violence. That is, Schmitt's *Entsetzung* marks a moment of suspension that is entirely within the cycles of what Benjamin calls mythical violence.

The English translation of the "Critique of Violence" in the *Selected Writings* also uses "suspension" to translate Benjamin's use of *Entsetzung* (202/251). A suspension of the law would indeed impoverish the kind of practical and political reasoning that could be done. It would let Rose's critique stick. For if the law is suspended, what could one reason with or about? But, as Christoph Menke argues, Benjamin should be read as using *Entsetzung* in a different sense. When Benjamin writes of the *Entsetzung* of law, he describes not its suspension but its "deposition," in Menke's translation, or, I would suggest, its "relief." It is "relieved" in the sense that one is relieved from office; it is also "relieved" as a city might be relieved from a siege. By the power of divine violence, Menke writes, the law is "deposed from the office it currently occupies, and *at the same time* released from a power besieging it."[36] Divine violence *relieves* the law from its role in the juridical order. It relieves it of binding power enforced by mythic violence. But divine violence also *delivers* law from its deep amalgamation with violence, much as the Apostle Paul describes the deliverance of the law in the Epistle to the Romans. Stripped of an alliance with violence, law is not overthrown but restored to its rightful form (cf. Romans 3:31). "The law is holy," Paul writes, "and the commandment is holy and just and good." But sin seizes an opportunity exactly in the goodness of the law and turns it toward the ends of death (7:12–13). Divine violence relieves law from this role. In its wake we "die to the law" (7:4). Divine violence therefore destroys the existing system of obligation. And, unlike the endless cycles of mythical violence, it does not establish a new system of obligation in place of the old. The relief of law invites instead a free response.

Reading Benjamin in conversation with Paul makes clear the ways that a political theology drawing on Benjamin can respond to Rose's main critiques. To say, as Rose does, that Benjamin does not offer criteria for discerning one historical moment as divine violence and another as merely mythical violence is to misunderstand the nature of divine violence. It is to assume that divine violence occurs in some discrete historical events but not in others. But such a view would collapse divine violence back into myth, for it would suppose a direct identification between divine and human action. Benjamin's notion of divine violence should not be understood as describing discrete acts that are, as it were, added to the history of human action. It might better be understood, as Agamben writes, by analogy to Benjamin's understanding of a pure language that is both other than and within everyday language:

> And just as pure language is not another language, just as it does not have a place other than that of the natural communicative languages, but reveals itself in these by exposing them as such, so pure violence is attested to only as the exposure and deposition of the relation between violence and law.[37]

The task is not to name which moments are identical to divine violence. It is rather to see divine violence—the moment when the fabric of the polity is torn open, when the goods, processes, and institutions of a juridical order are revealed to be finite—in the negation at work in every moment. And it is to see this negation, this secularization of the political, as participating, indirectly, in the work of redemption. It is to see law as a dialectical image that longs for the divine justice in which it still participates, however indirectly, in spite of itself. If the secular is not itself a "category of the Kingdom," it is still "a decisive category of its most unobtrusive approach."[38] Such a notion does not require criteria for identifying particular moments as moments of true divine violence. It requires instead a critical discernment that can hear the groaning of all creation. And, contrary to Rose's assessment, Benjamin gives ample resources for such discernment.

A better understanding of divine violence as the relief of law also makes clear that divine violence need not undo practical wisdom (phronesis) in the ways Rose says it does. Because Benjamin's divine violence does not destroy or even suspend law, it does not remove the law as a resource for political reasoning. The law is still there to give substance and content to practical and political reasoning. Thus, Benjamin's divine violence need not end in the arational decisionism of Schmitt. And because divine violence also delivers the law from its amalgamation with mythic violence, it makes possible a new kind of freedom in relation to the law. This is the freedom that reason needs to be fully reasonable. It is the freedom that politics needs to be genuinely political. Divine violence therefore frees people for a new relationship with the law, one that combines freedom and fidelity in ways that Benjamin learned to imagine by analogy to Kabbalah—the ardent reasoning about law that becomes possible when law has been relieved of its relationship with the violence of enforcement. Such freedom is not empty. And it is not a freedom only for reason. It is also a freedom of the law from the alliance with violence that distorts its inner character. The relief of law does not end phronesis but transposes it into a key marked by freedom and the love that freedom makes possible.

The relief of law sets phronesis free to seek the earthly happiness that Benjamin names as the right end of a secular order. All the arts and sciences that humans have developed to seek this happiness—and all the practical reasoning they involve—remain relevant. What changes is not the possibility of practical reason but the reasoner's relation to the ends practical reasoning seeks. Divine violence reveals the happiness of this age to be less than ultimate. This happiness runs, Benjamin writes, counter to the direction of redemption. Divine violence reveals it to be passing away. Thus Benjamin can describe the politics that pursue this happiness as a kind of "nihilism."[39] But that nihilism is not itself ultimate. It operates within a larger eschatology in which the pursuit of mortal happiness, precisely because it is fleeting, plays its part in the work of redemption. It is in groaning that creation is joined to the Spirit.

This eschatology also frames the phronesis made possible by divine violence. Benjamin offers a phronesis that, Taubes writes, fits with the *hōs mē* (as if not) passages of Paul's letters to the church in Corinth. "Those who deal with the world," Paul writes, should be "as though they had no dealing with it. For the present form of the world is passing away" (1 Corinthians 7:31). A person who knows the work of divine violence would not cease participating in the political life that divine violence has rendered mortal. But she would participate with a different sort of consciousness, seeking the goods of this world as one who is delivered from their pretensions and freed from their demands. She would understand both that the politics of this age cannot achieve anything ultimate and that, exactly in their limitations, they are joined to the work of redemption. She could reject the necessity of the state and still seek the earthly goods it can achieve. Delivered by divine violence, she would be capable of a rightly secular politics.[40]

The Hope of a Great Criminal

What would a notion of divine violence as the relief of law mean for the ways in which we remember John Brown? It would argue against those who reject Brown as a fanatic simply because he took up violent means outside the law. It is not that the Commonwealth of Virginia's laws against theft and murder were simply wrong. Rather, they had joined themselves not only to the violence of their enforcement but also to the violence that sustained a social order deeply dedicated to slavery. Divine violence reveals the depth of those alliances. And, in this monstrous case, it reveals the breadth of the gap between justice and law. Divine violence opens a space in which Brown can wrestle with the law in solitude, eventually taking on himself the responsibility for abstaining from it. Brown becomes visible, then, as what Benjamin calls a "great criminal." A great criminal "is not someone who has committed this or that crime for which one feels admiration; it is someone who, in defying the law, lays bare the violence of the legal system, the judicial order itself."[41]

To see Brown as a great criminal is not the same thing as seeing him as a freedom fighter. A freedom fighter might break an earthly law, but she or he does not do wrong. For a freedom fighter's violence can be inscribed into a narrative of liberation that justifies it as a necessary means for a good end. But a great criminal is, in the end, still a criminal. The commandment the great criminal breaks is still valid. "Thou shalt not kill" is not suspended, even in 1859. And breaking this still-valid commandment is not justified, as in so many arguments about the regrettable necessity of "dirty hands." If divine violence relieves the law and opens up the space in which Brown can deliberate, it does not then legitimate his actions. A sense of divine violence as the relief of law does not give resources for arguing that Brown was ethical, even in a very complex way. Rather, it shows the *limits* of ethics.

The actions of a great criminal are not justified because they conform to some deeper sense of the virtuous, the right, or the good, or even because they correspond to a divine will that is above every kind of virtue, right, or good. The great criminal cannot even claim the kind of justification that would come with a performance of divine violence, as Slavoj Žižek would suggest. Žižek understands that Benjamin's sense of divine violence does not legitimate acts of violence done in the name of some Divine Will. He sees that divine violence is "just the sign of the injustice of the world, of the world being ethically 'out of joint.'"[42] He understands that divine violence is not a sign that founds a new order but rather "a sign without meaning" (169). But Žižek then runs right past Benjamin's injunction against naming some particular moment as a moment of divine violence. We should, Žižek writes, "fearlessly identify divine violence with positively existing historical phenomena, thus avoiding any obscurantist mystification" (167). He makes some of these identifications himself, naming divine violence at work in the Red Terror of 1919, the Revolutionary Terror of 1792–1794, and the terror unleashed by John Brown in 1859 (167, 138). Žižek cheerfully admits that the violence in these moments has no divine sanction. There is, he writes, no "big Other" that guarantees them (169). This is a kind of nihilism but not the nihilism that is, in and in spite of itself, caught up in a redemption it does not create. It is total in a different way. And it is more certain of itself. Žižek's complete epistemological confidence in naming a moment that destroys the possibility of meaning makes for a curiously fundamentalist nihilism. But Žižek's nihilism runs only so deep. It is not hard to discern the criteria lurking behind Žižek's selection of these particular moments as moments of divine violence. And it is not difficult to imagine those criteria—like all such criteria—slipping into the forms of mythic violence. One need only read the history.

We would do better to resist the temptation to identify John Brown with a moment of divine violence. It is enough to know, as Benjamin says, that divine violence is possible. For the mere possibility of divine violence makes possible a critique of violence. If it does not justify Brown, it lets us see him as a great criminal, one who made plain the ways that the world was "out of joint." Such divine violence makes visible the limits of law and the limits of ethics that would become law. It relieves the law of the siege that mythic violence would impose on it and the office that mythic violence would establish for it. It renews the possibility of politics. It reminds us of how even great criminals can—in spite of themselves—find themselves caught up in God's great work of redemption. The significance of John Brown is not that all these things are fulfilled in his story but that in reading his story, we can learn again how to hope for them.

4 THE HIGHER LAW

ONE OF THE MOST IMPORTANT ICONS in American political imaginaries is kept on the second floor of the rotunda in the Kansas State Capitol. John Steuart Curry's monumental mural depicts bleeding Kansas as a "tragic prelude" to the Civil War (see Figure 4.1). The fallen bodies of two white soldiers, one in blue, the other in gray, establish a baseline for the painting. Bathed in the soft glow of fallen heroes, they reach toward one another, almost touching. Above them a frenzied tangle of bodies, black and white, struggles under Union and Confederate flags. In the near background, as if in a memory, settlers drive oxen pulling wagons. In the far background the earth itself cries out: a cyclone churns on the left as a prairie fire consumes the right. At the center of it all, with the bodies at his feet and the conflict under his outstretched arms, stands the abolitionist John Brown.

"I portray John Brown as a bloodthirsty, god-fearing maniac," Curry wrote in 1940.[1] Curry's Brown is not just any kind of fanatic. He is a distinctively *religious* fanatic. Even more specifically, he is a fanatic of the law. Brown's long beard and wild eyes cast him as a mad Moses who has come down from the mountain with a vision of the higher law and a desire to enforce it. He carries a Sharps rifle in one bloody hand and an open Bible in the other. The Alpha and Omega on the pages of his Bible suggest the apocalyptic content of the law he proclaims. And the sword and pistol on his hips underscore the means by which his prophecy will be fulfilled. Curry painted Brown as a violent prophet of a distinctly religious higher law.

FIGURE 4.1 John Steuart Curry (1897–1946), *The Tragic Prelude* (1937–1942). Kansas State Historical Society.

Curry's mural rode a tide of sentiment against Brown that had been rising throughout the 1920s and 1930s. White Southerners had long seen Brown as a dangerous fanatic. But the growing agreement of white Northerners represented a significant shift. From the time of Brown's raid on Harpers Ferry through the early days of Reconstruction, many white Northerners had celebrated Brown as hero and martyr. As Brown awaited hanging in 1859, Ralph Waldo Emerson said that this "new saint" would "make the gallows glorious like the cross."[2] But as Reconstruction gave way to Jim Crow, and as colonial ambitions and foreign wars gave new urgency to the project of national unity, whites in both the South and the North began to reconsider the Civil War. By the 1920s, these reconsiderations had become the norm. In the South, the band of writers known as the Fugitives breathed new power and respectability into the argument that the war had been caused by Yankee fanaticism. Robert Penn Warren crystallized this argument in his 1929 biography of Brown, which cast the abolitionist as the logical end point of New Englanders' extreme devotion to the abstract principles they called the "higher law." The Fugitives found echoes in the North. Revisionist historian Avery Craven matched Warren's portrait of Brown as an overzealous Northern fanatic with his own portrait of Edmund Ruffin as a temperate Southern traditionalist. In Craven's portrait, Ruffin's agrarian concreteness embodied a moderation that illumined Brown's abstract fanaticism by contrast.

An even more influential portrait of Brown as fanatic flickered on screens across the country right before Curry began work on his mural. *The Santa Fe*

Trail, directed by Michael Curtiz and starring Errol Flynn as J. E. B. Stuart, Ronald Reagan as George Custer, and Olivia de Havilland as the woman they both love, was one of the top-grossing films of 1940. The film depicted pro-slavery forces in Kansas as law-abiding citizens. African Americans, when they spoke at all in the film, expressed nostalgic longings for slavery. John Brown was the source of all the trouble. He was violent and religious in equal measure. He knelt to pray fearsome prayers. He shot an unarmed man. He plotted to bring down the nation. The army saved the day. Flynn's Stuart and Reagan's Custer might have disagreed about slavery, but they came together to fight the fanatical Brown—just as Northerners and Southerners would soon come together to fight German and Japanese soldiers cast as fanatics of a different sort. With pictures like these in circulation, it is clear that John Steuart Curry did not invent the image of Brown as a violent religious fanatic. He simply perfected the prevailing image of his time—and gave it the staying power of a wall in a state capitol.[3]

Curry's mural has been endlessly reproduced in scholarly studies, popular histories, and even tins of souvenir mints for sale at the statehouse in Topeka.[4] It continues to anchor memories of Brown and to orient American political imaginaries of many kinds. It establishes an enduring image of the solitary believer unleashing storms of righteous violence in the name of a higher law. Both those who praise Brown and those who see him as a terrible threat have tended to understand him as the religious warrior that Curry depicted.[5] Curry cast Brown as a kind of bogeyman that had to be suppressed. His mural helped secure the image of Brown that became a stock example for generations of critics of politics of the higher law. But that same image, once established, sometimes broke free from its curators' intentions. For people like Timothy McVeigh and the members of the Weather Underground the image of Brown as violent prophet of a higher law became an avatar to be inhabited.[6] It provided a ready-made role that promised an opportunity to share, through violent action, in the regeneration of the nation. As bogeyman or inspiration, the image of Brown as a violent prophet of the higher law plays an outsized role in American political imaginaries.

An image, however iconic, is not an argument. But it can shape political imaginaries in ways that make arguments more and less plausible. It can supply a concept that makes complex phenomena visible *as* something. Curry's image of Brown welds together the words Curry uses to describe him: "bloodthirsty," "god-fearing," "maniac." It helps us see bloodthirsty, god-fearing maniacs, even when a closer look might reveal details that do not easily fit that image. The three terms become linked in ways that give a hidden strength to arguments claiming that politics that appeal to a higher law—especially when that law is "religious"—are especially prone to violence. The image joins many other images, arguments, and institutional arrangements to give a commonsensical feel to political formations that separate religion and politics in the name of reducing violence.

An image is not an argument, but it can be argued with. In this chapter I make two arguments against Curry's image. First, I argue against attempts to identify John Brown's appeals to a "higher law" as simply "religious." Brown and other abolitionists clearly shared a sense of a higher law. That vision of a higher law was often interlaced with religious commitments. But Brown and others argued for their commitments to higher laws in ways that outran anything like what we usually call religion. Thus, a politics that bars religious reasoning would not eliminate the mythic violence that often accompanies appeals to the higher law. Second, I argue against the assumption that appeals to a higher law necessarily produce more, and more total, acts of violence. I recall examples of this-worldly politics that rejected any talk of higher law and still ended in justifications for total war. And I recall the witness of abolitionists and civil rights activists who rejected the violence of "carnal weapons" precisely because of their commitments to a higher law. Not all rejections of a higher law make for peace, and not all appeals to higher law end in violence.

The answer to violence in the name of higher laws is not less religious reasoning but better and deeper religious reasoning, the kind that can imagine the higher law as something other than a code to be enforced and history as something more than an endless succession of homogeneous moments to be wrenched into conformity with the law. From such an angle of vision, John Brown would look less like a bloodthirsty, god-fearing maniac and more like a flawed prophet who is caught up in a story of redemption that he cannot quite imagine.

A Declaration of Liberty

John Steuart Curry put a Bible in Brown's hand and a prophet's beard on his face to identify his violence as essentially religious. Critics of Brown have long reproduced this picture of him as a fanatical reader of the Bible, a fundamentalist autodidact who took some verses a little too literally ("Remember those that are in bonds") while seeming to forget others altogether ("Turn the other cheek"). Admirers of Brown have also stressed the significance of the Bible in his thought. Louis DeCaro, in a 2002 biography that treats Brown as a kind of "Protestant saint," describes a formative role for the Bible in Brown's vision. "As an evangelical Christian," DeCaro writes, "[Brown] not only read the Bible as God's word, he read the Bible as *God's word to John Brown*. He believed that the scriptures continued to speak to life situations, radiating fresh truth and directives without obscuring its original and primary meaning."[7] Curry and DeCaro offer radically disparate evaluations of Brown. But they agree in defining him as driven by devotion to a higher law revealed in the Bible.

The Bible *was* a significant source for Brown's understanding of the higher law. He drew inspiration especially from a passage from the Sermon on the Mount: "Whatsoever you would that men should do to you, you should do even to them."[8] Brown cited this "Golden Rule" throughout his testimony to the court. He put it at the center of his final speech, which was endlessly reprinted across the North. In this final speech he linked the Golden Rule to a string of other verses that were dear to abolitionists. And he made clear that together they constituted a higher law:

> This court acknowledges, as I suppose, the validity of the law of God. I see a book kissed here which I suppose to be the Bible, or at least the New Testament. That teaches me that all things whatsoever I would that men should do to me, I should do even to them. It teaches me, further, "remember them that are in bonds, as bound with them." I endeavored to act up to that instruction. I say, I am yet too young to understand that God is any respecter of persons.[9]

The breathless density of biblical references in this paragraph suggests the ways Brown thought about the higher law. He was not so much providing proof-text warrants for propositions as rolling in a sea of biblical phrases.

The Bible was important to Brown, but it was far from his only source. Without any hesitation, he blended biblical references with a wide range of other references—especially those sacred to the national memory of the United States. Writing from prison to a cousin who had expressed concern, Brown reminded him that their grandfather, Captain John Brown, had fought and died in 1776. He, too, "might have perished on the scaffold had circumstances been but *very little different*."[10] Brown's defenders would take up this point and make it again and again: Brown's resistance was just like that of the generation of 1776. In fact, it might have been even better, the Reverend Fales Henry Newhall argued, because Brown was fighting for the rights of others, not only himself.[11]

Brown combined biblical and nationalist references seamlessly. When investigators searched the farmhouse from which Brown launched the raid on Harpers Ferry, they found a huge cache of weapons, including rifles, pistols, pikes, and even heavy guns. They also found a document Brown had written, "A Declaration of Liberty by the Representatives of the Slave Population of the United States of America."[12] As the title suggested, Brown's treatise sampled and riffed on the Declaration of Independence from 1776. If its title made reference to sacred American political traditions, its material form called up more biblical echoes. The declaration had been written out on foolscap pages, which were then pasted one after another on a long, narrow band of white cloth. A rod had been attached to each end of the cloth so that the declaration could be rolled up like a scroll. Brown's higher law looked the part.[13]

It sounded the part, too. "When in the course of Human events" the declaration began, in a direct echo of the 1776 declaration (637). Like the authors of that document, Brown appealed to "Self Evident" truths: "That all men are created Equal; That they are endowed by their Creator with certain unalienable rights. That among these are Life, Liberty; & pursuit of happiness." And like the authors of the 1776 Declaration, Brown identified natural laws that could be known by reason with the laws of God. Brown's declaration justified the rising up of an oppressed people to "assert their Natural rights, as Human Beings, as Native and Mutual Citizens of a free Republic." From this talk of natural rights Brown could move directly into an appeal to "the unchangeable Law of God" (642). And in another verbatim quotation from the 1776 Declaration, Brown's declaration called for enslaved people "to assume among the powers of Earth the same equal privileges to which the Laws of Nature, and nature's God, entitle them" (637). In the reasoning of both declarations, the laws of nature and of nature's God are one and the same. If Jefferson and the other authors of the 1776 Declaration fused appeals to God and nature, reason and revelation, Brown added one more layer to the mix: in quoting the 1776 Declaration, he was not just appealing to the same sources but also appealing to the sacred text of the very government he was opposing.

All of these sources, and more, come together in the last lines of Brown's "Declaration": "'Indeed; I tremble for my Country, when I reflect; that God is Just; and that his Justice; will not sleep forever' &c. &c. Nature is mourning for its murdered, and Afflicted Children. Hung be the Heavens in Scarlet" (643). In these compact lines Brown quoted Jefferson trembling for his country that God was just. He made reference to Jeremiah's cry that Rachel was mourning for her children (see Jeremiah 31:15) but transposed the tune into a more deist key by replacing Rachel with Nature. And he adapted the opening line of *Henry VI, Part 1*. Shakespeare had given the Duke of Bedford lines of mourning: "Hung be the heavens with black," Bedford said to open the play. But Brown was ready to fight, not to mourn, so he concluded his declaration with a revision of Shakespeare's color scheme. "Hung be the Heavens in Scarlet," Brown wrote. The higher law would be established in blood.

Jefferson, Jeremiah, and Shakespeare, all in a paragraph, and with a reference to Nature-with-a-capital-N thrown in for good measure: Brown could blend these traditions so easily because, to his mind, they all testified to the same higher law. Truth was unified, and it took the form of a higher law. This emphasis on the higher law—not the biblical appeals that were one of its sources—defined Brown's thought. The range of references suggests a correction to Curry's portrait of a Bible-mad fanatic. An accurate portrait would show John Brown holding not just the Bible but also the Mayflower Compact, the Declaration of Independence, the Constitution of the United States, bloody relics of Bunker Hill, copies of the collected works of Jefferson and Shakespeare, and more. The defining feature of the violent politics of John Brown was not his commitment to a single sacred book but his conviction that he was called to execute the judgments of a higher law.

Treason Is Our Inheritance

In his promiscuous use of sources, Brown reflected some of the range and diversity of the sources other Americans of his day were using to justify their own understandings of the higher law. Methodist bishop Gilbert Haven called a long roll of New England preachers as his precedents before preaching a sermon on the higher law in 1850. The roll included the Reverend Jonathan Mayhew of West Church, Boston, whose own sermon on "the Higher Law" was "by the confession of John Adams . . . the opening gun of the Revolution."[14] Haven was right to argue that the habit of appealing to a higher law had a long history in North America. But the range of appeals is so wide that it cannot be consolidated into a single tradition. And the tradition is even wider than Haven's narrative of New England pulpits would suggest.

References to the higher law rang out in the first years of Puritan settlement in New England and then again around the time of the Revolution. They surged again a few decades later as the debate about slavery gained more and more intensity. African Americans, especially, used language of the higher law to frame criticism of slavery through the 1830s and 1840s. At its first meeting in 1837, the African American–led American Moral Reform Society (AMRS) argued that the laws of the land had no legitimate standing:

> The separation of our fathers from the land of their birth, earth ties and earthly affections, was not only sinful in its nature and tendency, but it led to a system of robbery, bribery and persecution offensive to the laws of nature and justice.
>
> Therefore, under whatever pretext or authority these laws have been promulgated or executed, whether under parliamentary, colonial, or American legislation, *we declare* them in the sight of Heaven wholly *null* and *void*, and should be *immediately abrogated*.[15]

Because the founding of civil government in Anglophone North America—in all its dispensations—had been linked to a system of slavery that was offensive to the laws of nature and justice, its own laws had no authority. The AMRS described the laws that enforced slavery as illegitimate "in the sight of Heaven," but the society did not rely on appeals to any distinctively Christian sources or doctrines. Instead, the AMRS built its case through a theory of legitimate government that was grounded in "the laws of nature and justice." The society's argument for a law that was higher than the laws of the land sounded more like the liberal John Locke than the Puritan John Cotton.

Black abolitionist and Presbyterian minister Henry Highland Garnet offered a more searing version of higher law reasoning in his 1843 "Address to the Slaves." He called enslaved people to resist slavery, even if resistance involved violence not sanctioned by any earthly law. He grounded this call in the positive duty of all people to obey the higher law. And he found this higher law, he said, in the Bible. God commanded people to worship only God, love their neighbors, keep the Sabbath, read the Bible, and train up their children in the ways of God. Slavery did not excuse people from these duties, Garnet said. "To such degradation [as slavery] it is sinful in the extreme for you to make voluntary submission. . . . The forlorn condition in which you are placed does not destroy your moral obligation to God." Garnet's politics of the higher law did depend on ideals from the Bible. And he did argue that violence might be necessary to allow people to obey the law. But Garnet made clear that violence had no positive capacities to establish the righteous state dreamed of by the law. It simply removed or defied the obstacles created by earthly powers.[16]

In 1843, when Garnet made his address, the number of white abolitionists who would have echoed his talk of resistance for the sake of a higher law was small. But references to the higher law surged among white Northerners in reaction to the Fugitive Slave Act of 1850. Passed as part of a bundle of compromises that included the admission of California as a free state, the Fugitive Slave Act gave slaveholders the right to pursue the people slaveholders called their property across state lines and into Northern states. It stripped African American people of legal rights to appeal detention and deportation. And— most offensive to white New England consciences—it forced Northerners to assist in the process. Before the Fugitive Slave Act passed, Northerners had been able to think of slavery as a system maintained in other places by other people. It was unfortunate but not necessarily something they could or should do anything about. The Fugitive Slave Act made manifest the North's connection to slavery and rendered that complacency impossible. While many white Northerners accepted the law, an increasingly large number resented and rejected it. They found their champion in William Seward, the freshman senator from New York.

On March 11, 1850, Seward rose to give his very first speech in the Senate. Just days before, Daniel Webster, one of the most powerful orators of his day and an emblem of New England rectitude, had disappointed Yankee abolitionists by arguing for the compromise that included the Fugitive Slave Act.[17] Webster's "Constitution and Union" speech was pragmatic. It accepted what it could not change and sought to do what good it could. It appealed, above all else, to the Constitution as the existing law of the land. The Constitution provided for slavery in the territories where it already existed, Webster said. But the Constitution did not authorize extension of slavery to new territories. The territories seized in the war with Mexico should therefore enter as free states. But respecting slavery where it was already established meant respecting the so-called property rights in slaves even across state lines. Thus Webster opposed abolition, supported the entry of new free states, and supported the Fugitive Slave Act. He proposed a reasonable compromise in the name of the Constitution, the law of the land.

Seward and others with abolitionist sympathies found this compromise not just unreasonable but appalling. "The Constitution regulates our stewardship," Seward said; "the Constitution devotes the domain to union, to justice, to defence, to welfare, and to liberty. But there is a higher law than the Constitution, which regulates our authority over the domain, and devotes it to the same noble purposes."[18] Seward appealed to a higher law established by "the Creator of the Universe." But his arguments depended less on references to the Bible than to

Burke, Montesquieu, and Machiavelli. From these sources Seward argued for a law that was higher than the Constitution. That higher law, he said, prohibited compromise with those who would hold their fellow humans in bondage.

Seward's "higher law" speech set the vocabulary for opposition to the Fugitive Slave Act. By one estimate, preachers delivered some two thousand sermons against the law in the early 1850s.[19] Lecturers delivered even more speeches in halls across the Northern United States and southern Canada. A common rhetoric of higher law dominated these sermons and speeches. But speakers used a wide range of sources as they argued for the existence of the law they said was higher than the law of the land. They gave different kinds of content to the higher law. They described different relationships between the higher law and the law of the land. And they discerned different practical implications from the existence of a higher law. The trope of a higher law could circulate so widely in part because it was open to so many different systems of belief and action. The only thing that held the appeals together was a loose sense of some authority beyond the one made manifest in the laws of the land and the almost incantatory power of the phrase itself.

Massachusetts native Gilbert Haven showed the power of this language in an 1850 sermon denouncing the Fugitive Slave Act that he entitled "The Higher Law." Haven was clearly inspired by Seward, but he made a very different sort of argument than the one Seward made. He opened with an expansive account of political life, arguing that civil government arose, in the Providence of God, as an "expression" of "the social element in man."[20] Civil law reflected those origins, grounding a good but not ultimate obligation. What Haven called the "moral law," though, arose as an expression of a higher human faculty, Conscience. Conscience was the "viceregent" of God (7), Haven said, and while it could be "rendered imperfect and obtuse by reason of sin," it retained a "force that is ever pressing it against all temptations" toward right discernment of an unchanging moral law (9). As Conscience was higher than the social element in humans, the moral law was higher than the civil law in society. Haven brought this political theology to ground in an application section that was marked as such in the old style. And the applications were clear. Listeners should refuse to do the things the Fugitive Slave Act commanded when they went against the higher law, continue to do what the higher law required even when the law of the land forbade it, and work steadily to change positive law to bring it into conformity with the higher law (15). As Haven moved toward his conclusion, specific application rose to broader exhortation: "In Christ, not in the Constitution, must we put our trust. On His law should we meditate, not on that which again nails Him, scourged and bleeding, to the fatal cross" (29). Haven's language was unmistakably theological. But at the heart of his argument was not a string of biblical texts but individual conscience. Haven made theological appeals to the higher law, but he looked nothing like Curry's image of John Brown.

African American preachers and speakers further expanded the range of appeals to higher laws against the Fugitive Slave Act in the early 1850s. J. W. Loguen, who became a bishop in the African Methodist Episcopal Zion Church, was himself a fugitive slave when he called the city of Syracuse to defy the laws of the land and declare itself a city of refuge.[21] Samuel Ringgold Ward declared in an 1850 speech in Boston's Faneuil Hall that "if the fugitive slave is traced to our part of New York State, he shall have the law of Almighty God to protect him."[22] Frances Ellen Watkins, who taught at the African Methodist Episcopal Zion Church's Union Seminary, mocked those who hid behind the claim that "we have no higher law than the Constitution" in an 1857 address to the New York Anti-Slavery Society.[23] Mary Ann Shadd, who after the war became the first woman to enroll in the law school of Howard University, called upon the higher law in an 1858 sermon in Chatham, Canada:

> As the law of God must be to us the higher law in spite of powers principalities selfish priests or selfish people to whom the minister it is important the [that?] we assert boldly that no where does God look upon this the chief crimes with the least degree of allowance nor are we justified in asserting that he will tolerate those who in any wise support or sustain it.[24]

The law of God condemned slavery, Shadd said, whatever the law of the land. And God could not tolerate defiance of the higher law.

Even those who supported the Fugitive Slave Act could make use of the rhetoric of the higher law. John C. Lord, the pastor of Central Presbyterian Church in Buffalo, New York, invoked the higher law in a sermon calling for obedience to the Fugitive Slave Act. Slavery had been established by God, Lord argued, so the law of God commanded people to comply with the law of the land in this case.[25]

Orestes Brownson, who left the transcendentalist movement for the Catholic Church, made a more subtle argument that reached the same conclusion. He denounced the ways that people like William Seward and Gilbert Haven appealed to the higher law. "The appeal to the supreme Lawgiver is compatible with civil government," Brownson wrote in 1851, "but the appeal to private judgment, or conviction, as to a higher law than that of the state, is not; for it virtually denies government itself, by making the individual paramount to it."[26] Brownson argued that relying on individual conscience as a guide to the higher law could end only in anarchy or tyranny. If every individual was left free to follow his or her own conscience, there could be no civil order. And if there was to be some order in such a society, it would have to be imposed by tyrannical force. True freedom, Brownson wrote, required a state to guarantee it. That state had to stand under a higher law in order to be legitimate. But the higher law could not be known by individual conscience, for that would only reinstall private judgment and dissolve the state. Instead, the higher law had to be known by the living authority of a church. Brownson may have denounced the role of conscience in Seward's "Higher Law" speech, but he "agree[d] entirely with Mr. Seward and his abolition and free-soil friends, as to the fact that there is a higher law than the constitution. The law of God is supreme, and overrides all human enactments, and every human enactment incompatible with it is null and void from the beginning and cannot be obeyed with a good conscience, for 'we must obey God rather than men.'"[27] Brownson rejected individual conscience as a resource for knowing the higher law even as he insisted on the higher law itself. He advocated a distinctively Christian version of the higher law, but it looked nothing like the vision of Gilbert Haven or Mary Ann Shadd. And it looked nothing like Curry's solitary individual with a book in one hand and a gun in the other.

Talk of the higher law surged again in the wake of John Brown's capture and execution in 1859. In a memorial sermon entitled "The Martyr's Death and the Martyr's Triumph," white abolitionist preacher George B. Cheever set up a series of oppositions between what the state said and what God said. "God says, 'Thou shalt not deliver unto his master the servant that has escaped from his master unto thee.' . . . The State says, 'Thou shalt oppress him; thou shalt deliver him up.'"[28] Cheever repeated the opposition again and again: "God says . . . The State says . . . " Cheever's rhetorical form made clear the conflict between divine and human laws. And when what God said did not match what the state said, the Christian had to listen to God:

> And whenever a great sin is enthroned in government and law, and any man, in the name of God, sets himself with God's Word against it, disobeying the unrighteous law, and teaching men to obey God's law above it, God's law against it, the conflict is irrepressible, for God will reign, and God's children must maintain his sovereignty, and the supremacy of his law, even unto death.[29]

Cheever saw Brown as one who disobeyed the unrighteous law of the state in order to obey the higher law of God. He then wrapped Brown's faithful disobedience in a larger story about the sovereignty of God.

Cheever joined a chorus that ranged far beyond ordained clergy. Henry David Thoreau preferred a lyceum podium to any pulpit, and he never would have spoken as Cheever did about the sovereignty of God, but he shared with Cheever the trope of the higher law. In "The Last Days of John Brown," an essay composed nine months after Brown's death, Thoreau described the effect of Brown's witness:

> The North, I mean the *living* North, was suddenly all transcendental. It went behind the human law, it went behind the apparent failure, and recognized eternal justice and glory. Commonly, men live according to a formula, and are satisfied if the order of law is observed, but in this instance they, to some extent, returned to original perceptions, and there was a slight revival of the old religion. They saw that what was called order was confusion, what was called justice, injustice, and that the best was deemed the worst.[30]

Brown lived by the higher law, Thoreau said, and he helped others do the same. He helped people get "behind" the human law to real justice. In doing so, he made the North "all transcendental."

Thoreau emphatically framed Brown not only as a model of transcendentalist courage but also as an extension of the tradition of the Puritans. In a New England society that was both eagerly and anxiously moving beyond Puritan forms of life, Brown offered a reassuring link to the past. With a gaunt body formed by asceticism and poverty, Brown looked like Thoreau's listeners thought a Puritan should look. Brown embraced the identity: he claimed, and Thoreau claimed on his behalf, that he was descended from Peter Brown, who had signed the Mayflower Compact.[31] But the deepest link was more substantial. In a sermon entitled "The Puritan Principle and John Brown," New England abolitionist Wendell Phillips reminded his hearers that the state of Massachusetts was founded in defiance of the edicts of the king and obedience to the higher law of God. The motto of these founders, Phillips said, "was not 'Law and Order'; it was 'God and Justice,'—a much better motto."[32] This motto, and the fidelity to a higher law that it implied, meant that "treason is our inheritance. The Puritans planted it in the very structure of the State; and when their children try to curse a martyr, like the prophet of old, half the curse, at least, turns into a blessing. I thank God for that Massachusetts!" (305).

Wendell Phillips called upon the traditions of New England. Gilbert Haven used language of the cross to argue for the importance of conscience. Henry David Thoreau stressed the decisive significance of individual conscience, but without any scaffolding from traditional Christian doctrines. Henry Highland Garnet called for violent resistance to achieve the freedom to follow God's law. William Seward spoke of Montesquieu and Burke. Frances Ellen Watkins mocked the authority of earthly laws. John Brown combined something from all of these sources, and more. Even among abolitionists, higher law talk ran from many different sources and in many different directions. There was no singular "higher law tradition." Higher law language defined instead a structured but relatively empty space that was charged with its own significance even as it was open to many different kinds of content and compatible with many different sorts of worldviews.

The diversity of appeals to the higher law reveals the distortion at work in Curry's icon—and the many political imaginaries it informs. Curry's portrait of Brown as a bloodthirsty, god-fearing maniac reduces a complex welter of ideas about the higher law to a single, religious source. It is hard to say just which of these many sources of higher laws are "religious" and which are not. The sources are often deeply intertwined, as in Haven's argument from conscience as the viceregent of God or Phillips's argument from God and Massachusetts. But it is clear that at least some versions of the higher law—those of Thoreau, Seward, and the AMRS, for instance, and even of Brown himself, at times— were rooted in sources beyond those associated most closely with groups that are usually identified as religions. The definition of "religion" can be thinned and expanded to include these sources, of course. "Religion" can be defined to include conscience, nature, and nation, especially if they function to legitimate claims about a higher law. But if anything that grounds an account of the higher law is religious, then the argument behind Curry's mural can slip into tautology: if religion is just whatever causes people to take violent action for a higher law, then the claim that religion leads to violence for the sake of a higher law just restates a point already smuggled in to the definition of religion.[33] Instead, we should insist on the fact that abolitionist appeals to the higher law took many forms and that some of these forms drew more on established religious traditions than others.

Refusing to conflate the higher law with religion has at least two implications. Analytically, this refusal argues against a functionalist definition of religion that calls "religious" anything that promotes a higher law. It argues for the retention of separate terms to describe religion and the higher law. An analysis will need both terms to name distinct social phenomena and understand the relationships between them. Practically and politically, refusing to conflate religion and the higher law means that the problem of violence done in the name of higher laws cannot be solved simply by limiting religions or insulating political processes from them. If religions are no longer cast out as identical with the problem, they might be able to provide resources for addressing it.

Ambivalent Faith

While many contemporary conversations collapse religion and the higher law into a single term, Andrew Delbanco's long essay, "The Abolitionist Imagination" (2012), maintains clear distinctions between religiously motivated politics and a politics of the higher law. Delbanco can see the ways that theologians like Reinhold Niebuhr resist politics of the higher law, even as he sees the potential of aggressively secularist movements, like Stalinism, to engage in violence for the sake of higher laws. The distinction helps Delbanco focus his critique. He is not arguing against religion in politics but against appeals to the higher law that can underwrite violence—whatever sources they might draw from, and whatever ends they might pursue.

Delbanco builds his case by looking back to consolidate a tradition of opposition to politics of the higher law. He defines a tradition that runs from Nathaniel Hawthorne and Herman Melville through Abraham Lincoln to American pragmatists who were reacting against the horrors of what they saw as a Civil War driven by idealisms on both sides. Delbanco's tradition continues on to mid-twentieth-century critics like Lionel Trilling who tried to find middle ground between hysterical anticommunists and head-in-the-sand fellow travelers with Stalin. This tradition, Delbanco writes, is defined by what Trilling called an aesthetic of "articulate ambivalence."[34] It is marked by a commitment to Arthur Schlesinger Jr.'s "vital center" (40). It features an openness to compromise, a refusal to demonize opponents, and a willingness to wait for gradual change. Delbanco defines these virtues with relatively thin language. Most of their content, and the strongest arguments for their goodness, comes through contrast. Playing off the title of Trilling's *The Liberal Imagination* (1950), Delbanco describes the liberal tradition by setting it against what he called "the abolitionist imagination." Abolitionism, he writes, "may be regarded not as a passing episode but as a movement that crystallized—or, as we might say today, channeled—an energy that has been at work in our culture since the

beginning and is likely to express itself again in variant forms in the future"
(22–23). Abolitionists include not just people like John Brown and Frederick
Douglass but anyone "who identifies a heinous evil and wants to eradicate it—
not tomorrow, not next year, but now" (23). Abolitionists in every age appeal to
higher laws, in the broadest sense. Those laws give abolitionist politics urgency
and clarity. By their very form, higher laws make compromise difficult. The liberal tradition Delbanco defines, on the other hand, embraces doubt, ambiguity,
and compromise. It rejects politics of the higher law.

Delbanco describes a history of ebb and flow between liberal and abolitionist traditions. One high-water mark for the liberal tradition, Delbanco argues,
comes in the middle decades of the twentieth century. The work of figures
like Trilling, Schlesinger, Edmund Wilson, Richard Hofstadter, and Reinhold
Niebuhr enjoyed both wide influence and academic respectability. One could
add the names of liberal anti-utopians like Isaiah Berlin, Raymond Aron, and
Hannah Arendt to Delbanco's list. And the Fugitive and Revisionist histories
of the Civil War—along with the critique of religious fanaticism in *The Santa
Fe Trail* and John Steuart Curry's Kansas statehouse mural—helped lay the
groundwork for this midcentury moderation. But, Delbanco writes, "this cen-
trist perspective—we might as well call it a liberal aesthetic—could not, and
did not, survive the Cold War or the concurrent academic culture wars" (40).
The 1960s, 1970s, and 1980s saw less ambivalent celebrations of movements
for emancipation. There was a real shift—to cite an example Delbanco does
not name—from C. Vann Woodward's deflationary essay on Brown in 1960 to
Stephen B. Oates's biography, written just one decade later, that replaced questions about Brown's sanity with careful attention to his theology.[35] Woodward
would not grant Brown the dignity of being a devil, portraying him as little
more than a half-mad horse thief engaged in conflicts that never attained fully
public significance. Oates, on the other hand, offered respectful attention to
Brown's religious commitments. The differences between these two influential
works offer further support for Delbanco's narrative of oscillation. There was a
clear movement from a midcentury rejection of higher law talk as madness and
ideology to a post-1960s willingness to engage such talk as serious and significant—especially if it was linked to a movement for liberation.

Now, Delbanco argues, the tide has turned again. A string of prominent
works since the turn of the millennium has shown more ambivalence about
higher laws and higher causes, especially in accounts of the Civil War. What
Delbanco calls the "full-throated Unionism" of a book like James McPherson's

Battle Cry of Freedom (1988) has been replaced at the center of the field by the deep ambivalence of books like Louis Menand's *The Metaphysical Club* (2001), Drew Gilpin Faust's *This Republic of Suffering* (2008), Harry S. Stout's *Upon the Altar of the Nation* (2006), and David Goldfield's *America Aflame* (2011).[36] None of these recent books offers anything like an apology for slavery. But all of them question the cost of the conflict and the morality of both sides. Delbanco's survey overlooks some significant exceptions to his thesis. Books like David S. Reynolds's *John Brown, Abolitionist* (2005) and Evan Carton's *Patriotic Treason* (2006) make vigorous cases for John Brown's politics of the higher law. John Stauffer's subtle *Black Hearts of Men* (2004) does not directly affirm an abolitionist politics of the higher law, but it does discern the ways those politics helped bring black and white abolitionists into relationships that transformed understandings of race. The presence of such prominent books suggests the incompleteness of Delbanco's story about the pendulum's swing back to this-worldly and pragmatic politics. In ignoring them, Delbanco's analysis does not just describe the arc of the pendulum but also gives it a push. If politics in America are moving in the direction Delbanco suggests, he has helped to make it so.

Resistance to talk of higher laws has been on the rise, Delbanco writes, in part because the most prominent public speakers of religious language have shifted from civil rights leaders to "jihadists abroad and the Christian right at home" (45). While Delbanco does not engage in any close study of such figures, at least some of them do give evidence for his argument. Paul Hill, for example, cast himself as an agent of the higher law when he murdered John Britton and James Barrett outside the Pensacola Ladies Center in 1994. Britton, a physician, worked part-time at the center and provided abortions for women there. Barrett served as his bodyguard. After Hill shot the men, he cited John Brown as a precedent for his actions. He hoped that the Pensacola Ladies Center would become for anti-abortionists what Harpers Ferry was for abolitionists. And he quoted Brown's 1859 testimony into a new context when he told the jury that condemned him to death that they could "mix my blood with the blood of the unborn and those who have fought to defend the oppressed."[37] Paul Hill took up the mantle of the John Brown that Curry painted. In doing so, he became a perfect illustration for Delbanco's argument against the higher law.

Hill justified his killings by appealing to what he called the Moral Law of God. The Sixth Commandment, he said, did not prohibit all killing. It prohibited the killing of *innocents*. But, Hill argued, claiming the Westminster Catechism as precedent, it not only allowed for the killing of guilty people but also implied a positive obligation to use "the means necessary for protecting the innocent from harm—including lethal force." The commandment not to kill became a commandment to protect innocent lives even if it meant taking the lives of others. "This duty exists," Hill wrote, "even if horribly unjust laws, which sanction murder, and forbid the use of these means, are in force. Under these circumstances, we must obey God rather than men."[38] The Moral Law of God, Hill believed, required the killing of Barrett and Britton.

Delbanco would surely disagree with Hill's justification for his actions. But he would agree with Hill's account of the parallels between violent anti-abortion activists and violent abolitionists like Brown. "And the parallels should remind us," Delbanco writes, "that all holy wars, whether metaphoric or real, from left or from right, bespeak a zeal for combating sin, not tomorrow, not in due time, not in Lincoln's phrase, by putting it 'in the course of ultimate extinction,' but *now*" (48–49). Delbanco proposes instead a little less conviction and a little more patience with history, one another, and ourselves. Like Daniel Webster, Delbanco would turn our gaze from higher laws to the slow, difficult task of working together to improve the laws we already have.

The pragmatic vision of Delbanco has great appeal in an age when violence in the name of higher laws seems to be coming from all directions. He is right to see through the sheen of particular political causes down to the structure of appeals to the higher law. Too often evaluations of the ends determine evaluations of the higher law. A critic who opposes slavery but supports the availability of legal abortions, for instance, might be warm to appeals to the higher law when they come from John Brown but condemn them as fanatical when they come from Paul Hill. The higher law can become something to invoke when it serves our agendas and to attack when it does not. The pragmatism of Delbanco is more principled. It sees the common structure of appeals to higher law. And it warns against the structure itself.

Delbanco is right to be ambivalent about most appeals to the higher law. And the principled nature of his critique lifts it above simple partisanship. But his thoroughgoing, consistent ambivalence begins to imply claims of another order—not just about this or that appeal to higher law but about the whole category of such appeals. It denies that the category exists on its own terms. It allows that appeals to the higher law might do some social good, if carefully controlled (the abolitionists, Delbanco acknowledges in an echo of Reinhold Niebuhr, did at least expand a collective sense of what might be possible).[39] But a principled ambivalence knows in advance that even appeals to the higher law that might do some good are not what they say they are. It understands them rather as the deeply held interests of competing groups. As interests, however deeply held, they are mundane, this-worldly things, the kinds of things that can and should be subject to bargaining. This is a strong claim that is linked to a strong political program. It fits with institutional arrangements—like a simple privatizing of religion or an insistence on a neutral public reason—that have difficulty acknowledging the absolute quality of their own foundations. A piecemeal ambivalence that takes each appeal to the higher law as it came might avoid such moves. But Delbanco's principled ambivalence refuses the very possibility of a higher law.

Violence and the Higher Law

Andrew Delbanco's resistance to the whole idea of a higher law depends on an assumption that politics of the higher law are more likely to produce more violence. There is an intuitive appeal to this line of argument: it seems commonsensical that ultimate values would lead to ultimate violence, especially because the charge has so often been repeated. And this can happen, as in the case of Paul Hill, the murderous anti-abortion activist, or Gerrit Smith, the white abolitionist whose commitment to "Bible civil government" led him to supply weapons to John Brown in hopes of sparking a wider war. A higher law *can* incite violence, as in the case of the proslavery mobs and militias that killed more people than the abolitionists did, or the Southern theologians who rooted support for slavery in laws of God that transcended whatever came out of Washington.[40] Delbanco could gladly grant all of these cases, even if it means pulling proslavery mobs under the awkward umbrella of an "abolitionist imagination." For his real argument is not against abolitionists but against appeals to higher laws for any purposes. He sees the ways that these appeals can lead to violence without limit. But he misses the ways that appeals to a higher law can restrain violence. And he misses the ways that ambivalent, pragmatic, earthbound arguments for the rule of law can also legitimate violence without limits this side of total victory.

William Tecumseh Sherman, for instance, had nothing like an abolitionist imagination. He refused both the narratives that made war into a theater of glory and the higher laws that sustained those narratives. "War is cruelty," he wrote to the mayor and city council of Atlanta in September 1864, "and you cannot refine it." The city had surrendered, and Sherman's troops occupied it. He ordered the mayor and council to remove all occupants from the city.

They asked that he spare property and noncombatants in the name of peace. "I want peace," Sherman wrote, "and believe it can only be reached through union and war, and I will ever conduct war with a view to perfect and early success." Perfect and early success, Sherman had come to believe, required a strategy that included destruction of anything that could be used to support the enemy's war effort. Whether these tactics met the threshold for "total war" or merely, as Mark Grimsley argues, "hard war," they clearly overrode significant constraints on violence by appealing to military necessity.[41] Sherman stressed that he undertook these measures neither for the sake of personal gain nor for the sake of some higher law: "We don't want your negroes, or your horses, or your houses, or your lands, or any thing you have," he wrote, "but we do want and will have a just obedience to the laws of the United States. That we will have, and, if it involves the destruction of your improvements, we cannot help it." On November 14, in the name of military necessity and the rule of law, Sherman's troops set fire to Atlanta as they set out for Savannah.[42]

Sherman's tactics reflected a growing consensus between Lincoln and his generals. However deep and sincere Lincoln's opposition to slavery, it was not a desire to eliminate slavery that led him to approve a strategy that approached total war. As James McPherson argues, the Union strategy escalated steadily from 1861 to 1864 in response to a series of military setbacks. Commitments to abolish slavery did not lead this escalation but trailed behind it. Abolitionist commitments had a chance, early in the war, to play the leading role. In September 1861, Generals John C. Frémont and David Hunter declared the slaves in the areas under their control to be free. Lincoln revoked these declarations of martial law, worrying both that they were issued without proper authority and that they would provoke the secession of the border states that retained slavery but did not leave the Union. As the war escalated, it became clear that slaves were a significant resource for Confederate forces and that freed men and women could do much to help the Union cause—both materially at home and in the battle for public perception abroad. In a slow series of measures, Lincoln expanded emancipation and the threat of emancipation until finally, on January 1, 1863, he proclaimed that all enslaved persons in areas that were in rebellion were now "forever free." He claimed the authority for this declaration as commander in chief, framing it as "a fit and necessary measure for suppressing said rebellion." The Emancipation Proclamation was one "necessary measure" in a larger strategy that included seizure, liberation, or destruction of anything that could be used in the war effort—from enslaved people to the entire city of Atlanta.[43] It would be wrong to dismiss the Emancipation Proclamation as nothing more than a cynical measure to win the war. But it would be wrong, too, to imagine that fanatical commitment to an abstract ideal of emancipation demanded the strategies that transgressed old limits on the way to mass destruction. Politics of the higher law did not produce such "hard war." Rather, hard war included politics of the higher law as one measure among others.

The pattern of escalation in the Civil War exposes a first fault line in Delbanco's assumptions about the higher law and violence. Sherman's commitment to the rule of existing law—not his pursuit of a higher law—drove escalation of the conflict beyond customary limits on violence. Thus, sequestering or dissolving all talk of higher law, as Delbanco advocates, would not necessarily have prevented the emergence of something close to total war. On the contrary, when political processes refuse talk of higher laws, then prevailing interests, laws, and customs can become insulated from thoroughgoing critique. They can attain what Walter Benjamin called "mythic" qualities all their own. The language of "necessity" can quickly be taken over by the state's own imperatives for survival. Such transformations can offer deep legitimation for violence that is undertaken for ends that prevailing laws approve so long as it is done by agents that prevailing laws authorize. That legitimation can extend to violence with no limits this side of victory. Here I don't mean to argue that politics without reference to higher laws are associated with "more" violence. I am wary of both the morality and the accuracy of attempts to quantify violence. I mean rather to make an argument about the ways violence is legitimated and the kind of license legitimation gives. And I mean to argue that the elimination of any kind of appeal to a higher law can provide the shade that allows mythological justifications of violence to flourish in the soil of pragmatism, realism, and necessity. Union troops pushed past traditional limits on violence not because of John Brown's pursuit of a higher law but because of William Tecumseh Sherman's realistic sense of military necessity.

Purging politics of appeals to higher laws does not necessarily make for peace. And making appeals to higher laws does not necessarily lead to violence. In describing the abolitionist imagination, Delbanco gives little attention to the nonresistance of William Lloyd Garrison, who was perhaps the most prominent white abolitionist leader of the 1840s and 1850s. And he makes no mention of the Quakers who played such a significant role in the abolitionist movement, especially in its earliest years. In the name of an Inner Light, they denounced both slavery and violence against it.[44] For many abolitionists, commitment to a law above the positive law of the land did not bring violence but peace.

Delbanco overlooks a similar case in his narrative of the twentieth century. In describing the flourishing of the liberal aesthetic, Delbanco lists Martin Luther King Jr. with Reinhold Niebuhr as an appealing user of religious language in the public sphere. But Delbanco does not attend to the relevant differences between them. Niebuhr can fit relatively easily into Delbanco's midcentury consensus of people like Trilling, Schlesinger, and Warren. His "Christian realism" rejected the higher law, at least as something that could be known in ways that could provide direct warrants for action in this world.[45] King, on the other hand, appealed time and again to a higher law—most famously in the "Letter from Birmingham Jail."

King's 1963 letter was addressed to moderate white religious leaders who displayed all the virtues of Delbanco's aesthetic of ambivalence. As tensions began to rise in Birmingham, eight leaders of Protestant, Catholic, and Jewish communities in Alabama wrote a public letter they dubbed "A Call to Unity." The authors of the letter were not fanatical segregationists. On the contrary, all eight of them had signed an earlier public letter condemning the extremism of Governor George Wallace's January 1963 inaugural address. Wallace had vowed to resist federal law in the name of "segregation today, segregation tomorrow, and segregation forever," and these white religious leaders had responded with what they called "An Appeal for Law and Order and Common Sense." Now, on April 12, 1963—Good Friday—they again called for law, order, moderation, and unity in relation to Martin Luther King, Fred Shuttlesworth, and other leaders of the mass demonstrations in Birmingham. Positioning themselves against the "extreme measures" of both Wallace and King, they were almost perfect analogues to the heroes of Delbanco's narrative, the people he described as "sympathetic to the crime of slavery, but squeamish about the abolitionist response."[46] The authors of "A Call for Unity" acknowledged what they called "racial problems" and expressed their sympathy for "the natural impatience of people who feel that their hopes are slow in being realized." But they criticized the demonstrations as "directed and led in part by outsiders" and "unwise and untimely." They put their hope in "a new constructive and realistic approach." They counseled patience. Patient, realistic, able to see good and bad in both sides, and stressing the need to obey the laws of the land, the eight white clergymen displayed a perfect example of an ambivalent politics that rejected appeals to higher laws on both sides.[47]

King, on the other hand, displayed what can only be called an abolitionist imagination. He had just been arrested for breaking the earthly laws the moderate clergymen defended. He read their letter in a newspaper smuggled to him in jail. He started drafting his reply almost immediately, writing on the newspaper itself for want of other supplies. King's reply was at once courtly and fierce. Against the call for law and order, he argued that work for justice might require breaking some laws and then accepting the penalty that came with such actions.[48] Just laws deserved to be obeyed. But unjust laws had no authority. "How does one determine when a law is just or unjust?" King asked. "A just law is a man-made code that squares with the moral law, or the law of God. An unjust law is a code that is out of harmony with the moral law" (174). King then filled in the content of those categories with a variety of formulations. An unjust law degraded human personality. It substituted what Martin Buber called an "'I-it' relationship for an 'I-thou' relationship." It imposed a burden on a minority that it did not impose on a majority (175). Such laws, King wrote, citing Augustine, were "no laws at all" (174).

The abolitionist imagination, Delbanco writes, surfaces whenever someone identifies "a heinous evil and wants to eradicate it—not tomorrow, not next year, but now."[49] This was exactly the immediacy that worried the moderate white religious leaders. King swept their calls for patience aside, arguing that he had "yet to engage in a direct action that was 'well timed' in the view of those who have not suffered unduly from the disease of segregation" (173). Justice required immediate action. African Americans had already waited, King wrote, for more then 340 years. Then, in one long, powerful sentence, he called the roll of the costs of waiting. Those costs were as brazen as lynch mobs and as subtle as "living constantly at tiptoe stance, never quite knowing what to expect next." They were as systemic as mass poverty and as personal as having to explain to a daughter why she could not go to a public amusement park. "There comes a time," King wrote, "when the cup of endurance runs over, and men are no longer willing to be plunged into the abyss of despair" (173–174). King wanted to end racial injustice in the time frame that Delbanco used to define the abolitionist imagination: "not tomorrow, not next year, but now."

Appealing to a higher law, calling for immediate change, and naming the collusion of ambivalence with injustice, King cannot count as evidence for the goodness of Delbanco's moderation. Indeed, the example of King counts against the assumption that undergirded so much of Delbanco's worry about the abolitionist imagination. For King shows that an appeal to a higher law need not lead the one who makes the appeal to violent action. King's sense of the higher law led him instead to a deep and costly commitment to nonviolence. The significance of that commitment did not register with the white moderate authors of "A Call to Unity." In staking out their own role in the middle, their rhetoric placed King and Wallace in analogous positions:

> Just as we formerly pointed out that "hatred and violence have no sanction in our religious and political traditions," we also point out that such actions as incite to hatred and violence, however technically peaceful those actions may be, have not contributed to the resolution of our local problems.[50]

The nonviolence of King and the Birmingham movement was only "technically peaceful" to the ambivalent white liberals. Their rhetoric positioned it as analogous to the violent resistance called for by George Wallace—and soon to be unleashed by Bull Connor. Such ambivalence was not wisdom. It could not even grasp the significance of the difference between singing a spiritual and swinging a truncheon. The liberal aesthetic of Delbanco has many virtues, including a rightful call to humility in judging the past. But acknowledging the difficulty of the tests posed in 1963 does not change the fact that, at a crucial moment, an aesthetic of ambivalence led thoughtful people to misjudge a situation badly. Contrary to their expectations, a politics of the higher law did not underwrite violent action but faithful witness. The worst violence happened in the name of law and order. Appeals to a higher law *did* produce extremism, but some kind of extremism was the only appropriate response to the moment. After all, as King wrote, Jesus was an extremist for love, and Amos was an extremist for justice. Lincoln and Jefferson were extremists, too, in King's accounting. And now, he wrote, "the South, the nation, and the world are in dire need of creative extremists" (179–180). King saw the potential for a politics of the higher law.

Code Fetishism

Mythological justifications for violence pose a significant problem, just as John Steuart Curry saw. But I have tried to argue that the roots of these justifications are not inherent in religious traditions like Judaism, Christianity, and Islam, as Curry's mural and too much contemporary commentary would suggest, but in a misshapen politics of the higher law that can be fueled by many different sorts of ideologies or comprehensive worldviews. And I have tried to argue that dissolving talk of a higher law into a pragmatic, this-worldly ambivalence, as Andrew Delbanco suggests, does not eliminate the risk posed by mythic violence. On the contrary, it can silence voices that might interrupt the chatter by which a sense of contingent necessity assumes more absolute forms. What we need is neither an endorsement of whatever kind of higher law supports our own political projects nor a ban on higher laws that becomes ideological in its drive to exterminate ideology but critical deliberation about the nature and function of appeals to higher law. For this, we need to cultivate the capacity for reasoning together about the *form* of a higher law. That kind of reasoning is the work of political theology.

The question of the form of any candidate for a higher law is often submerged under a rough and unreflective consensus. Discussions of the higher law from very different camps have tended to imagine the form of that law in similar ways. Paul Hill, John Brown, and Andrew Delbanco, for instance, all saw the higher law as the *same kind of thing* as positive, earthly law. Such higher laws take the form of codes of obligations and prohibitions. These codes are in the imperative mood; they are commands. And those commands, in turn, presume a gap between the way things are and the way things should be. The promise built into the form of the command is that following it will help close that gap.

This basic form of code can undergird a huge variety of visions of the higher law. A code can prohibit or oblige any number of things. It can be a realistic goal or an ideal that is impossible to attain. It can be easily known or beyond human comprehension. It can impose agreeable rules or impossible demands. If it is construed as code, the higher law can accommodate consequentialist or deontological logics. It can proceed from God, nature, history, the structure of human consciousness, or any number of other sources. Arguments about the higher law have seen every possible combination of these positions, and then some. These differences have often obscured a shared sense that the higher law, like positive law, takes the form of code.

Assumptions that a higher law takes the form of code have fit with and propelled a wider phenomenon Charles Taylor calls "code fetishism" or "nomolatry." Taylor describes code fetishism as the belief that "the entire spiritual dimension of human life is captured in a moral code." He traces its rise over several centuries, showing the ways it has been driven along by what he called the "Reform" impulse at the heart of Western Christianity. Successive moments of Reform—stretching long before and long after the time identified as the Reformation—have sought "to make people over as more perfect practicing Christians through articulating codes and inculcating disciplines." In time, "the Christian life became more and more identified with these codes and disciplines." The codes, or bundles of codes, ceased to be just the means of reform; they often became the substance of Christianity itself. A complex form of religious life came to be understood as codes of ethics.[51] And those codes eventually acquired lives of their own. Especially as they were written down, they broke free from background beliefs and practices in a process that Aleida Assmann has called "excarnation."[52] They could even break free from any kind of connection to orthodox Christianity, as codes of God became codes of nature's God and eventually codes derived from a natural order that could be defined without any reference to God. The flexibility of code not only let it stand on many different kinds of sources but also let it take on many different kinds of content. What has proven most enduring is neither the faith behind the code nor the content of any particular code but the sense that the highest good could be expressed best in the form of a code.

The form of code can seem infinitely adaptable, a neutral vehicle that can accommodate most any vision of the good life. But the genre itself exerts a significant narrowing influence, as prophets from Saint Augustine to Marguerite Porete to Shakespeare's Falstaff to Friedrich Nietzsche to Dorothy Day have seen. For if fulfillment of the law means conformity with a code, however enlightened, what room is there for things whose nature seems to require a different kind of freedom, things like festival, worship, and the raptures of human and divine love? For the state, code fetishism has meant that visions of the common good have often involved exertions of biopower to bring citizens up to snuff. For the church, code fetishism has often turned the Beatitudes, those great indicative declarations of blessedness, into lists of things to do. It has shown the ability to make Psalm 119—a long declaration of love for the law—into the self-satisfied song of a prig. Nomolatry has made sermons feel "relevant" only when they end in exhortations of some kind, whether to give your life to Christ, live your best life now, or get to know the sources of your food. One could argue that John Brown was at his most tedious when he sought to perfect, distribute, and fulfill his understanding of the higher law as a code. Even his followers showed mixed enthusiasm for his codes. The most astonishing moments in his life came not in conformation of his world to the words on his scroll but in the rich neighbor-love that flourished in the little community of black and white households that lived on the edge of law in a remote corner of the Adirondacks. If devotion to an egalitarian code had something to do with the formation of that community, its strongest relationships took forms that fulfilled that code by transcending it rather than corresponding to it.

The form of code makes not only for limited lives but also for violent ones. For if the higher law is something like the perfection of public policy, and if fulfillment of the law is the perfection of earthly conformity to this heavenly rule, then believers in the higher law can understand themselves as called to discern the law and then devise plans to make the world a little more like the law. And because correspondence of social realities to codified ideals is the kind of state that might be achieved through violence, violence lurks always as an option. The nature of code therefore invites violent action for its fulfillment. *This* was the error of Brown's scroll: not its conviction that there was some blessed state that stood in judgment of the evils of slavery but its insistence that this state could be expressed in—and enforced as—a code of laws like the ones on the books.

Concern about the violence of higher laws understood as better codes has produced a variety of reactive strategies. The most direct response simply rejects any politics of the higher law, as Andrew Delbanco does. But, as I have argued earlier, stripping away a higher law to leave mundane, ambivalent pragmatism is no sure guard against ideologically legitimated escalations of violence.

Another set of responses, sometimes claiming both religious and "realist" legacies, has proposed retaining some notion of a higher law but then insisted that we cannot attain it because it is beyond our knowledge, beyond our moral capabilities, or both. But pushing the higher law over horizons of knowledge or ability tends to sap any practical significance from the distant ideal. Therefore these realisms, in practice, tend to collapse back into something like the completely immanent pragmatism Delbanco described. They are always prone, as Charles Taylor has argued, to "a sudden burst of confidence in procedural reason (never in short supply in modern culture)."[53] That confidence can run past limitations on knowledge or moral ability and justify enforcement of the once-distant code. It is not just that overconfident preachers, North and South, cheered on the Civil War in the name of a partisan God. It is that an ambivalent Christian realist like Wilfred McClay, in the name of a God whose will transcends human history, could put some swagger in his statement of enthusiasm for war on Iraq. In an essay written shortly after 9/11, McClay argues that "every human enterprise is inadequate and destined for shipwreck." And because of this—not in spite of it—he writes, "When the President says, 'Let's roll,' I'm ready."[54] Such realism claims to check the violent tendencies of a higher law. But it is perfectly capable of licensing mythic violence of its own.

Yet another strategy for managing the violent potential of the higher law as code couples greater confidence about the ability to know the higher law with a principled refusal to do violence for the sake of fulfilling that law. This strategy informs a confident Christian social ethics that includes something like a rider clause forswearing personal violence. But this strategy still presumes an ideal that takes the form of code that some kind of violence will be required to enforce. It typically assigns that violence to the state. Even if it would limit violence in wars abroad and criticize excessive violence in enforcing policies at home, it still presumes a necessary role for state violence in the establishment and maintenance of justice. And it is just that notion of "necessity" that opens the door to mythic justifications for violence.

This array of bad choices can seem like the only ones we have. Each of them promises to eliminate the mythic violence legitimated by a higher law, and each of them ends up grounding mythic violence in another way. But this array defines the field of possibilities only if we assume that the higher law takes the form of a code that can be fulfilled through perfect enforcement. When the higher law is reduced to a code, these are the options that make sense. Their poverty reveals the real cost of secularization: not declining numbers of members of religious institutions but this constriction of the imagination, this reduction of beatific visions to policy proposals, this loss of the ability to think of a higher law as anything but a better code.

A Medley of Unordered Letters

I want to take seriously the danger of violence in the name of a higher law. But the answer to that problem is not that we can never know enough, nor that we can never be pure enough, nor that the code of a higher law should be accompanied by excarnate prohibitions of violence. The better reasons not to take up violence to enforce a higher law involve a deeper shift in our understandings of the nature of the higher law and what it would mean for it to be fulfilled. They require an understanding of the higher law as something more than a code with better content.

Giorgio Agamben presses toward such an understanding in what he calls "the messianic fulfillment of law." Agamben, the editor of Walter Benjamin's works in Italian, draws upon Benjamin to describe deep cycles of collusion between law and violence. Whether established by conquest, revolution, or even a social contract that inevitably denies full participation, law is established in violence. Violence establishes law, and law, in turn, legitimates the violence that upholds the law. The law, Agamben writes through a commentary on the Apostle Paul's letter to the church in Rome, is not bad in itself so much as seized by the power of sin. Consequently, "the opposition between messianic law and the law of exile cannot be an opposition between two laws of identical structure, which merely contain different prohibitions."[55] What Agamben calls the "messianic law," and what I have been calling the "higher law," is not just a better version of this-worldly code. And messianic hope is not hope for the culmination of the cycle of law and violence in a law so perfect it cannot be improved and a violence so perfect it no longer needs to be performed. The hope Agamben calls "messianic" is rather for the *interruption* of this cycle of law and violence. It is the hope for something like what Benjamin called the "relief" (*Entsetzung*) of law, the *deliverance* of law, the deep decoupling of law and violence. Such hope will require imagining the fulfillment of law as something other than the perfect execution of a perfect code.

Understandings of law as code shape contemporary social imaginaries so deeply that it can be difficult to conceive the law in any other way. Agamben gives two images that help evoke the hope he is trying to describe. Drawing on Benjamin, who was in turn drawing on traditions of Jewish mysticism, Agamben cites a passage in which Moses Cordovero described the original Torah as a series of letters that had been shaped from the "divine light." In its purest form the Torah is just this manifestation of divine presence. It is not a code to be enforced but a gift to be enjoyed. Agamben sees this tradition running through Matthew 5:17–18, when Jesus says that he has come not to destroy the law but to fulfill it, and through Paul's letter to the church in Rome, which also speaks of the "fulfillment" of the law. The fulfillment of the law, Agamben says, "contains neither commandments nor prohibitions but only a medley of unordered letters."[56]

Fulfillment of the law looks not like the perfect enforcement of perfect policy but like an array of letters that have been delivered from their alliance with coercion, and even with meaning, to manifest divine presence. The painter Paul Klee developed an analogous vision in his 1938 painting *Gesetz* (Law; see Figure 4.2). The forms in the painting look like letters in some ancient script. They call to mind signs of the zodiac, notations from a musical score, and even human faces that let the law look back at the viewer. The letters have a dynamic quality, as if they might quiver on the canvas when the viewer looks elsewhere. No strong arrangement determines the path of the viewer's gaze—the letters could be encountered in many possible orders and constellations. For all the vitality of these letters, they cannot be assembled into code. They can't even be read. They can only be seen, beheld. The form of this law invites not enforce-

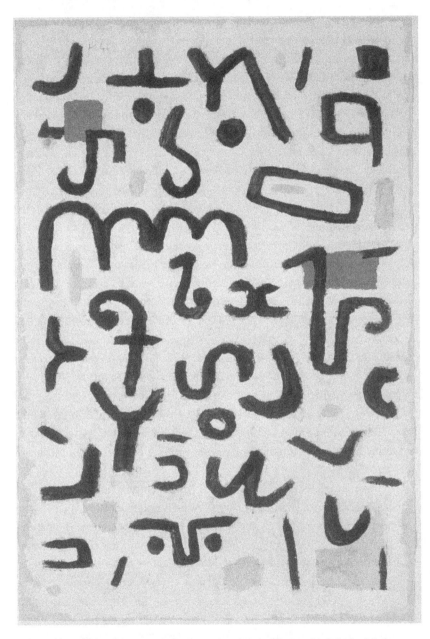

FIGURE 4.2 Paul Klee (1879–1940), *Gesetz* (1938). Munich, Pinakothek der Moderne. Photograph © Bayer & Mitko—Artothek.

ment—what would that even mean?—but study, contemplation, and delight. This is the law as a "medley of unordered letters."

In a more recent work Agamben gives another image for what he calls "the messianic fulfillment of law." "One day," he writes,

> humanity will play with law just as children play with disused objects, not in order to restore them to their canonical use but to free them from it for good. What is found after the law is not a more proper and original use value that precedes the law, but a new use that is born only after it. And use, which has been contaminated by law, must also be freed from its own value. This liberation is the task of study, or play.[57]

Agamben sketches hope for a law that has become like a tool that has fallen out of use only to be picked up by children and played with as a toy. Like a found object, the fulfilled law is broken out of its ordinary use and so from its alliance with force. Separated from force, law becomes an object of study, even play. The higher law becomes our deepest delight.

Agamben's account of the "deactivation" of law sees the significance of forms of life that cannot be commanded into being. And it has the great advantage of undoing the drive to do violence in the name of the law. It dissolves that drive at its deepest level. A person who shared Agamben's vision would forgo violence not because she lacked the ability to know what she should be enforcing, or because her cause was insufficiently pure, or because she thought the law prohibited violence. Instead, she would not take up violence to fulfill the law because something about the nature of fulfillment made it impossible to achieve fulfillment through violent action. Violence just wouldn't make sense. Agamben's politics of the higher law, then, would not involve a theocratic enforcement of the higher law but a practical, mystical delight in the presence of God made manifest in a law delivered from its alliance with force.

Agamben's images of the fulfillment of the law in luminous letters or tools-become-toys help ease the hold of code on our abilities to imagine law. And Agamben's account of law without force exerts particularly strong critical power in an age marked by the proliferation of force without law, a condition that defines what Agamben calls the "state of exception." Agamben's ideal both brings the state of exception into sharper focus and helps us imagine alternatives. But Agamben's particular understanding of fulfillment of the law as "deactivation" or "negation" ends in an aestheticizing of the law that undercuts all talk of justice. He insists that his account is not "antinomian," and this is true. He is not negating the law per se.[58] But the law survives in Agamben only by making the transition from a moral sphere to an aesthetic sphere. The normative qualities of law—the qualities most deeply aligned with force, but also with justice—are not relativized so much as eliminated. Consider Klee's painting of the luminous letters of the fulfilled law. We might delight in them. We might play with them. We might study them. But how could we involve them in anything like deliberations about justice? Agamben's work helps break the hold of code fetishism. But it also clarifies the need to find ways to think about justice that do not reduce immediately to codes that need to be enforced.

The Indicative of Reconciliation

Agamben is right to focus on Benjamin's sense of messianic fulfillment as the "relief" of law. And he is right to see that this quality of having been relieved distinguishes "higher law" in the sense of a fulfilled, delivered, and renewed law from a "higher law" that is nothing more than a code with better content. To work within Benjamin's language, this relief distinguishes justice (*Gerechtigkeit*) from law (*Recht*). But the best description of the effect of this relief is not the turning of the moral into the aesthetic, as Agamben's images suggest, but a turning of the imperative of law into the indicative of divine justice.

Peter Fenves emphasizes the indicative quality of justice for Benjamin by locating it in relation to Kant's categorical imperative. Kant describes a moral standard that he understands as impossible for people to attain, given the limits of this age. But the impossibility of meeting the demand does not undermine its categorical quality. It remains an imperative, an impossible demand. Like Kant, Benjamin describes a justice that cannot be attained in this age. But this is not because of failings of knowledge or will but because justice is of *another order of magnitude* than any kind of earthly politics. As Fenves argues, contrasting Benjamin with Kant on the question of distributive justice,

> It is not simply that there is a scarcity of goods, which makes it impossible to distribute them on the basis of a neutral principle; rather, there is a fundamental mismatch between the number of claims and the number of goods. The former is of a higher power than the latter, for even if there were an infinite number of goods—as if paradise were a matter of material plenitude—the claims would "outnumber" the goods, since no particular claim carries greater weight than any other, such that it would tilt the scale in favor of one potential possessor over another.[59]

It is not just that the claims of people outnumber the goods available. It is that the goods themselves have a claim to what Benjamin calls "the good right of the good." That claim—a claim rooted in the goodness of creation—makes justice not just contingently impossible (the kind of thing that higher productivity might correct) but of another order entirely. Thus, Fenves argues, it is not just that the demands of justice are impossible to fulfill; it is that "the category of justice cannot be expressed in terms of demands at all."[60] Justice, in this sense, is not an obligation for action. It is a state of being. It takes not the imperative mood but the indicative. And when it is pressed into the form of an imperative, it falls into what Benjamin calls "law."

For the purposes of this chapter, I will leave aside the question of whether Agamben or Fenves offers a better interpretation of Benjamin's text. For my argument does not depend on whatever authority would come from continuity with Benjamin, and my purpose is not to reconstruct the meaning of his text, let alone to translate it into some other idiom. It is rather to let conversations with Benjamin and others break the spell of a secularized imagination, to renew the possibilities for thinking about a higher law—a divine justice—that does not colonize every sphere of life under the sign of "should," that can imagine indicatives not made by human hands, and that does not therefore slip into justifications for violence. I take up the work of developing those possibilities now on the other side of a gap and in the language of a distinctly Christian political theology.

Christian political theology has too often worked within conceptual frameworks that identify the higher law with some kind of code. To help think past those frameworks, I would sketch a picture of the higher law marked by four qualities: an *indicative* mood that serves to *negate* absolute obligations in this age in ways that invite a *free response* in history that is *permeated by the presence of God*.

Understanding justice as an *indicative* rather than an imperative relieves it from its deep alliance with violence. An imperative might be enforced, whether on someone else or on oneself. An indicative, on the other hand, just *is*. Such a higher law would need no more enforcement than the law of gravity. But the shift from imperative to indicative would not rob the higher law of its distinctly moral qualities. A higher law in the indicative mood would still give a picture of justice, a vision of relationships in the New Jerusalem. But it would not demand action to establish that city. Jesus does not give people a plan for bringing in the Kingdom of God but announces that the Kingdom is at hand. Mary does not return from the tomb waving a list of things to do but proclaiming that Christ is risen. Paul writes that God was in Christ, reconciling the world to Godself, naming the indicative quality of a past event that continues into the present. The great creeds of the church are entirely in the indicative. We can, of course, fashion imperatives from any of these indicatives. But the derivative, made quality of those imperatives matters. The higher law, the new commandment, is not first of all a code that might be enforced. It is first of all a declaration of a change in the way things are.[61]

The higher law may take the form of an indicative, but it does not relate to this age as an empirical description of the facts on the ground. To say that the Kingdom of God is at hand is not to describe the world's present and perfect conformity to that vision. The indicative of the Gospel relates to the world as *negation*. Following Benjamin's understanding of divine violence as the mode in which justice relates to this age, I understand negation as the mode in which the higher law relates to this age. The indicative of the higher law is not present as a simple description; it is present through its negation of earthly law. It breaks the structures of obligation of earthly laws not just by proposing better content for those laws but by declaring an indicative of fulfillment that undoes the absolute quality of the whole category of earthly law. The divine violence of the higher law relativizes not just every particular "ought" and "should" but the whole imperative mood. The proclamation that the Kingdom of God is at hand does not bring with it a new set of imperatives, for such imperatives would betray the gift they announce. The proclamation of the Reign of God instead relativizes the full spectrum of people's obligations. Because the Kingdom is at hand, obligations to Caesar, to families, and even to one's own life lose the sheen of absoluteness. And because the sign of the Kingdom is the cross, new obligations do not arise to fill the little gaps left by the old. In the cross Jesus does not squeeze himself into Caesar's throne. He does not just offer a new and improved edition of Roman law. In the cross Jesus relativizes not just particular claims to authority but the whole category of earthly law. The indicative of the higher law breaks the absolute hold of every earthly imperative without establishing new ones in their place.

The nature of this negation becomes clearer in conversation with Russell Jacoby's distinction between two kinds of utopian literature. A "blueprint utopia," he writes, gives a plan for a perfect society that invites violence for its realization. This is the utopia of code. What Jacoby calls an "iconoclastic utopia," on the other hand, does not give positive content that is supposed to be enforced. Shrouded in "mysticism and silence," it exerts its influence simply by negating the pretensions of this age. But such an empty utopia is always in danger of slipping into a kind of neo-Kantianism that becomes, in practice, indistinguishable from Delbanco's entirely immanent pragmatism. The higher law I mean to sketch here has positive content: the wolf lies down with the lamb; the law is written on people's hearts; the dwelling place of God is with humans, and God shall wipe every tear from their eyes, and death shall be no more. Because the content of these visions takes an indicative form, it does not license the violence of what Jacoby calls a blueprint utopia. And because there is something to these visions, even if known only in hope, they do not function as a blanket rejection of all claims to value, as iconoclastic utopias can. Because these vectors of negation have their source in some determinate hope, they have direction.[62]

Gershom Scholem was right to discern something freeing in the divine violence worked by the messianic fulfillment of law. What he called "messianic apocalypticism"—a tradition both Jews and Christians have inherited, developed, and shared in their own ways—opens the well-ordered house of law to an "anarchic breeze."[63] Neither Jewish nor Christian hopes end in an anarchy of relativism or nihilism, let alone in one of the forms of self-seeking libertarianism that so often claim the venerable black mantle of anarchism today. Messianic hope describes the fulfillment of the law, not its destruction. The fulfillment of the law provides a deep ground of every kind of value. But because it does not take the form of code, its form does not command obedience. Instead, the indicative of fulfillment invites *a free response*. The response is marked not by obedience but fidelity. "It is because fidelity is creative," as Gabriel Marcel saw, "that, like liberty itself, it infinitely transcends the limits of what can be prescribed." Something about the nature of fidelity demands freedom. Fidelity cannot be prescribed even by a code with perfect content. But it can be freed, enabled, invited. The higher law dissolves imperatives in the fulfillment of the indicative, thus making possible the freedom that is a condition of the fidelity that the higher law invites. And because fidelity is a free response, Marcel wrote, it "reveals its true nature, which is to be an evidence, a testimony."[64] A code commands obedience; the higher law, on the other hand, invites faithful, free responses, which become testimonies to God's great indicative of reconciliation.

Faithful, free responses have the quality of testimonies not only because they point toward the fulfillment of law but also because they come from the fulfillment of law. For it is the negating power—the divine violence—of that law that breaks the hold of earthly obligation and makes possible a free response. The fulfillment of the law is therefore *present* in the responses it makes possible, not in the way in which a code would be present in a world that conformed to it but in the way that the Ascension of Jesus—the absence of Jesus—allows him to be present with new depth and power to the church. Jesuit historian Michel de Certeau elaborates on this dynamic:

> The Christian language begins with the disappearance of its "author." That is to say that Jesus *effaces himself* to give faithful witness to the Father who authorizes him, and to "give rise" to different but faithful communities which he makes possible. There is a close bond between the absence of Jesus (dead and not present) and the birth of the Christian language (objective and faithful testimony to his survival).[65]

Faithful testimonies "never repeat the gospel," Certeau writes, "but they would be impossible without the gospel." Just so, faithful performances in response to the higher law never simply embody that law. But they would be impossible without it.[66] The messianic fulfillment of law—the great indicative of reconciliation—is distinct from every particular response just as the sovereign is distinct from the political order. The messianic fulfillment of law makes every free and faithful response possible, so permeates each and all of them with a presence that is never simply identical to them.

Imaginations shaped by code tend to locate the presence of God in relation to a correspondence of this world to some heavenly standard. Perhaps the power of God makes perfect obedience possible. Perhaps the will of God works around human agency to make the world correspond to code by other means. Or perhaps, because the world never seems to correspond directly to our understanding of the higher code, God is never really present in this age at all. While these accounts of divine presence differ in significant ways, they share a sense that presence depends on a relationship of identity, and that identity could be measured by a code. They also tend to share a sense that the code implies an imperative—measure up!—and that violence might need to be part of the repertoire of means to bring about the correspondence of reality to code that would mark the presence of God.

An accent on the indicative of divine reconciliation, though, allows us to imagine the presence of God in a very different way. God is present not where the world lives up to some imperatives that God has given but in the fact of free responses to the messianic fulfillment of law. If some or all of those responses fail to measure up to the ethics implicit in fulfillment, it does not mean that the law is any less fulfilled or that God is any less present. For the presence of God does not depend on relations of identity. On the contrary, to say that God is gracious is to say that God remains present to creatures and institutions that are *not* identical to God. This presence-without-identity is the ground of a hope rooted in the messianic fulfillment of law.

Messianic Politics

I have tried to suggest a theological understanding of the form of the higher law that stresses its indicative quality, its relation to the present age as negation, its invitation of free response, and its manifestation of divine presence without identity. This vision of the higher law makes possible a messianic politics that is a perfect inversion of theocratic politics. For theocratic movements, politics are prior to the fulfillment of a higher law. They seek to bring the world into conformity with a divinely given code. They drive toward the goal of bringing politics to an end. Politics—with words or with weapons—is just a means to make the world correspond to the standard set by code. When that correspondence has been achieved, and achieved so perfectly that it cannot be undone, politics comes to an end.

If, on the other hand, the law is "higher" because it has already been fulfilled, then all these patterns are reversed. There is no need to seek to establish a law that is already fulfilled. And the already-accomplished messianic fulfillment of law is not the end of politics but the beginning. The fulfillment of the law does not undo the desire for politics, for politics, as Aristotle saw, is not just a means to other ends but a constitutive part of human flourishing. Politics continues as collective deliberation about the nature of free and faithful response. And because the fulfillment of the law manifests itself in this age as divine violence, politics proceeds with new freedom. The richest forms of political life are possible only when people are free to do more than conform their societies to preexisting codes, whether those codes claim to be set by earthly or divine powers. The fullness of political life requires a freedom on the other side of binding code. Because people are born into a world already ordered by codes of many kinds, some kind of emancipation is necessary for political life to begin. The divine violence of the higher law does this work. It does not bring politics to an end; it makes politics possible.

The hold of code on American social imaginaries means that contemporary American Christian ethics is steadily tempted by a theocratic logic. When

Christian ethics sees its task as discerning God's will for the world, devising a set of policies that approximate that will, and then figuring out ways to argue for those policies in the polities that would have the power to enforce them, a theocratic logic is at work. Commitments to democratic process sit uneasily with this logic. Commitments to a pluralist society that involves people who would resist the implementation of the divinely sanctioned code are perhaps even more difficult to sustain. Both kinds of commitments require amendments to the basic theocratic impulse, like so many epicycles in a Ptolemaic account of the solar system. Those epicycles have the shaky standing of small corrections to a strong central vision. When the higher law is conceived as a kind of code, theocratic politics exert a steady pull.

John Brown gave in to that pull when he picked up a rifle to enforce the code on his scroll. William T. Vollmann is right in his identification of what he called "John Brown's Maxim: *If you refuse to follow the Golden Rule, then I have the right to use terror to impel you to follow it.*"[67] Brown performed theocratic politics of the purest kind. He built on centuries of precedent in prying one verse out of a whole body of thought and turning it into a Golden Rule, a master bit of code. The process of excarnation left behind a whole paragraph of verses that suggested a very different kind of politics. In Luke's version of what he calls the Sermon on the Plain (Luke 6:17–49), the so-called Golden Rule appears amid commands to "Love your enemies, do good to them which hate you, bless them that curse you, and pray for them which despitefully use you." Turn the other cheek. If someone takes your cloak, let them have your coat, too. For God "is kind to the unthankful and to the evil. Be ye therefore merciful, as your Father is merciful." The so-called Golden Rule is nested within a longer recitation of the higher law. Turning the Golden Rule into a divine warrant for violence requires ignoring all of these adjacent verses. It also requires ignoring the larger logic of the Sermon on the Plain. The sermon is occasioned by a Sabbath healing that, from Luke's perspective, reveals Jesus to be Lord of the Sabbath, the messianic fulfillment of law. And it begins with a torrent of indicative blessings. The Golden Rule—and all the imperatives that follow—are not a higher code but a description of the new life given in the fulfillment of law. As such, they cannot be enforced. They are given not as blueprints for a better society but as gifts to be received and enjoyed.

If Brown's own motives were theocratic, we still might understand his actions within a frame of messianic politics. For the higher law of the Sermon on the Plain meets Brown's world not as a new set of imperatives but as a divine violence that negates every imperative. It negates the authority of the slavery-sustaining laws of Virginia and of the United States. It renders them, in Martin Luther King's words, no laws at all. And it demands a free response. One could imagine the raid on Harpers Ferry as such a response—not commanded by a higher code but chosen in response to the messianic fulfillment of law that negated every earthly authority. One could frame it as a desperate act of politics in a desperate time, an act valuable chiefly *as politics*, as speech, as a saying of that which could not be said in a way that could finally be heard. Framing the raid with reference to divine violence does not justify it. On the contrary, it involves stripping away Brown's theocratic justifications, leaving the raid exposed again to judgment. But framing the raid in light of this notion of divine violence does help make it legible. If it was not justified by some divinely sanctioned code, it was made possible by a higher law that revealed the whole edifice of laws sustaining slavery for the organized violence that they were. And if Brown's response was not identical to the work of God, something of that work was present in and in spite of this response that slipped into theocratic violence. The raid becomes visible as something like what Benjamin calls a dialectical image. It is a dialectical image of the messianic fulfillment of law, faithful testimony in spite of itself.

Seeing the raid as a fallen, faithful witness to the messianic fulfillment of law shows its continuity with other parts of Brown's life. He lived outside the laws of his day not only in his acts of violence but, perhaps even more radically, in his daily relations with African Americans. In a time when few whites had much to do with African American people who were not serving them, Brown stayed in the homes of Stephen Smith Esq. of Philadelphia, Isaac Holden of Chatham, the Reverend and Mrs. James Newton Gloucester of Brooklyn, Frederick Douglass of Rochester, and many others.[68] He studied the tactics of Toussaint L'Ouverture. He sought advice from Harriet Tubman. He did not hesitate to trust his life to fellow raiders Oswald Anderson, John Anthony Copeland Jr., Shields Green, Lewis Leary, and Dangerfield Newby. He was a treasured neighbor of Lyman Epps, who sang at his funeral. As W. E. B. Du Bois wrote, Brown "worked not simply for Black Men—he worked with them; and he was a companion of their daily life, knew their faults and virtues, and felt, as few white Americans have felt, the bitter tragedy of their lot." Brown was, Du Bois wrote, "the man who of all Americans has perhaps come nearest to touching the real souls of black folk."[69] Such rich relationships were possible only because the divine indicative of redemption had broken the authority of the earthly codes that forbade them. If these relationships never fully escaped the power of racism, they still represented an astonishing response—and not only by Brown—to the messianic fulfillment of law. If an egalitarian code played some role in making these relationships possible, they quickly transcended what even the best code could prescribe. Brown bore his most transparent witness to the higher law not when he sought to enforce it but when he lived the life it already made possible.

5 THE POLITICS OF PARDON

CALLS FOR THE PARDON OF JOHN BROWN started rolling in to the office of Governor Henry Wise almost as soon as Brown was arrested. The most promising of these calls suggested pardon on the grounds of insanity. A verdict of insanity appealed to Northern Republicans for the ways it saved Brown's life—and opened up some breathing space between his politics and their own. Northern papers made the case for insanity. Some supporters of Brown from Akron, Ohio, sent a telegram promising evidence that mental illness ran in Brown's family. Wise heard these arguments. He considered having Brown examined for mental illness but in the end decided not to risk what such an examination might find. Brown himself rejected the idea completely, calling the idea that he was insane "a miserable artifice and pretext." "I am perfectly unconscious of insanity," Brown said, "and I reject, so far as I am capable, any attempts to interfere on my behalf on that score."[1] Brown got his wish. The call for pardon on the grounds of insanity gained no traction. Within weeks, Brown was hanging from a gallows in Charles Town, Virginia.

On December 2, 2009, exactly 150 years after Brown's execution, David S. Reynolds wrote an essay for the *New York Times* that made a very different sort of case for pardon. In the essay Reynolds, author of the most comprehensive contemporary biography of Brown, urged President Barack Obama or then-Governor Tim Kaine of Virginia to pardon Brown. Reynolds did not argue that Brown was insane. On the contrary, Reynolds had taken great pains in his biography of Brown to establish the abolitionist's sanity. Reynolds made his case not in the name of mercy but in the name of justice. He argued that Brown rose above the racism of his day to give his life for the cause of ending slavery. While Brown's attack on Harpers Ferry did not succeed in a strategic sense, Reynolds wrote, it did help launch the war that brought emancipation to millions of enslaved people. The raid made Brown a hero in the North. People like Frederick Douglass and Ralph Waldo Emerson expressed deep admiration, admiration that should lead us to give Brown the benefit of the doubt. Reynolds readily conceded that Brown had "some blotches on his record." But, he argued, the murders in Kansas happened in a time of "pre-emptive and retaliatory violence that most historians now agree were in essence the first engagements of the Civil War." Moreover, Reynolds wrote, we have found ways to admire other flawed figures from that period. Abraham Lincoln, for instance, "shared the era's prejudices." Andrew Jackson shared not only in prejudices but also in the formation of policies that led to the death and forced migration of thousands of Native Americans. Compared to such men, Brown's wrongdoing faded into the disfigured background of the normal. Reynolds concluded, "Justice would be served, belatedly, if President Obama and Governor Kaine found a way to pardon a man whose heroic effort to free four million enslaved blacks helped start the war that ended slavery."[2]

Reynolds made his case for pardon in the name of justice. Because of the centrality of justice to the argument, the case for pardon depended on showing that Brown was right in some sense. Reynolds did not make a simplistic argument for the morality of Brown's actions. He acknowledged Brown's violence. He did not justify that violence so much as minimize it by putting it in context. And he did not make his case in absolute terms but through comparisons to other leaders who were admired in spite of their failings. With moves like these, Reynolds made a subtle argument for the morality of Brown's actions. If Reynolds's ethical argument for Brown was complex, the underlying logic of his understanding of pardon was clear: if Brown could be shown to be right, then, in the name of justice, he should be pardoned.

Reynolds's vision of pardon is appealing, for it promises to suture law and justice back together. When Brown raided Harpers Ferry, the logic of this argument runs, he acted in accord with a justice that transcended any law. It was the law of the time that was wrong when it judged Brown guilty. A pardon offers a chance to right that wrong and let the verdict of the law catch up to the standard of justice. Pardon on these terms would involve reversing a past decision. But it would not require making a real exception to the highest ethical standards, as pardons sometimes do. Pardons that make exceptions raise difficult questions of fairness: If an exception is made for one person, why not another? They also raise questions of singularity: Why should *this* case be an exception to the general rule? Reynolds's logic avoids such questions by proposing no exceptions. On the contrary, it would correct a past decision that now, in hindsight, appears as an exception to the standard set by justice. A pardon on the grounds that a person was right or justified seeks to eliminate old exceptions, not create new ones. Pardons on these terms are not so much exceptions to the rule of justice as revisions to the code of law. They do not challenge an understanding of ethics that stresses universal and exceptionless norms. Rather, they fit snugly within it. Because this ethical framework is so prominent in contemporary social imaginaries, pardon on these terms feels reasonable. If Reynolds could show that Brown was right, then the established persuasiveness of this framework would practically complete the case for Brown's pardon.

I share Reynolds's hope that Brown will be pardoned, and I would do more to stress that the scope of pardon should be broadened to include all those who participated in the raid. While Brown undoubtedly played the leading role in planning and executing the raid, he always acted as part of a network of relationships. In October 1859 he acted as part of a band of raiders that also included Jeremiah Anderson, Osborne Anderson, Oliver Brown, Owen Brown, Watson Brown, John Cook, John Copeland, Barclay Coppoc, Edwin Coppoc, Shields Green, Albert Hazlett, John Kagi, Lewis Leary, William Leeman, Francis Meriam, Dangerfield Newby, Aaron Stevens, Steward Taylor, Dauphin Thompson, William Thompson, and Charles Tidd. There are times when Brown should be singled out, as in considerations of American national memory, where he plays an outsized role. But when talk turns to pardon, he must be considered with the men who fought with him and in many cases died beside him. The best cases for pardon will extend to argue for all the raiders.

I also want to suggest a different rationale for pardon than the one Reynolds describes. Reynolds's pardon in the name of justice fuses sovereign power with everyday politics. It sets precedents that end up reinscribing the "mythic violence" I diagnosed in Chapter 3. In this chapter I trace these effects of pardon that is performed in the name of justice. I then try to give an account of my hope for a very different kind of pardon, one that can maintain a distinction between sovereignty and politics. This kind of pardon would negate the application of past rules without mystifying the production of new rules. It would be rooted in a willingness to reason about singularities, even to declare exceptions, to laws that remain valid. Such pardon would separate the question of whether the raiders should be pardoned from the question of whether their actions were right. It would outrun the categories of ethics.

In describing the need for pardon as an exception, I do not seek to destroy the framework that thinks about law and ethics as norms that take the form of universally applicable rules. I believe that the widespread acceptance of this framework is a significant historical achievement. It overturned the possibility of rule by royal caprice. It developed an ideal of equality before the law. It enshrined fairness as a cardinal virtue of systems of justice. These are some of the most important values in our culture, and they are worth great effort to preserve and extend. I hope to strengthen the framework that helped secure these gains by restoring it to its limits. When it operates without any sense of limit, when it mistakes itself for the whole, it can grow feral. It can begin to undermine its own core values. Naming an exception checks some of this tendency of universal norms to sprawl into ideology. The exception, as exception, does not destroy a framework that stresses equal justice before the law. On the contrary: the exception redeems the rule.

Democratic Suspicions of Pardon

The roots of the appeal of pardon in the name of justice run back through the very long processes that replaced rule by decree with a rule of law. Pardon has rightly been seen as a relic of monarchy. William Blackstone, distilling centuries of English legal traditions from his vantage point in the 1760s, made the deep, old connection between pardon and monarchy clear. He called pardon "the most amiable prerogative of the crown." From the time of Henry VIII it had belonged exclusively to the king or queen. Indeed, Blackstone wrote, it was "that act of his [the monarch's] government, which is the most personal, and most entirely his own." This profoundly personal act brought compassion to a system of law that otherwise lacked it by necessity. The laws needed to be framed without compassion, Blackstone wrote. Lawmakers had to set general rules for the common good. These laws set procedures and standards in place that then had to be followed without compassion. Judges and juries had to limit themselves to findings of law. All of these actors could play their parts with confidence only because they knew that the monarch would exercise pardon to prevent abuses. The monarch would ensure that justice was joined to mercy, as promised in the coronation oath. Such pardons required that the monarch stand above the law in some sense, even possessing the ability to display what Blackstone called "a tacit disapprobation of laws." It was just this power that grated against democratic ideals. "In democracies," Blackstone wrote, "this power of pardon can never subsist," for the executive branch was conceived as administering the laws, not declaring exceptions to them. Mere administrators could not offer pardon, for they stood within the law themselves. Because their authority derived from law, they had no authority to declare exceptions to the law. Pardon was therefore as alien to democracy as it was native to monarchy. Thus, Blackstone concluded, the ability to provide for pardon, and so join mercy to justice, was "indeed one of the great advantages of monarchy in general, above every other form of government."[3]

Thomas Paine disagreed with William Blackstone about the advantages of monarchy, but he agreed that pardon had no place in a democracy. "For as in absolute governments the King is law," Paine wrote in his pamphlet *Common Sense*, "so in free countries the law ought to be King; and there ought to be no other." The law alone should rule, Paine argued, and no individual should have the power to declare an exception. Pardon should be dismantled along with the monarchy that sustained it.[4]

Other thinkers with democratic sympathies sought to leave more room for some kind of pardon. John Locke, for instance, considered pardon under the category of "prerogative" in his *Second Treatise of Government*. Locke recognized that "the good of the society requires, that several things should be left to the discretion of him that has the executive power."[5] Because a legislative body could not foresee every relevant circumstance, and could not always act quickly enough to amend and refine the laws, executing laws with "inflexible rigor" would undermine the common good. The executive needed some prerogative, which Locke defined as a "power to act according to discretion, for the public good, without the prescription of the law, and sometimes even against it" (§ 160). Locke took care to offer a genealogy of prerogative that tied it clearly to popular sovereignty. Prerogative did not descend from ancient rights of kings, he wrote. It arose as a community recognized that its own well-being required some delegation of powers to an executive who could act "where the law was silent, and sometimes against the direct letter of the law, for the public good" (§ 164). Because prerogative was rooted in the people's sense of their own good, the people could curtail it without infringing on the rights of the executive. For the executive had no rights to prerogative apart from the public good.

Locke used prerogative to name a whole category of actions, from convening Parliament to acting quickly in a crisis. He made his case for pardon as a member of this category. Locke argued that

> a man may come sometimes within the reach of the law, which makes no distinction of persons, by an action that may deserve reward and pardon; 'tis fit the ruler should have a power, in many cases, to mitigate the severity of the law, and pardon some offenders: for the end of government being the preservation of all, as much as may be, even the guilty are to be spared, where it can prove no prejudice to the innocent. (§ 159)

Like Blackstone, Locke recognized a need for pardon in the order of society. And like Paine, Locke resisted attempts to grant pardon power to a monarch who stood above the law. Locke tried to reconcile his instincts by devising a potent but uneasy combination that retained executive pardon, but only as a power delegated by the people for the sake of the public good.

The traditions represented by Locke, Paine, and Blackstone all seem to have influenced Alexander Hamilton's consideration of pardon in Federalist No. 74. Writing in the United States in 1788, Hamilton had to acknowledge the skepticism of someone like Paine. Because of arguments like Paine's, Hamilton could not take pardon for granted, as Blackstone did. But he could begin his argument for pardon with an echo of Blackstone's sense that pardon was required for justice to be done. "The criminal code of every country partakes so much of necessary severity," Hamilton wrote, "that without an easy access to exceptions in favor of unfortunate guilt, justice would wear a countenance too sanguinary and cruel." Justice demanded the possibility of an exception. The real question was who should have the power to make such an exception. Like Locke, Hamilton argued that the power should be vested in an executive, one Hamilton called a chief magistrate, for one person could exercise better judgment—and feel responsibility more keenly—than a committee. But, just as Locke wrote, the power of the magistrate was of a different kind than the power of the monarch. It was rooted not in ancient privileges but in the public good. The real purpose of pardon, Hamilton argued, was the restoration of "the tranquility of the commonwealth." This was especially true in cases of treason. Hamilton's understanding of pardon was rooted not so much in respect for individual rights as in a sense of what it would take to sustain and heal the body politic.[6]

Hamilton's arguments eventually helped secure a place for pardon in the United States Constitution. Article II, Section 2 of the Constitution gives the executive the power "to grant Reprieves and Pardons for Offenses against the United States except in Cases of Impeachment." George Washington established an early precedent for exercising this power, pardoning the leaders of the Whiskey Rebellion on his last day in office. Since that time the president's power to pardon has been secure but never quite comfortable. Pardons are often accompanied by the stink of scandal. Even in the best of cases, problems like those Paine named endure. Pardon smacks of royal prerogative. It grates against our collective understandings of equality and fairness. It seems to undermine the rule of law. It lives in what Austin Sarat called "law's barely chartable borderland." On the one hand, pardon is clearly established in both statute and precedent. It is within the law. On the other hand, it names the need for powers that go beyond anything the law can prescribe. As Sarat argued, "Law cannot quite contain the exception, nor can it renounce the effort to do so." So pardon endures as an established but unstable part of contemporary politics.[7]

The double status of pardon within the law and beyond the law leaves the standard language of jurisprudence always struggling to discuss it. In particular, the questions before the courts keep slipping between ordinary modes of legal reasoning and modes of discourse more familiar to theology. In the Supreme Court's decision in *U.S. v. Wilson* (1833), for instance, Chief Justice John Marshall called pardon "an act of grace."[8] Marshall's language made the connection explicit, but it was present more subtly in legal questions about matters such as whether pardon could be refused, whether it could be made conditional, whether it had to follow some due process, whether it could become effective by decree or through a kind of contract, and whether it was a "private" act of the executive, subject only to his or her own counsel, or a "public" act that was responsible in some sense to the general welfare.[9] One need not accept the fullness of Carl Schmitt's "sociology of the concept" to note the structural similarities between these questions and the questions Christian theologians have asked about the grace of God for twenty centuries. This is the register in which reasoning about pardon keeps finding itself. Maps of the borderlands of law are drawn most clearly in the language of political theology.

Pardon without Exception

David Reynolds's proposal for pardoning John Brown might seem like the kind of pardon most fitting for a democratic republic committed to the rule of law. After all, it requires no exception to the standard of justice. It simply promises to apply that standard more uniformly across time. Thus, the executive still seems to play a role that is primarily administrative, even if that administration is in the service of a moral standard above the law. And the rule of law is not threatened but strengthened, as the law shows its ability to make progress toward a higher standard through the correction of past mistakes. If the logic of such a pardon would not convince Thomas Paine, it does more than any other to address his concerns. This is a form of pardon that fits readily with modern social imaginaries.

But pardon in the name of justice also creates at least two different sets of problems. First, it invites distortions of the historical record as the morality of the person in question is exaggerated in order to strengthen the case for pardon. In pleading Brown's case, for instance, Reynolds wrote, "Unlike nearly all other Americans of his era, John Brown did not have a shred of racism." This strong claim invites questions of clarification. Did Reynolds intend "nearly all other Americans" to refer only to white people? If not, did he mean to suggest that African Americans, Native Americans, and other minoritized groups were marked by racism? If he did mean to suggest that members of these groups were racist, what did he mean by "racism"?

Reynolds's claim also invites questions from the historical record. There is no doubt that Brown managed to imagine the world, and his place in it, in ways that were not as determined by prevailing racial categories as the visions of most white people of his time. Brown could imagine meaningful kinship—the kinds of ties one might kill and die for, but also the kinds of ties that make for deep neighborly relations—across racial lines. This sense of kinship was extraordinary in Brown's day and remains remarkable in ours. But one can recognize the extraordinary nature of Brown's vision and actions without saying that he "did not have a shred of racism."[10] While he worked closely and consulted respectfully with African Americans, he also did his best to retain control in most of these collaborations. He invited African Americans to sign the "Resolution" of the League of Gileadites, but he drafted the document and served as the leader of the league. He convened a constitutional convention in Chatham that included thirty-four African American delegates and twelve white delegates—but, again, he dominated the process of drafting the constitution, and there was never much doubt who would be named commander in chief of the provisional government. He invited African American people to join the raid on Harpers Ferry and trusted them with his life, but he made the plans and he gave the orders. And, as contemporary artist Kara Walker has argued in her works, Brown was not immune to the gratifications offered by the paternalist ideal of the benevolent white man doing for black people what they could not do for themselves.[11]

Brown was not even above putting on the persona of an older African American man to lecture free African Americans about how they needed to change their lives. In 1847 or 1848 Brown wrote an essay he entitled "Sambo's Mistakes" for the *Ram's Horn*, a black-owned abolitionist newspaper. In the essay he wrote as if he were a free black man, "Sambo." In Sambo's voice Brown wrote to acknowledge the mistakes he had made. He confessed to reading "silly novels & other miserable trash," joining "the Free Masons, Odd Fellows, Sons of Temperance," buying "expensive gay clothing," and, above all, seeking the favor of whites by "tamely submitting to every species of indignity contempt & wrong instead of nobly resisting their brutal aggressions from principle."[12] While the rhetoric of confession shaped the surface of the essay, it was not the confession of a contrite heart. It was criticism and exhortation from one who presumed to know better than the ones he was addressing. It not only slipped into paternalism but also relied on caricature and stereotype to form its list of mistakes. It then put on a black identity to give the charges additional authority. Pseudonymous writing was more widely practiced then than now, and Willis Hodges, the black editor of the *Ram's Horn*, knew Brown and knew that he had written the piece.[13] But can it be said that the author of "Sambo's Mistakes" "did not have a shred of racism"? And if the pardon of Brown depends on certain superlatives of his character, how could pardon be extended to the other raiders?

What matters most for the argument of this chapter is not digging up traces of racist clay in the feet of our image of Brown but figuring out why a historian as excellent as Reynolds would feel the need to make such a total claim. At the least, we can say that the historical record does not *demand* a claim like this. What does invite this kind of claim is the logic of pardon at work in Reynolds's argument. If Brown should be pardoned because he was right, then someone making a case for Brown's pardon would have reasons to argue that Brown was as right as a person can be. If there are some "blotches" on the record that need to be offset, then areas of moral strength would need to be cast in even stronger terms, perhaps even extending to claims to be free of the tiniest taint. Reynolds's logic of pardon does not require such excessive claims. But it does make them attractive. It leads away from the truth telling on which the deepest forms of pardon depend.

A second problem with this logic of pardon comes in the ways that it establishes legal and ethical precedents. If the raiders are pardoned because they were right, and if the arguments that they were right rely on norms that have a general form, then others can argue from these same norms to justify their own acts of violence. For instance, if the raiders are pardoned because they killed a few people in a struggle against an unjust system, then their pardon sets a precedent that invites imitation. Paul Hill made just this kind of argument after killing a doctor who provided abortions and that doctor's bodyguard. Timothy McVeigh and the Weather Underground also appealed to Brown as a precedent for justifying terrorist violence. Arguments that name criteria showing that the raiders were right, and then justify a pardon for the raiders using these criteria, make an implicit promise to legalize actions that meet those criteria.

This same dynamic of ethical arguments creating precedents is at work in other cases in which acts of prerogative expand to become new norms. In setting up courts to regulate transgressions of domestic and international laws, the Obama administration has established a pattern of providing lawlike, precedent-setting justifications for extralegal violence. While these courts are not issuing pardons, their work shares a structure with pardon. Like a pardon, the work of these courts is a legally sanctioned spot for deliberation about moving beyond or even against the rule of law. And when these courts base their decisions on generalizable criteria—on the kinds of norms that define what we usually mean when we speak of "ethics"—they set meaningful precedents. Pardon and other prerogatives, when executed in the name of a justice that can be described by generalizable norms, avoid the problems associated with exceptions. But they create problems of precedent.

The real problem is not just that some of these precedents might be unwelcome. It is that this mode of pardon enables a sovereign act to create rules that have enduring authority. This fusion of sovereignty and politics—of the exceptional and the everyday—is the signature of mythic violence. The problem becomes visible in the ways that a pardon in the name of justice disrupts relations between the different branches of government. If a governor or president were to pardon the raiders out of a belief that the raiders were right and the law was wrong, then the executive would in effect be invalidating one law and replacing it with another. Even if the laws that convicted the raiders remained on the books, a pardon in the name of justice would have the effect of installing a new legal standard. In establishing that standard, the executive would usurp the lawmaking function of the legislature. A pardon presented as an exception would avoid this kind of usurpation, for the exception would not become a rival law, even in function. It would not share the genre of law. As an exception, it would not set a precedent. It *would* display a strong version of what Hamilton and Locke called prerogative. But it would not displace laws already made, and it would not make anything like a new law. It would leave the separation of powers intact.

Ironically, the mode of pardon that seems to fit most readily with modern social imaginaries—pardon for the sake of a lawlike justice—can undermine values and institutions that these visions of political life hold to be essential. As Søren Kierkegaard saw, understanding Abraham's violent intentions against Isaac as a terrible exception does more to strengthen ethics than the effort to pull Abraham's violence within a system of exceptionless norms. Just so, a pardon of the raiders as an exception can do more to strengthen the laws and institutions of a nation committed to the rule of law than a pardon based on the idea that the raiders were right according to the standard of what the law should be.

Brown biographer Tony Horwitz had the right instincts when he asked was it "possible for Brown to have been right, but others who cite his example to be wrong?"[14] The best way to make sense of this instinct is not to seek out some generalizable criteria that can distinguish the Harpers Ferry raiders' violence from the violence of others. This effort would run the risks that come with pardon in the name of justice. And it would run right past the enduring evil of violence for whatever cause. A better mode of pardon would not try to make a case that the raiders actions conformed to some ethical rule. It would not set a precedent. It would negate the power of a rule to order relations without exception. It would not argue that the raiders were right. It would declare that they were forgiven.

The Cities of Cain

Pardon should be understood not as the work of reconciling law to justice but as the sovereign naming of an exception to law. Such pardon—as Locke and Hamilton saw—involves the exercise of a kind of prerogative. It does not involve the power to change statutes, build up case law, or even set ideal standards that laws should approach, as Reynolds's pardon in the name of justice would suggest. Pardon that names an exception does not change the content of law. It instead says where, when, and to whom the law applies. It performs the work of relating the law to a world that is beyond the law.

As the sovereign declaration of an exception, pardon might seem to threaten the rule of law. It *does* tear a hole in the fabric of law's claim to completeness. But just that naming of a limit makes clear that there is a boundary to law. And the boundary makes clear that there is something other than the sum total of laws.

In negating the law's application in one instance only, the exception relates a larger system of law to a reality beyond itself. "In the exception," as Carl Schmitt wrote, "the power of real life breaks through the crust of a mechanism that has become torpid by repetition." For the exception—when it is understood as an exception, and not, as Reynolds's logic would imply, a de facto amendment— declares that the law applies in every case except this one. As a singular event, Schmitt wrote, "the exception in jurisprudence is analogous to the miracle in theology."[15] The miracle does not invalidate the ordinary laws of nature. It does not even amend them. Its status as a miracle ratifies those ordinary laws in their present form, for to say that an event is a miracle is to say that it is an exception to laws that ordinarily hold true. That which law cannot conceive, that which is alien to the form of law, thus helps secure law's relationship to the world. The aporia of an exception disrupts the completeness of the system of laws. But it secures the *rule* of law, for it establishes the relationship between law and that which is beyond the law.

Schmitt saw the way that an exception related a set of rules to a world beyond the rules, but he failed to see the need for discontinuity between the exception and the politics that arose in its wake. The exception Schmitt had in mind was a season of extralegal violence like the one that marked the führer's rise to power in Germany. In Schmitt's vision, that exceptional violence would establish the authority that would issue the laws that would make ordinary politics possible. But, as Walter Benjamin saw, such a "mythic" account of a political order misses the need to name a radical distinction between the exception and what follows. Schmitt was right to stress the role of an exception in the origins of politics but wrong to think that the originating extralegal action should take the form of violence that erected a new authority. For when an act of violence founds the authority that establishes the laws, institutions, customs, and characters that constitute a political order, that founding violence continues to radiate throughout the order. The laws and institutions perform endless repetitions of the founding violence. And just that repeated, radiating violence undermines the possibility of free, constructive dialogue and the possibility of politics in the fullest sense.

Schmitt's story of the role of violence in the founding of a political order reads like a bowdlerized retelling of the story of the founding of Rome: Romulus killed his brother, Remus, and gained the power to promulgate the

laws that established the city. Violence beyond the law established the authority that then established the law. Within that body of law, the story goes, politics could flourish. But the story explains only how Romulus established power
over others. He did it first through murder and then through the promulgation
of laws. The deep continuity between these acts makes the laws an extension of
the murder. The founding murder resounds through the laws. Thus the story
explains the emergence of *rule* but not the emergence of the free, creative, reasoned exchanges of *politics*.

The narratives in the first chapters of Genesis tell a different story about a
different kind of exception. They, too, begin with fratricide. They tell the story
of how Cain killed his brother, Abel, but in Genesis this killing established
nothing beyond Cain's guilt. Cain might have had superior force for a time, but
that was all. He had no legitimacy, no claim on people beyond whatever force
he could muster. His murder did not let him found a city; on the contrary, it
made the ground itself cry out against him. It condemned him to life as "a fugitive and a wanderer on the earth" (4:12). Anyone he met could and should kill
him in the name of justice. His violence founded nothing except an endlessly
swirling cycle of revenge, mythic violence that endlessly recapitulated the initial murder. This cycle stopped, the story says, when God put a mark on Cain
and forbade retribution. That pardon was an exception to the rule of revenge.
It declared a rupture, a break with the past, a new beginning. In the wake of
that pardon, Cain built the city of Enoch, somewhere east of Eden (4:16). As
Genesis tells the story, this is the beginning of civilization. Murder begets only
murder. It is pardon that enables the founding of the city.

A founding pardon might feel more palatable to contemporary readers than
a founding murder, because it seeks to end violence rather than perpetuate it.
On one level this is true. But the violence involved in God's pardon of Cain
should not be missed. God did not just offer God's own personal pardon of
Cain, as if the matter were a private transaction between them. A private pardon
might have saved Cain's soul, but it would not have enabled him to found the
city. God's pardon made politics possible because of its public dimensions. In the
stories of Genesis God secured those public dimensions with the promise of violence. "Whoever kills Cain," God declared, "will suffer a sevenfold vengeance"
(4:15). This was a promise not just of violence but of violence outside the law. For
the pardon of Cain was as far beyond whatever laws and customs prevailed at
the time as were the murderous acts of Cain and Romulus. In Genesis God not
only acted outside the law but vowed to uphold that act with violence.

The real difference between the stories of Romulus and Cain is not the presence or absence of some kind of sovereign violence but the relationship of that sovereign violence to the politics of the city. Romulus himself possesses sovereign power and uses that power to perform the extralegal act that founds the city. He then gives the laws. There is a deep continuity between the extralegal violence and the giving of the law, and they are held together in the person of the sovereign. This continuity of sovereign power and political power is what gives the violence its mythic quality. Unlike Romulus, Cain possesses no sovereign power. He is not the agent of the extralegal act that breaks the old order of obligations but the *recipient* of that act. When he founds the city of Enoch, he acts not as sovereign, nor even as an agent of the sovereign, but as one set free to respond to sovereign grace. There is an infinite discontinuity between the sovereign power that named an exception to the old order and the political power that developed a new form of life in the opening created by that exception. This discontinuity marks the sovereign grace of pardon as a moment of what I have been calling divine violence.

Pardon makes politics possible. Pardon declares an exception to mandated violence, and that exception opens up new possibilities. Those new possibilities center on the pardoned one. As Blackstone wrote, the effect of pardon is to make the offender "a new man."[16] It does not change the law so much as the identity of a person under law, and so the obligations owed by and to that pardoned individual. The pardon of Cain does not legalize murder; it does not even make a case that Cain's act fulfilled certain criteria that make it a precedent-setting instance in which murder might be justified. On the contrary, the pardon of Cain, as an exception, ratifies the law as it stands. The pardon of Cain does not change the law against murder. It changes the standing of Cain in the network of relationships around him.

The power of this change should not be underestimated. While it does not create a new law, it does create a new polity. The effects of pardon begin with the individual person being pardoned, but because they have to do with what that person owes to others and what is owed to that person, they have a much wider significance. The effects of pardon extend to the whole network of relations in which the pardoned one exists. Pardon interrupts old patterns of relationship—even, or especially, those demanded by ethics—and makes it possible to create new patterns. Pardon makes possible not just a new life for Cain but a new city on the plain.

The pardon of Cain does not determine the shape of the new patterns it makes possible, just as a miracle does not create new laws of physics. The mark of Cain declares an exception to existing laws without establishing a new law. It demands the response of a new form of life without prescribing what that response should be. It demands the free, creative, human work of politics. But these politics do not unfold against a legal and moral landscape rendered barren by some antinomian blast. The politics of the city of Cain do not have to pull themselves up by their bootstraps from the vast emptiness that Hegel called "bad infinity." For the pardon of Cain is not an abstract suspension of every law. It is the very concrete declaration that this person will not be subject in this case to the punishment prescribed by this law that otherwise holds. An exceptional pardon does not determine what comes after it. It does not have that kind of positive content. But its negation does have direction, for it is the pardon of a particular crime. In this combination of particularity and open-ness, the pardon I am trying to describe functions like what Theodor Adorno called "determinate negation."[17]

The determinate negation of pardon makes new social orders possible without determining the form they will take. The significance of pardon is clear enough in the case of a country like South Africa, where contested con-cepts of pardon have played a role in every stage of the process of refound-ing the nation. But pardon has also played a significant role in less obvious cases. It is not too strong to say that contemporary Europe emerged in the wake of the explicit and implicit pardon of Germany. That pardon did not determine the course that led to the European Union, a common currency, and other institutions designed both to readmit and contain Germany. But the pardon did serve as a necessary precursor to all that has followed. Later I sketch the ways that pardon shaped life in the United States after the Civil War. Both the particular pardons offered and the pardons withheld helped set a course the nation still follows today—for better and for worse. As even this short list of examples suggests, pardon can take many forms. It can require truth telling, oath swearing, disarming, or other conditions—or set no con-ditions at all. It can impose a long probationary period or offer immediate membership with full parity. It can be achieved through multiparty contract or unilateral decree. Many kinds of acts can be gathered under the name of pardon. But they all involve withholding some kind of violence that would otherwise be due. If they are acts of pardon, they involve an exception to ethics—what is due—and a rupture with the past. They make what Charles Taylor called an "upward thrust," a decision that does not just settle for a spot of fairness on a horizontal line between two parties with conflicting claims but moves in a vertical dimension with the hope of "a new horizontal space where the resolution will be less painful or damaging for both parties."[18] With this upward thrust, acts of pardon open new planes on which the give and take of everyday political life can begin again in renewed forms.

The gift of pardon is that it breaks the binding hold of codes of ethics; the risk of pardon is that it will not rise above what those codes could offer but sink beneath them. The power to pardon has often been abused. It has served as the occasion for cronyism. It has provided cover for actions that allowed guilty people to continue to perpetrate crimes. It has been used in ways that undermine the trust and sense of common life that help hold a society together. If pardon has sometimes transcended ethics, it has also sapped the stuff on which ethical life depends without offering a better alternative. Seeing these risks, we can be tempted to pull pardon back within the ethical, as David Reynolds tried to do. But, as I argued previously, this turns exceptions into precedents. When exceptions become precedents, the sovereign power that declares an exception is fused with the everyday stuff of politics. The violence of the founding act echoes throughout the polity in waves of mythic violence. Breaking those waves requires the risk of a pardon that sets no precedents, an exception that neither fits with an existing system of ethics nor founds a new one. The risks of such pardon are real.

The enervating, cruel, and ultimately apolitical repetition of code makes clear the need to retain some possibility of pardon as exception. But the risks of pardon make just as clear the need to develop modes of reasoning about the exception. This deliberation cannot invoke reasons that imply or rely upon universalizable standards, for these would make the code only more baroque without naming a true exception. The required deliberation must be willing to transcend the horizontal plane of existing code. It must be able to reason about the singularity of an exception. It must be able to reason about sovereignty. We might call such discourse political theology, a rationality of the upward thrust. If it cannot be prescribed in even a new and improved set of rules, it can be displayed. The remaining sections of this chapter seek to display such reasoning. They combine attention to concrete particularities and transcendental hopes. They involve both history and eschatology, ethics and theology. And they invite rebuttal. The possibility of rebuttal makes the larger point: If the reasoning of political theology does not proceed according to a code of method and rules of evidence, it can still involve meaningful arguments. Even the question of pardon helps make politics possible.

An Exception for the Raiders

Though the arsenal at Harpers Ferry stood on federal land and the raiders in the blockhouse were captured by federal marines, they were charged and tried by the Commonwealth of Virginia. Governor Henry Wise moved swiftly and decisively to secure jurisdiction, and President James Buchanan showed little interest in stopping him. The state brought three charges in *Virginia v. Brown*: treason against the Commonwealth of Virginia, first-degree murder, and incitement of slaves to rebellion. In a trial that lasted a little more than one week Brown was convicted on all three charges and sentenced to hang. The other trials followed suit. Just one month later the sentences were carried out.

One could argue that the raiders' conviction should be overturned because Virginia lacked jurisdiction to try the case. Brown's lawyers made this argument. They pointed out that Brown was not a citizen of Virginia, had never lived for any length of time in Virginia, and had carried out his raid against federal property standing on federal soil.[19] They were right to argue that the trial should have been held in federal court. The point is not a mere technicality, as the boundaries between federal and state sovereignty were central to the issues of the day. But this defense evades the harder questions raised by the possibility of pardon. The raiders were surely guilty of treason against the United States (and just as surely would have been glad for the attack on Harpers Ferry to contribute to the overthrow of the Commonwealth of Virginia as it was constituted at that time). Their attack resulted in multiple deaths, whatever the jurisdiction. And small bands of the raiders had gone out to set enslaved people free, put weapons in their hands, and asked them to fight the powers that sustained slavery. If this should not be a crime, it was defined as one at the time. These facts were not in dispute then, and they are not now. It is little wonder that the jury could convict the raiders so quickly. The real question is not whether the raiders were guilty of crimes as defined by the laws of their day but whether they should be pardoned for them now.

David Reynolds's case for posthumous pardon in the name of justice is most persuasive in relation to the charge of incitement of slaves to revolt. After the Thirteenth Amendment made slavery illegal, current law, established through ordinary means, does not recognize incitement of slaves to revolt as a crime. Thus, pardoning the raiders on this charge, even in the name of justice, would not declare an exception that established a precedent that defined new law. It would not fuse sovereignty and politics. It would only recognize the law that had already been established.

Such arguments cannot be made in relation to the charges of treason and murder. The law still defines treason and murder as crimes. Pardon in the name of justice would establish precedents that would amount to amendments to the norms defining these crimes. Those precedents would be dangerous. Even those of us who reject the absolute claims of the state would have qualms about a precedent-setting principle that would justify taking up arms against the state whenever it was in the wrong. This is all the more true for the charge of murder. Pardoning murder in the name of justice would set a precedent that would open the door to the arguments of Paul Hill, Timothy McVeigh, the Unabomber, and anyone who believed in a cause. But, as I argued earlier, the real problem is not just the particularities of these individual precedents. We might decide, on the whole, that we could live with them. The real problem is the way that pardon in the name of justice—sovereignty justified and exercised within the realm of ethics alone—foments mythic violence. Seeing this dynamic highlights the relevant difference between the three charges against the raiders. It matters that the law no longer defines incitement of slaves to revolt as a crime but does still forbid treason and murder. Pardon in the name of justice would be appropriate for the charge of inciting slaves to revolt, but not for the charges of treason and murder. The question of this chapter thus becomes sharper: Should Brown be granted an exceptional pardon for treason and murder?

A truly exceptional pardon would not declare that the raiders were right. It would declare that they were forgiven. Such a pardon would spring from the deepest reserves of freedom. It could not be mandated, not even by the relatively weak form of a practical syllogism. It could not be demanded by desert, for the norms that established desert would link sovereign power to subsequent politics in ways that would just establish a new mythic violence. But pardon could be freely chosen through a form of reasoning attuned to singularity, a form more like erotics or aesthetics than an ethics of generalizable norms.

In this reasoning about the singular, a sovereign power could decide to pardon the raiders as a way of saying No to the power of the slave system to define the social order. In the language I have been developing in this chapter, such a pardon would perform a determinate negation of the mythic violence of slavery. That violence *still* courses through the laws, institutions, and ethical life of the United States. It runs so deep that it cannot be rooted out by actions that conform to the standards of the social order it has helped create. Actions that are ethical by the standards of the order reiterate its mythic violence in deep ways. Even actions that appeal to an ethic that stands in judgment of the order can reiterate its violence when they focus on giving perpetrators what they are due. As Nelson Mandela and Martin Luther King Jr. saw, even just retribution can extend the power of mythic violence to control a polity. Addressing mythic violence—what Christian theology would call "original sin"—requires a more radical break, a break that does not forget the past but also does not let the past control the present. It requires an act of grace, an exception. Such a pardon would deliver the raiders from the place of Remus, the brother who had to be slain to secure the city. But it would not transform them into Romulus, the vindicated brother whose murderous act resonated through all the laws of Rome. It would, rather, inscribe on them the mark of Cain, the murderer who is nonetheless part of the city.[20]

Such a pardon would not set a precedent. It would not change the law. It would only change the place of the raiders in the network of relations and memories that surround them. And this change would be significant. If a pardon would not justify the raiders, it would transform them from fanatics who had to be expelled and executed into members of the polity who deserve to be reckoned with. The story of the Civil War would be transformed if the raiders took their place alongside others pardoned for treason and (implicitly) murder. The national memory would shift significantly if John Brown were remembered less like Timothy McVeigh and more like Robert E. Lee.

Abraham Lincoln saw this analogy, at least in 1859. Speaking in Kansas just one day after Brown's execution, Lincoln paired Brown with potential proslavery rebels. Brown was right about slavery, Lincoln said. But even being right "cannot excuse violence, bloodshed, and treason." So, Lincoln warned his hearers, if "you undertake to destroy the Union, it will be our duty to deal with you as old John Brown has been dealt with."[21] Lincoln named a likeness of crime and promised a likeness of punishment. But the pardons issued during and after the war have not yet recognized this likeness. Lee has been pardoned, but Brown and the Harpers Ferry raiders have not. To argue that Brown and Lee broke some of the same statutes is not to name a simple ethical equivalence between them. There are significant ethical differences at stake, and the weightiest of these differences—those related to slavery—tilt the ethical scales decisively in Brown's favor. I do not pair these two in order to justify the pardon of Brown. Pardoning Brown because he was ethically superior to someone already pardoned would only slip back into pardon in the name of justice and the mythic violence it underwrites. I make the juxtaposition only to suggest the kind of difference the restoration of Brown to membership in the polity would make.[22]

Pardoning Brown as Lee was pardoned would transform the nation's under-standing of itself, for it would change the narrative of the Civil War, which has become the story of the nation's second founding. Pardoning the Harpers Ferry raiders as a negation of the slave system would reject any stories about fanati-cal abolitionists forcing war upon noble, moderate, peace-loving slaveholders. It would acknowledge slavery itself as a state of madness and war, all the more fanatical because it was established in law and custom. A nation that could tell these stories about itself would be very different from one that sees the Blue and the Gray as two armies of valiant men fighting over states' rights and whether economic policy should favor agriculture or domestic manufacturing. Pardoning Brown as Lee was pardoned would tell a more truthful story and make possible a more just politics.

As appealing as a politics on the other side of such a pardon might be, they should not be used to justify pardon as a means to the end of a better politics. For that logic would treat the pardon not as a singularity but as a member of a set of actions that could achieve a good end. Means are never true singulari-ties, even when it seems as if there are no other ways to achieve the desired end. The very idea of "means" to an end suggests at least a potential plurality and interchangeability. Pardon as a means to better politics thus slips into the ethi-cal frame just as surely as pardon in the name of justice. If pardon in the name of justice emphasizes deontological reasoning—the raiders should be pardoned because they were right!—pardon as a means to renewing the polity emphasizes a more consequentialist mode—the raiders should be pardoned for what that pardon would make possible! Both kinds of pardon would set precedents. Both would knit sovereign power to a subsequent politics. Because of this continuity between sovereign exception and everyday politics, pardon for the sake of a bet-ter politics would reiterate mythic violence just as surely as pardon in the name of justice. Describing the polity pardon would make possible, then, does not justify an exceptional pardon any more than describing good effects on a person's health might justify love. It simply makes clear the difference pardon would make.

An exceptional pardon requires sovereign freedom. And while I have tried to gesture toward the kind of reasoning such freedom might involve, even rea-sonable sovereign freedom still runs the constant risk of tyranny. The key, as Immanuel Kant saw, is the standing of the sovereign in relation to the crime to be pardoned.

Kant was deeply committed to a worldview structured by a framework of universalizable norms, and correspondingly suspicious of sovereign exceptions.

But even Kant saw the need to allow some room for pardon. His wariness kept him alert to potential abuses of pardon. Kant called pardon "the slipperiest" of all the rights of a sovereign, for, he wrote, it involves "doing injustice in the highest degree." Kant argued that the sovereign should "absolutely not" exercise pardon power in relation to crimes that subjects committed against one another, for this "failure to punish (*impunitas criminis*) is the greatest wrong against his subjects." The sovereign could offer pardon "only in case of a wrong done *to himself* (*crimen laesae maiestatis*)."[23] Kant's standard rightly recognized the enduring dignity of individuals in relation to any sovereign. The claims of wronged individuals should not simply be dissolved in sovereign desire for a better polity. The sovereign could pardon only crimes that were against the sovereign, Kant wrote. Exceptional pardon required appropriate standing.

Even by Kant's restrictive standard, the governor of Virginia or the president of the United States would have legitimate authority to pardon the offense of treason. Treason is the purest form of an offense against the sovereign. If an executive could pardon only the wrong done to the sovereign, she or he could still pardon the whole of treason.

Murder is another matter. In the very first hours of the raid on Harpers Ferry, the raiders killed Hayward Shepherd, a free African American man who handled baggage for the B&O railroad. In the course of the fighting they went on to kill three white men from Harpers Ferry, Thomas Boerly, George W. Turner, and Fontaine Beckham. And in the final, pitched battle for the blockhouse they killed Marine Luke Quinn. The number of those harmed by the raiders also included those wounded and those taken hostage. Pardon in the name of justice would justify all this damage, whether because the people injured and killed deserved it in some sense, or because it was done with right motives, or because it was on the way to a greater good, or for the sake of some other rationale. Arguments like these ease the pressure of questions about the standing of the sovereign, for they would remove the moral weight from the raiders' crimes. But pardon as an exception recognizes the enduring wrong of killing, even killing of people who are defending an evil system. Pardon as an exception therefore cannot dodge Kant's arguments about the limit of sovereignty. How could an executive have the power to pardon real crimes against those she had sworn to protect?

The sovereign, as Kant argued, could rightly pardon only those crimes that were against the sovereign's own person. The murders at Harpers Ferry, like all violations of the law, *were* crimes against the sovereign. This idea is at the center of the distinction between criminal and civil law. Because the government brings the charges in a criminal trial, the raiders were prosecuted by Virginia and hanged for crimes against Virginia. This was true not only for the charge of treason but also for the charges of murder. Thus, the Commonwealth of Virginia—or the United States, acting where it should have acted before—would have standing, even within Kant's standards, to pardon the raiders for murder as a crime against itself. Such a pardon would not negate the claims of the victims and their families. The victims would retain the right to bring claims for damages in civil court, for a sovereign pardon could not negate those claims without becoming tyrannical.

A sovereign pardon would not justify the raiders. It would not exonerate them. It would not absolve them of their responsibilities to their fellow citizens. It would simply pardon their crimes against the state as a refusal to let slavery's cycles of violence continue to determine national memory. And it would, like the pardon of Cain, make possible a different set of relationships and so a different kind of polity.

Between Two Proclamations

Offering an exceptional pardon to the raiders would interrupt the mythic violence generated by slavery in a way that a pardon in the name of justice would not. In particular, an exceptional pardon would denounce slavery as the root of the violence that broke out in Harpers Ferry and then, on a cataclysmic scale, in the Civil War. This alone would be significant work. Our national narratives would be different if we could clearly name slavery—rather than religious fanaticism, an individual's insanity, transcendentalism, the abolitionist imagination, or some other Yankee malady—as the root cause of the violence that ran from Kansas through Harpers Ferry to Appomattox and beyond. But an exceptional pardon would not just say that slavery was wrong. Pardon in the name of justice could do that. An exceptional pardon would also refuse the power of conflicts about slavery to continue to order our collective life. Pardon in the name of justice, on the other hand, would be one more episode in those struggles. Introducing a break into the cycles of violence in conflicts over slavery would be significant work. But it would also leave significant work undone. It would not address those who perpetuated and suffered from the monstrous crime of slavery itself.

An exceptional pardon of the raiders would therefore fit closely with the course the United States has already charted. The nation has used pardon to heal the wounds of treason and murder from the conflict over slavery, while leaving slavery itself abolished but untreated. It is worth distinguishing these two issues—violence *about* slavery, on the one hand, and the violence *of* slavery, on the other—for the processes of addressing the two were pulled apart, even set against one another, in politics after the Civil War. The difference in the ways these crimes have been addressed does much to define life in the United States today.

Abraham Lincoln took on both issues with executive proclamations that served as bookends for the decisive year of 1863. On the first day of that year he issued the Emancipation Proclamation, which declared that all people who were enslaved in territories still in rebellion were now and forever free. It further committed the US military to maintaining that freedom. The proclamation helped bring slavery to an end, but it did not even begin to deal with the legacy of slavery. By itself, it was like a command to stop a flogging that left untended the wounds from centuries of flogging. If the proclamation was a good and necessary first step, it was also incomplete.

The relatively short course of Reconstruction established the work of the Emancipation Proclamation but did not expand that work in ways that endured. Lincoln had issued the proclamation as an extension of his powers as commander in chief of the armed forces. Emancipation received a more secure legal footing in the Thirteenth Amendment, which Lincoln, calling up echoes of one of the oldest practices of sovereign power, called a "King's cure for all the evils" besetting the nation.[24] But, like the Emancipation Proclamation, the Thirteenth Amendment only brought slavery to an end; it did not deal with the legacy of slavery. The Fourteenth and Fifteenth Amendments continued this trajectory. Together they secured citizenship for African Americans and established the right to vote whatever a citizen's "race, color, or previous condition of servitude." The amendments aimed at legal equality going forward. The Civil Rights Acts of 1866 and 1875 extended this legal equality even further, at least in statute. But they did not address inequalities in the economic sphere that had arisen in centuries of slavery. And they did not address the moral offenses of the acts that created and sustained slavery. Reconstruction saw an end to legal slavery, but it did not declare slavery a crime. By the end of Reconstruction, the terms of national reconciliation neither demanded penitence nor promised pardon for slavery.

The treason of Confederates, on the other hand, *was* recognized as a crime. Naming it as a crime invoked a logic that meant that it could not be dealt with just by forcing it to stop. Naming secession and war as acts of treason committed the government to some combination of punishment, demands for penitence,

and pardon. Lincoln saw the need for pardon for the sake of national regeneration, and he began the process of pardon with a proclamation at the other end
of 1863. In December the Proclamation of Amnesty and Reconstruction offered
pardon to Confederates who would take an oath of loyalty to the United States.
Citing the power to pardon granted to the president in the Constitution, Lincoln exercised sovereignty to declare an exception to the law. He promised restoration of rights and property—with the explicit exception of the "property" of
enslaved people—to any who would take a loyalty oath. When a number equiva-
lent to 10 percent of the people registered to vote in the 1860 presidential election took the oath, a state could reorganize itself for readmission to the Union.
The so-called Ten Percent Plan did not extend to everyone. It did not offer the
possibility of pardon to those who had held office in the Confederate government, those who had served as high-ranking officers in the military, those who
had resigned seats in Congress or military commissions to join the rebellion,
and select other groups of people.[25] But the offer of pardon was expansive, and it
gave rise to a river that would only get wider over time.

After Lincoln's assassination, Andrew Johnson pushed to widen the pardon
offered for treason. He proclaimed an immediate pardon for all Confederates
who owned less than twenty thousand dollars' worth of property and had not
served at the highest levels of the military. He offered those excluded by the
initial offer an opportunity to petition for pardons, which he granted readily—
sometimes at a clip of more than one hundred in a single day.[26] Section 3 of the
Fourteenth Amendment barred from public office those who had once held
office in the United States and then broken their oaths of loyalty to the Constitution by joining or supporting insurrection. But even this limitation was
largely undone by the Amnesty Act of 1872. By the time Republicans in Congress agreed to withdraw federal troops from the South in a bargain that would
settle the disputed election of 1876, pardon for treason was effectively universal.

Lincoln's twin proclamations of 1863 set the template for national reconciliation. The Emancipation Proclamation declared an end to slavery under certain conditions, but it did not name slavery as evil and did not treat slavery
as a crime. It included no provisions for punishment, reparations, pardon, or
some combination of these three. No enduring forms of punishment, reparations, or pardon for slavery emerged in the course of Reconstruction. Instead,
the forward-looking, rights-oriented logic of the Emancipation Proclamation played itself out. Emancipation was extended through a series of acts and
amendments that aimed to secure civil rights going forward. They tried to leave

slavery behind, making it no longer permissible while leaving it unpunished and unpardoned. The logic of Lincoln's proclamation from the end of 1863 set a very different course. The Proclamation of Amnesty and Reconstruction named treason as a crime and offered pardon as a response. Over time, that pardon expanded in legal statute and deepened as social fact. Much of life in the United States today is framed within the lines that extend these proclamations of 1863. Slavery is outlawed, and civil rights are at least promised to all citizens. But the legacies of the slave system live on in every sphere of society. The legacies of the war over slavery, on the other hand, have largely been healed and left behind. The completeness of their pardon is memorialized every time Civil War battles are reenacted by people who know, at the end of the day, that they are on the same side.

The legacies of Lincoln's proclamations of 1863 should not be read as if they were independent phenomena that just happened to take different courses. The intransigence and ongoing political power of former Confederates and their Northern allies created a very literal trade-off between attempts to deal with the legacies of slavery and attempts to reconcile whites from the North and the South. As the withdrawal of federal troops from the South to secure acceptance of the results of the disputed presidential election of 1876 made clear, the price of reconciliation between whites has been the refusal to punish or even to pardon slavery as a crime. Frederick Douglass discerned the trade-off even as the deal was being done. In an 1875 address entitled "The Color Question," Douglass named the reconciliation that was taking place. "So sure as the stars shine in the heavens, and the rivers run to the sea," he said, "so sure will the white people North and South abandon their quarrels and become friends." Douglass was sure that reconciliation between whites was coming, but he was not at all sure that it would be good for African Americans. "If war among the whites brought peace and liberty to blacks," he asked, "what will peace among the whites bring?"[27] The years since Douglass's speech have been filled with grim answers to his question.

The answers to Douglass's question have unfolded within the bounds suggested by Lincoln's 1863 proclamations of emancipation for slaves and amnesty for Confederates. These always intertwined proclamations have helped create a social and political space marked by an ideal of legal equality between blacks and whites that has often not been realized, on the one hand, and a gradual but real reconciliation of whites from the North and the South, on the other. Americans still live in the space defined by these two proclamations.

Pardoning the raiders as an exception would not change the basic contours of this space. It would further negate the power of violence over slavery to shape life in the United States. And it would help shift the narratives that define the meaning of the Civil War and the nation that arose in its wake. These are not small things. But a pardon of the raiders would extend the offer of reconciliation to only a few more people who killed other people in the conflicts over slavery. It would not address slavery as a crime.

Refusing Cheap Grace

Because the nation has not addressed the crime of slavery and its legacies, slavery still marks national life in definitive ways. It can be tempting, then, to consider pardon for slavery as a way of breaking the hold this crime still has on our life together. Pardon would at least name slavery as a crime. And it might have the power to stop the spirals of mythic violence that arise from this evil woven so deeply into the founding of the United States. If the state could pardon treason and murder by the men who raided Harpers Ferry, could it not also pardon slavery?

No.

Even if the state could pardon slavery, I could not make the case. As a white man, a beneficiary of slavery in more ways than I know, I lack the standing to make an argument that slavery should be pardoned. I could at most offer confession and then hope for pardon in reply. I would offer such confession. But I would refuse any pardon offered by the state.

Pardon by the state would be unjust. It would be unjust because of the magnitude of the crime. Millions of people were seized. Millions more were killed. Millions more were born, came of age, and died in slavery. Rape was so common that social customs evolved to accommodate it; torture was so ordinary that its implements could be bought and sold in public markets. Every effort was made to destroy cultures, the better to force people into new roles. Households, companies, cities, states, churches, universities, societies, and nations were built on the backs of the people enslaved by this system. The crime was so deep that a list like this one, however infinitely extended, falsifies it by failing to recognize how deep it runs. For this crime, pardon is impossible, unthinkable.

Pardon would also be unjust because the dehumanizing violence of slavery continues in many forms. If the Thirteenth Amendment made slavery illegal, it did not end the legacies of slavery. It did not stop the rise of Jim Crow. It did not prevent waves of lynching. It has not stopped systematic mass incarceration and growing economic inequality. It would defy justice to offer pardon for slavery when it is so deeply continuous with ongoing wrongs.

Pardon would also be unjust because those who need pardon have not consistently and publicly told the truth about the crime. Almost none of those involved directly in the slave system managed to name what they had done. And those who, by sins of omission and commission, have perpetuated and benefited from the legacies of slavery have acknowledged their connections to the crime only in sporadic statements. Meanwhile, textbooks hide brutality under silence and euphemism. National myths of meritocracy and innocence suppress more disturbing—and truthful—accounts of reality. Everyday interactions are expected to proceed as if nothing happened.

Reparations should be paid, but even they would not make pardon just. The damage done runs beyond what even the wealth of the richest nation in the history of the world could reach. Even after massive reparations, pardon would still offend justice. To say that reparations could not make complete atonement for the crimes of slavery is not to argue that reparations should not be demanded and paid. On the contrary, even reparations that would not completely repair the damage done could do great good. They could acknowledge a wrong. They could help individuals who suffer from a legacy of harm. They could help establish what justice is possible in this world. But they would still leave a gap that it would be unjust for pardon to bridge.[28]

Pardon for slavery would be unjust. But earlier in this chapter I argued for a pardon of the Harpers Ferry raiders that both exceeded and fell short of the norms of justice—pardon as an *exception* to justice. Jacques Derrida, considering arguments about the impossibility of forgiving the violence done in the Shoah, argues, "There is only forgiveness, if there is such a thing, of the unforgivable."[29] Injustice is a necessary feature of forgiveness that makes an exception, for no exception would need to be made to forgive actions that could be forgiven within the framework of ethics. Derrida writes,

> If one is only prepared to forgive what appears forgivable, what the church calls "venial sin," then the very idea of forgiveness would disappear. If there is something to forgive, it would be what in religious language is called mortal sin, the worst, the unforgivable crime or harm. From which comes the aporia, which can be described in its dry and implacable formality, without mercy: forgiveness forgives only the unforgivable. One cannot, or should not, forgive; there is only forgiveness, if there is any, where there is the unforgivable. (32–33)

In a string of works from the last decades of his life, Derrida resisted what I have called pardon in the name of justice. Because such pardon ultimately reduces to ethics, Derrida argues, it loses any distinctive quality that pardon might otherwise have. Pardon then becomes nothing more than the recognition that should be offered to one wrongly judged or a kind of therapy that a nation might undertake in order to heal its wounds. In both of these cases, pardon reduces to ethics. But real forgiveness, Derrida argues, outruns the limits of ethics. If the state could never pardon slavery in the name of justice, could it offer pardon as an exception in which sovereign grace ran beyond the limits of ethics?

No.

It would be redundant to call an exceptional pardon unjust. It is unjust by definition. If exceptional pardons can ever be offered, they will be offered in ways that violate the norms of justice. To call them "unjust" is simply to call them by their name. But justice does not exhaust the categories for thinking about pardon. A state pardon for slavery would not just be unjust; it would be tyrannical. For no earthly sovereign has the standing to pardon the slavery practiced in the United States. Kant was right to say that the state could perform the injustice of pardon only in relation to crimes against itself. This is not just one more criterion within a framework of generalizable norms. Rightful standing does not, as Kant saw, reconcile exceptional pardons to justice. The question of standing relates not to the justice of pardon but to the definition of the act, which centers on a wronged party offering forgiveness to the one who did the wrong. Even exceptional pardons require that the one offering pardon have standing to offer the pardon. If the person or power offering pardon lacks the standing to offer that pardon, it is something other than pardon.

The state can offer pardon for treason and murder to people like John Brown and Robert E. Lee because the treason and murder these men performed were against the law and thus, in some real sense, against the state. But slavery was not against the law. On the contrary, the laws of both states and the federal government tied themselves in knots to accommodate slavery. The state as it was constituted then cannot claim injury. And, without the kind of radical discontinuity that founds a new state that represents those who were injured—the kind of discontinuity brought by the revolution in Haiti, for instance—the state lacks the standing to pardon slavery now. State pardon for slavery would be the embodiment of what Dietrich Bonhoeffer called *billige Gnade*, cheap grace, the kind of grace people bestow upon themselves. It would not be pardon at all.[30]

A Politics of the Open Wound

The United States lacks the sovereign standing necessary to pardon slavery. The body politic therefore staggers with an open wound. A clearer sense of the depth of this wound and how we might live with it becomes visible from the vantage point of a political theology that can imagine a sovereign pardon that makes an exception to frameworks of immanent moral obligation. Without some notion of a sovereign exception, we could imagine pardon for the Harpers Ferry raiders only if we could justify their violence. But such justifications would only add new strength to the waves of mythic violence that still flow from the originating sin of slavery. Moreover, a politics that cannot imagine an exception to immanent moral obligation could not name the need for an exceptional pardon for slavery. It would miss the need for the only kind of pardon that is possible. The need for such a pardon is not diminished by the fact that it cannot be offered. And seeing this need, this open wound, brings a richer understanding of why national life displays the problems it does and what kind of politics it might take to mend them. With a concept of exceptional pardon, we can see that the United States lives in need of a grace it cannot give itself.

Political theologies with roots in many different traditions could offer resources for understanding this situation. To insist on the need for theological thinking is not to suggest that religious traditions and institutions can heal wounds that the state cannot. The churches in the United States, for example, cannot perform the necessary act of pardon any more than the state can. Churches with white majorities are too deeply implicated in the crime to pardon it. And both black- and white-majority churches lack the standing to offer pardon on behalf of the many millions gone, especially as many of those millions did not identify themselves as members of any church, let alone as members of some one church that could speak for all. No church body possesses the authority that would come with representing all those harmed by slavery. No church could speak for all those who would need to be involved in an act of pardon. The church confronts, in itself, both the need for pardon and the inability to pronounce it.

If pardon for slavery could be given, it could be given only by a sovereign power that had the standing that came from suffering. If we dare to hope that God might have the power to offer such a pardon, then we commit ourselves to a distinct vision of God. For pardon could only be given by a God who had been seized in the night, chained in the hold of a ship, sold at auction, separated from family, raped at gunpoint, worked to death, and buried in an unmarked grave. It could be given only by a God who had found ways to survive, even to thrive, when these things were impossible. It could be given only by a God whose law was broken by every moment of the slave system. It could be given only by a God bound so closely to all those who suffered that it would not compound the sin to say that God endured the suffering in God's own flesh. And if such a God decided to offer pardon, it could come only by God's free decision in God's own time.

Hoping for this kind of sovereign pardon does not offer new legitimation to any political or ecclesial body. Rather, it interrupts the profane sovereignties that sustain and are sustained by the many kinds of mythic violence generated by slavery. It suggests instead a politics of penitence for those of us who have perpetuated and benefited from the mythic violence that arose from slavery and a politics of piecemeal repair for all those who long for a shared life not defined by these legacies. To call the politics of repair "piecemeal" does not mean that every effort must be small in scale. I would argue that the aims should include significant reparations, the kind that could be accomplished only by national policy. But even reparations on this scale would be piecemeal, for they would be partial, incomplete, and in need of later supplement and correction. On the other side of the realization that we need a sovereign we cannot create, concern for immanent moral obligations returns—but with a different character. A politics of penitence and piecemeal repair would not seek to establish a justice that lay beyond its power. It would have the character of active, persistent yearning for a response it could not generate. Acts like organizing, resisting, working toward justice, bearing witness through suffering, performing acts of mercy, and preaching good news all would have the character of prayer.

This vision of politics insists on a distinction between what earthly politics can accomplish and the Reign of God. But it does not depend on an abstract, generic argument about the impossibility of attaining ideals, or the imperfection of all human institutions, or the radical otherness of God. Rather, it makes a concrete, historically specific, contingent claim about one massive and particular evil in the life of one particular polity. It therefore invites something more than rummaging through the rubble to make whatever ethics we can. It invites a politics of determinate negation, a politics that resists the ongoing power of slavery to define our collective and individual lives.

In this political vision, the Reign of God is neither a paradise that has been lost nor an ideal that lies over the horizon of history. The Reign of God is a present reality. Even now the ax is lying at the root of the trees. As Walter Benjamin saw, divine power manifests itself in this age only destructively. The Reign of God is visible in this age in the need for a pardon that no earthly power can grant. Thus the Reign of God is present as a sign of judgment. That judgment is itself a kind of grace. It is a sign that the evil of slavery cannot go on forever. It is a sign, fearsome and hopeful, that God will not leave us alone.

6 NOT YET THE END

MANY OF JOHN BROWN'S CONTEMPORARIES saw him as a man out of time, a Puritan of the old school living in the age of steam engines and sewing machines. The description did not perfectly suit the man. It forgot his up-to-date speculations in business and—no small thing—his views on race. But Brown did share with many Puritans a typological understanding of history. He believed some events or people (types) prefigured others that fulfilled them (antitypes). Brown was constantly trying to discern the typologies at work in his time. His practical reasoning was guided not just by immanent moral obligations but by his sense of the larger arc of history and where he fit within that arc. Typology informed his daily decisions. He made those decisions with a steady eye to theological accounts of history.

The hurly-burly pluralism of ethics today makes any generalization risky. But it seems safe to say that contemporary forms of moral reasoning rarely involve *typology*. If the word arises at all, it most likely describes a presentation of the kinds, classes, or types of some phenomenon. Ethics as it is usually practiced today assumes that situations can be understood and evaluated without attending to any sign qualities they might have. It is not just that modes of discourse like typology can be ignored but that they *must* be ignored for properly ethical analysis. This pattern holds across a wide range of approaches. Ethicists who emphasize the consequences of actions look to the ways these consequences play out in this world, not to the role of an event in some kind of salvation history. Those who stress the qualities of the act regard the act as it is performed in this world, not as a sign of some higher reality. Those who focus on the virtues that actors might form or exhibit look at the lives of actors in themselves, not as types of other figures. In each case an immanent frame delimits the field of what should be considered. This pattern has such influence that it expands to include many explicitly religious ethics. Some Author beyond history might give the norms by which ethics should proceed. Some Spirit might nurture the motives or abilities for living according those norms. But the subjects to be evaluated are still complete in themselves and thoroughly of this world.[1]

A familiar parable gives an account of how modern ethics came to see the world in this way. Theorists like Marcel Gauchet and Charles Taylor may disagree on the details, but they share in telling a story in which a God-soaked, mystically charged cosmos that is full of sacramental significance eventually gives way to a disenchanted world in which what Taylor calls "buffered selves" take actions that participate in regular, observable, and mundane networks of cause and effect.[2] Raymond Geuss picks up this familiar story, arguing that a sense of ultimate obligation persists across the transition from a sacred cosmos to a secular and self-contained universe. The shift to an immanent frame does not destroy people's sense of obligation. Rather, it works a shift in the nature of the obligations people feel. If people in more theocentric times asked what God commanded them to do, people in this secular age ask what we ought to do—where the content of "ought" is supplied by some kind of more-or-less religiously adorned ethical evaluation of this-worldly realities.[3]

Geuss describes the new, ethical sense of obligation as retaining many of the defining qualities of the old. Like claims about the will of God, claims about ethics are ultimate. They subordinate all other claims. And as God's will was universal, reaching to every aspect of life, so ethics applies to every kind of decision. "With secularization," Geuss writes, "the ethical realm is construed not merely as freestanding, but also in some sense all-encompassing: I can and must ask the basic ethical question in *any* context in which I find myself in which action might be called for; no domain stands outside the scope of ethics" (45). When the ethical perspective is not just ultimate but also universally relevant, moral philosophy comes to dominate the whole of practical reasoning.

Geuss turns to Hegel, Nietzsche, Adorno, and Heidegger to diagnose this condition and suggest an alternative. His diagnosis names two problems in particular. Treating ethics as both ultimate and all-encompassing—like older

notions of the will of God—has the virtue of subjecting all areas of life to critique. This virtue was especially prominent in the early stirrings of bourgeois
society. Over time, though, as the institutions and ideas that would resist this
perspective grew weaker, it came to take more and more of the field for itself.
And now it can be difficult to find anything more to say about a decision after
we have decided whether it is right or wrong. It becomes difficult to imagine a
moment in which we might decide that an action was wrong by the standards
of whatever our ethics were but still "worth doing" in some sense that makes
a claim on us. That is, it becomes difficult to imagine kinds of value that cannot be translated into ethical values. Of course, ethics can and has expanded
to include other kinds of value. But, as I argued in the Introduction, an ethical
perspective changes the goods that it expands to include. Goods like the love
of neighbors, the health of bodies, or the beauty of a song change when they
become morally obligatory. And the fact that we feel the need to expand our
ethical perspectives to include these other kinds of goods only confirms Geuss's
basic insight about the central place of ethics in the modern world.

Geuss also points to the problems that come with assuming the relevance
of an ethical perspective to all situations. As Adorno writes in *Minima Moralia*,
"Wrong life cannot be lived rightly" (*Es gibt kein richtiges Leben im falschen*).[4]
When the world, the choices available to us, the ways we think about those
choices, and even our positions as choosers are "radically implicated in evil,"
Geuss writes in his explication of Adorno, then "demands that philosophy be
connected with any kind of injunction to perform specific actions are themselves both forms of repression and an incitement to evil" (56). In such situations we should not pursue the imperatives of ethics. We can only assert what
subjectivity we have by tracing the ways that we have come to be implicated in
this damaged life. In a world so fallen that our best actions only reiterate existing patterns of violence, the promises of ethics are profane.

The better response to such a world, Geuss writes, proceeds through thick,
concrete histories of the situations in which we find ourselves. Geuss appeals to
Hegel's critique of Kant, noting the need not just for history but for historical
studies infused with a philosophy of history. We need, Geuss writes, not a new
and improved version of Plato but "a Thucydides who philosophizes" (232).

The philosophy of Thucydides would not see history as driving toward a
great reconciliation that mocks the suffering of the world, as Geuss believes
that Hegel's does. Geuss argues instead for a Thucydides who philosophizes
with a vision of history like Adorno's, in which history ties itself in knots that

at best bear witness to a redemption they do not achieve. History then hopes for a radical transformation that is fundamentally discontinuous with historical projects. Not even the best ethical imperatives can command moral agents to accomplish this transformation (56). It is, in Adorno's language, "messianic." It is discontinuous not only with our projects but even with the hopes we know how to formulate. Real hope comes not in our dreams of better worlds but through our shudders at the horrors of this one. It comes through determinate negations of concrete moments of damaged life.

The pessimism of Geuss and Adorno is too complete. Their own arguments are the best arguments against their understandings of the world, for they both do much more than trace the outlines of the fractures in our lives, and they do so in ways that are not only intelligible but even beautiful. The fact that they can think such thoughts at all is the best argument against the totality of their despair.[5] The fall disfigures the image of God in human creatures but does not completely erase it.

Geuss and Adorno may overstate the completeness of human depravity, but they are right to recognize the problems that arise when ethics tries to pre- scribe right actions for a world gone badly wrong. And they are right that the best responses to "wrong life" involve not moral imperatives but philosophical histories of how things went so wrong. Consider, for example, the kinds of questions a person working out of the just war tradition might use to evaluate the raid on Harpers Ferry. The raid came in a time of state-sanctioned slavery, a form of life so wrong and so pervasive that it not only damaged people's moral vision but also put them in situations in which the application of an ab- stract morality—even one that might be good in other circumstances—would lead to collusion with established evil. Answering questions from the just war tradition in the simplest way would lead to such collusion. More critical an- swers would require not just additional historical facts but also a larger vi- sion of the shape and direction of history, as these sketches of questions and answers suggest:

- Did the raid have a reasonable chance of success? While the raid was not a work of insanity, it was unlikely to succeed in any of the various goals that have been ascribed to it. But arguing that the raid had little chance of suc- cess only validates the overwhelming control that slaveholders and their government wielded over the means of violence. And if the raid did not succeed in its short-term goals, it did help start the war that ended slavery. But then the war gave way to Reconstruction, which gave way in turn to Jim

Crow, which was overturned by the civil rights movement, which has seen some of its achievements undermined by both deliberate actions and unintended consequences. Given these long-term outcomes, should the raid still be counted as likely to succeed? What time frame should we use? And what should count as success?

- Did the raiders discriminate between combatants and noncombatants? On the one hand, the raiders killed people who were not in uniform, including some who had not taken up arms to fight them. On the other hand, Brown, following John Locke, argued that slavery was already a state of war. Law-abiding citizens of a state or nation committed to slavery were already engaged in warfare against enslaved people. As if to provide a perverse illustration of this argument, the Fugitive Slave Act of 1850 made the capture and return of escaped slaves the responsibility of every law enforcement officer in every state. Ordinary citizens and other residents were forbidden to offer aid to escaping slaves and required to turn them in. People suspected of having escaped from slavery could be convicted on the word of a claimant. They had no opportunity to testify on their own behalf and no right to a trial by jury. If the citizens of Harpers Ferry lived according to these laws and worked to enforce them, were they noncombatants in a war over slavery?

- Was the raid undertaken in self-defense? The raiders initiated the attack, and none of them faced immediate bodily harm. But one of the raiders, Dangerfield Newby, wanted to free his wife and seven children, who were being held in slavery in Warrenton, Virginia, about sixty miles from Harpers Ferry. His efforts to purchase their freedom had been rebuffed. Was the raid not a kind of last resort in self-defense for Newby? And if ties of kinship can justify acts of self-defense, can they not expand to include Brown, who sincerely regarded enslaved people as his sisters and brothers? A simple refusal of kinship ties because Brown was white risks reinscribing the racial categories that were themselves part of the evil.

- Did the raiders have competent authority to wage war? Not by any usual standard. But it is worth reversing the question. Did the militias that mustered against the raiders have competent authority? The constitution of the Commonwealth of Virginia had been written and approved in votes that were open only to white men. It had established slavery as the law of the land. Could such a constitution grant competent authority to wage war, especially a war to defend slavery? The raiders had recently participated in a multiracial convention and passed a provisional constitution of their own that served to authorize their raid. Were the two constitutions different in a way that should decide the argument about who had the right to use force in relation to slavery?

The list of questions could go on. The questions do not reveal some fatal flaw in just war ethics. They do reveal an incompleteness that becomes more profound when "wrong life" dominates a situation. They show the need to supplement moral philosophy with thick, critical historical narratives. To keep the criteria of just war from simply reflecting damaged life in a slave state, we need to ask questions that get at concrete historical realities. And those questions cannot be strictly empirical (what bit of data would tell us whether slavery was a state of war?). The questions instead need to engage the facts as they are embedded in larger accounts of value. To keep ethics from reiterating damaged life, we need a Thucydides who philosophizes, just as Geuss and Adorno saw.

Francis Lieber, the German American political philosopher who in 1863 formulated a code to guide US forces in the conduct of war, came to a similar conclusion about the raid on Harpers Ferry. The Lieber Code represented a significant establishment of just war thinking in the center of American military policy. Lieber was perhaps the Civil War era's most important embodiment of the type of moral philosopher that Geuss identified with Plato. Lieber developed, implemented, and refined codes of ethics. But when it came to the raid on Harpers Ferry, even Lieber started to sound more like Thucydides. Writing to a friend just two days after Brown was executed, Lieber expressed his admiration for Old Brown. "He died like a man," Lieber wrote, "and Virginia fretted like an old woman." Lieber respected the man, but he had no illusions about the raid. It never had much chance of success. It killed civilians. It hadn't been undertaken with proper authority. But it had a significance that outran any moral or even prudential evaluation. That significance was rooted in its place in a historical narrative. "The deed was irrational," Lieber concluded, "but it will be historical."[6]

The best thinking about the raid on Harpers Ferry will follow Lieber through and beyond discourses of ethics to consider the historical significance of the raid. The facts of the history of the raid are as settled as such things can be. But the historical significance of the raid remains open to dispute. Whatever significance the raid has varies with the understanding of history that makes sense of it. The facts of the raid will have one kind of significance if they are inscribed into a triumphal narrative like the one Geuss attributes to Hegel, in which hope is fulfilled in history. The same facts take on a very different significance if they are placed together in constellations that bear witness to their hopes only as they are negated, as in Adorno's philosophy of history. Both views of history—and many more—have already been at work as Americans have thought through the significance of the raid on Harpers Ferry. We do not need to import philosophies of history into the conversation. We only need to make explicit the ones that are already there.

They Could Not Hang His Soul

Brown and his contemporaries were writing his life into larger historical visions even before his death. The most triumphal narratives scarcely acknowledged his death at all. George W. Light, in his poem "John Brown's Final Victory," described "the martyr, Brown," who now "wears the hero's crown." The rhyme was irresistible, almost providential. It suggested Brown's ultimate victory over the forces of evil:

> Summoned to his home celestial,
> From their brief control,
> All the hemp of ruthless tyrants
> Could not hang his soul.[7]

Whatever the hangman's rope did, Light wrote, it did not kill noble John Brown.

Henry David Thoreau sounded a similar theme in his oration "The Last Days of John Brown." He concluded with this account of Brown's "translation":

> On the day of his translation, I heard, to be sure, that he was *hung*, but I did not know what that meant; I felt no sorrow on that account; but not for a day or two did I even *hear* that he was *dead*, and not after any number of days shall I believe it. Of all the men who were said to be my contemporaries, it seemed to me that John Brown was the only one who *had not died*. I never hear of a man named Brown now,—and I hear of them pretty often,—I never hear of any particularly brave and earnest man, but my first thought is of John Brown, and what relation he may be to him. I meet him at every turn. He is more alive than ever he was. He has earned immortality. He is not confined to North Elba nor to Kansas. He is no longer working in secret. He works in public, and in the clearest light that shines on this land.[8]

Thoreau's retelling of Brown's death went beyond the language and concepts of ethics. Thoreau did not just believe that Brown died for a good cause. He believed that Brown died as part of a historical process so right, and so certain of success, that he did not die at all. He was more alive than ever he was before.

Samson of Osawatomie

More sober interpreters saw Brown as part of that same triumphant march of history to the light but felt obliged to acknowledge the reality of his death. The biblical story of Samson helped shape many of those interpretations. Interpreters focused especially on the end of the Samson cycle. As the book of Judges told the story, Samson made a mistake in trusting Delilah, who cut off his hair and, with it, Samson's great strength. This enabled the Philistines to capture Samson and put out his eyes. But Samson's hair grew back in prison, and he slowly regained his strength, if not his sight. When the Philistines brought him out of prison and chained him to the pillars of their temple, Samson was strong enough to pull those pillars down. The whole temple collapsed, killing Samson and the Philistine leaders alike (Judges 13–16).

Frederick Douglass picked up on this typology, writing that Brown, "like Samson . . . has laid his hands up on the pillars of this great national temple of cruelty and blood, and when he falls, that temple will speedily crumble to its final doom, burying its denizens in its ruins."[9] Abolitionist preacher Fales Henry Newhall told the story with more exclamation points. When the Philistines captured Brown, they shouted, "Ha! it is he! It is Samson of Ossawattomie! Praised be Baal! Glory to Dagon!" They locked him up in Charles Town, but Brown's testimony from captivity only made him stronger. "But O!" Newhall cried, "How the old hero's locks grew in that dusky prison air!" When they led him to the scaffold, they bound him to their temple. And, the sermon concluded, he brought the temple down. "'Let me die with the Philistines,' cried Samson of Ossawattomie. Ah! see the vast fabric totter! hear the Philistines shriek! To-day there are dropping over all the land the first falling fragments from the great crash of American Slavery."[10]

Brown himself used the story to interpret the significance of his death. Over the years he had understood his life through several biblical figures. As Moses, for instance, he had led slaves to captivity and issued a new and higher law. But Samson loomed larger and larger in his mind as he awaited execution. Like Samson, he had made a tactical error. He stayed too long at Harpers Ferry, and this mistake led to his capture. Brown had a sense that he had failed as Samson failed. He also had nurtured a hope that he might be vindicated as Samson was vindicated. Brown articulated this hope in a November 1859 letter to the Reverend Heman Humphrey:

> "He shall begin to deliver Israel out of the hand of the Philistines" [Judges 13:5].
> This was said of a poor erring servant many years ago; and for many years I have

felt a strong impression that God had given me powers and faculties, unworthy as I was, that he intended to use for a similar purpose. This most unmerited honor He has seen fit to bestow; and whether, like the same poor frail man to whom I allude, my death may not be of vastly more value than my life is, I think quite beyond all human foresight.[11]

Brown was not absolutely certain that his death would break the power of the slave state as Samson's death had broken the power of the Philistines. But he was certain that God was working to end slavery, and he was certain that his death would play a role in that process. In another letter from the last month of his life he again compared himself to Samson. And then he wrote, "As I believe most firmly that God reigns; I cannot believe that any thing I have *done suffered or may yet suffer will be lost*; to the *cause of God or of humanity*: & before I began my work at Harpers Ferry; I felt assured that in the *worst event*; it would certainly PAY."[12] Because God reigned, Brown believed, his *own* death would play its part in God's plan. One way or another, it would *pay*.

The Samson story could acknowledge the reality of Brown's death in a way that Thoreau and Light did not. It could even acknowledge Brown's mistakes. And Brown's version of the story, at least, had a much stronger sense of the sovereignty of a personal God than Thoreau described. But all these interpretations shared a vision of the meaning and direction of history. All of them understood Brown as part of a larger historical process that was driving inexorably toward the just end of the abolition of slavery in the present age. All of them saw a deep continuity between Brown's intentions, at their best, and this coming consummation of history. All of them saw Brown's violence as "paying" into this historical process. Thus, all of them defended Brown through something more than claims that his ends could justify his means. They told stories in which Brown's connections to the work of a sovereign power in history authorized his actions. They therefore fused sovereignty and politics into what Walter Benjamin called mythic violence.

Paid in Blood

Samson's story was not the only bit of the Bible on John Brown's mind as he sat in the Charles Town jail. Even in his last days, he worked through multiple stories and images as he tried to make sense of his life. Throughout that life, and especially at the very end, he articulated a worldview in which blood paid the price of sin. Long before he came to national attention, Brown kept a record of the misdeeds of his son John along with an accounting of the number of lashes it would take to pay each one off. The main purpose of the whippings was to atone for sin, not to offer any kind of deterrence or instruction. The most important audience for the whippings was not John Jr. but God. Brown's purpose became clear one day when he administered some of the lashes to John Jr.—and then asked his son to give the rest to him. It was the payment that mattered, not the pedagogy, and Brown could make the payment in his own blood as well as his son's.[13] Brown carried this same worldview to his understanding of slavery, citing Hebrews 9:22—"without the shedding of blood there is no remission of sin"—as early as 1855 in an argument for violent action against proslavery forces.[14] As in the punishment of John Jr., such violence was not the means to some earthly state of affairs. It was an offering to God. It was not instrumental but sacramental. This was the worldview that infused the note Brown wrote on the way to his execution. When he wrote that "the crimes of this guilty, land: will never be purged away; but with Blood," he was not calculating the violence required to abolish slavery, and he did not think that the blood had to come only from proslavery bodies. He was describing the demand for blood of a just and terrible God. And he believed that his own blood could begin to pay down the debt a sinful nation owed.[15]

Brown has not been alone in understanding his death as part of a larger story of blood atonement for sin. The radical abolitionist and pacifist Henry C. Wright wrote,

> The sin of this nation . . . is to be taken away, not by Christ, but by John Brown. Christ, as represented by those who are called by his name, has proved a dead failure, as a power to free the slaves. . . . The nation is to be saved, not by the blood of Christ, (as that is now administered,) but by the blood of John Brown, which, as administered by Abolitionists, will prove the "power of God and the wisdom of God" to resist slaveholders, and bring them to repentance.[16]

Like Brown, Wright retained a worldview in which blood atoned for sin and generated renewal. And like Brown, Wright did not limit the blood that could do this work to that of Jesus Christ. The resulting theology combined a penitential, substitutionary understanding of atonement that many liberal theologians in the United States would have rejected with a low Christology that they would have affirmed. Salvation required blood, in this view, but the blood of Jesus was not exclusively powerful. It was, rather, an example that revealed the structure of an economy that would require future transactions.

The economy of blood redemption that Henry Wright used to make sense of John Brown's death found fuller and more prominent expression over time as people tried to make sense of the cataclysmic violence of the Civil War. Writing in January 1865, Harriet Beecher Stowe recalled the visions of Nat Turner. Turner, Stowe wrote, "saw the leaves drop blood and the land darkened." And these visions had come to pass.

> The work of justice which he predicted is being executed to the uttermost. But when this strange work of judgment and justice is consummated, when our country, through a thousand battles and ten thousands of precious deaths, shall have come forth from this long agony, redeemed and regenerated, then God himself shall return and dwell with us, and the Lord God shall wipe away all tears from all faces, and the rebuke of his people shall he utterly take away.[17]

Like Wright and Brown, Stowe described a vision of history in which death "redeemed and regenerated" the nation. If Wright stressed the saving power of the blood of John Brown, Stowe ascribed saving power to the blood of "a thousand battles" and "ten thousands" of war casualties. Stowe would have been glad to consider Brown among that band of holy martyrs. But now he, like Jesus, was one among the thousands.

Just a few long, bloody months after Stowe's essay appeared in the *Atlantic Monthly*, the formal hostilities of the war came to an end. Reflecting on the toll of the war later that spring, the liberal theologian Horace Bushnell argued that the blood shed during the war had renewed the nation. Like Brown, Bushnell described the significance of the blood with economic metaphors. "These grim heroes therefore, dead and dumb, that have strewed so many fields with their bodies,—these are the price and purchase money of our triumph."[18] The bodies of the dead purchased not only victory over the rebels but also a new life for the nation. The dead "have done for us a work so precious," Bushnell said, "which is all their own,—they have bled for us; and by this simple sacrifice of blood they have opened for us a new great chapter of life" (326). The nation had been consumed with commerce, but the dead put its collective mind on higher things. The nation had been divided, Bushnell said, but the dead "cemented and forever sanctified" national unity. And the nation had been young and capable only of thin and shallow feelings. But, Bushnell said, the dead "have given us the possibility of a great consciousness and great public sentiments" (330). Before the war scholars could feel sublime feelings only by studying the classics. But the dead of the Civil War gave rise to new depths of feeling that were distinctly *American*. They gave Americans the kind of history that a great nation enjoys. Because of the dead, Bushnell said, "we are not the same people that we were, and never can be again" (331).

All of this depended on blood. In what Bushnell called "the true economy of the world," true greatness and real nobility come "as outgrowths only of blood" (325). Bushnell went on to explain this economy:

> The reason is that, without the blood, there is really nothing great enough in motive and action, taking the world as it is, to create a great people or story. If a gospel can be executed only in blood, if there is no power of salvation strong enough to carry the world's feeling which is not gained by dying for it, how shall a selfish race get far enough above itself, to be kindled by the story of its action in the dull routine of its common arts of peace? (332)

Bushnell's description of the true economy of the world required no supernatural mechanisms. Humans just were the kinds of creatures who got caught up in the trivia of commerce and other everyday affairs. But death, especially on a massive scale, lifted our focus to higher things. Bushnell described a naturalistic mechanism, but he needed a theological register to name the depth of the change death brought. It was a gospel executed in blood. It redeemed the nation.

If the dead redeemed the nation, they also had an ongoing claim on its life. Because of the dead, Bushnell said, politics took on a new dimension of significance.

> Government is now become Providential,—no more a creature of our human will, but a grandly moral affair. The awful stains of sacrifice are upon it, as upon the fields where our dead battled for it, and it is sacred for their sakes. The stamp of God's sovereignty is also upon it; for he has beheld their blood upon its gate-posts and made it the sign of his passover. (341)

The dead made politics sacred in a new way. Their sacrifice demanded that "we take their places and stand in their cause" (349). It is a law of nature, Bushnell said, that the living come to stand in the place of the dead to carry on their work. In this case, the living had to continue a politics that rooted out the last claims of states' rights and thoroughly abolished slavery. Those redeemed by death had an obligation to take up a politics of redemption.

Horace Bushnell's talk of blood redemption can seem centuries away. But Drew Gilpin Faust has argued that contemporary historians have tended to assign a similar significance to the Civil War. War provides conventions that order acts of violence into narrative forms, Faust writes. Those narrative forms make possible dramatic events and rich character studies. They invite large claims about the significance of the war in defining or revealing American national character. They also supply a sense of direction and purpose to history—and a kind of justification for the violent acts along the way—almost in spite of an author's intentions. The entry of social historians into the field of Civil War studies has not changed this reality, Faust writes.

> We are both moved by the details of the war's suffering and terror and captivated by the unsurpassed insight the war offers into the fundamental assumptions and values of historical actors. Despite our dispassionate, professional, analytic stance, we have not remained untouched by war's elemental attractions and its emotional and sentimental fascinations. We count on these allures to build a sizeable audience for our books. In both the reality and irony of our fondness for war, we are not so unlike the Civil War generations we study.[19]

Something like Bushnell's vision of the redeeming power of war lives on in the narrative structures that order even seemingly secular histories of the war.

Narratives of the redemption worked by the Civil War have great descriptive power. Harry Stout's *Upon the Altar of the Nation* wants to count the cost of that redemption, but it does not deny the significance of what happened. "The Civil War taught Americans that they really were a Union," Stout writes, "and it absolutely required a baptism of blood to unveil the transcendent dimensions of that union."[20] Stout describes what happened; he does not offer an uncritical endorsement of the process. The blood of six hundred thousand *did* give new life to the nation, just as Bushnell and Stowe said it would. But one can recognize the empirical significance of this dynamic without believing that it is "the true economy of the world," as Bushnell did. We can recognize that "war is a force that gives us meaning"—as a recent book by Chris Hedges argued—and then use that recognition to question just what kind of meaning war gives and what kind of "us" it forms.[21]

Christian political theologians have especially strong reasons to argue with the vision of national atonement that Brown, Wright, Stowe, Bushnell, and some contemporary historians share. In framing the bloodshed of the war as a redemption of the nation, they offer what can only be called a sacramental theology. If the structure of this theology comes from Christian traditions, the particular content of it breaks decisively with those traditions. Orthodox Christianities have long affirmed that the work of God in Jesus Christ—however it might be realized—is in some sense *sufficient* for the salvation of the world. And if the blood of Christ is sufficient, then further blood sacrifice is not required. Here René Girard is right: Christ is the sacrifice that breaks the system of sacrifice. The God who gives Godself in Jesus Christ does not demand more blood. God is not Moloch.[22]

Christian theologies also give reasons to reject Bushnell's understanding of the one for whom atonement was made. Over the years Christians have argued that atonement might be made for many different subjects: individual disciples, the church, all humanity, or the cosmos. But whoever is the subject of redemption, it is not the nation *as nation*. For Bushnell, on the other hand—as for Brown, Wright, Stowe, and many more—the blood of the war did not redeem one of these traditional subjects. It redeemed America.

These narratives of blood redemption create continuity between a moment of sovereign violence and the politics that arise in its wake. In Bushnell's language, the dead demand that "we take their places and stand in their cause." That continuity legitimates what I have been calling, following Walter Benjamin, a mythic violence that recapitulates the founding violence in actions, laws, and social structures. Redeemed in blood, the nation is obliged to take on the redeemer's role. As the historian Jackson Lears argued, convictions about the redeeming power of the Civil War made possible "stories of an exceptional nation reborn into its modern form, cleansed of its original sin of slavery and ready to shoulder its redemptive responsibilities in the drama of world history."[23] Some of the oldest narratives of European settlers in North America gained new traction. Indeed, even Reverdy Ransom's sermon on "The Spirit of John Brown," preached in the early years of the twentieth century, drew a straight line from the redemption begun at Harpers Ferry to the work that needed to be done in Manila Bay. When understood as a sacrament, the cleansing violence of the Civil War purified America for the work of empire.

The Emperor

The sacramental views of violence in history described by John Brown, Henry Wright, Harriet Beecher Stowe, and Horace Bushnell broke through the frames of ethics for considering violence. They described bloodshed as part of a work of redemption that would renew the nation in this age. Thus they underwrote a mythic violence that translated John Brown's body into the eternal cause of liberty. This translation did not happen only in sermons and essays. It also took a decidedly corporeal form. Brown's body was dressed with a fresh collar that hid the terrible work the rope had done. It was enclosed in a coffin and delivered to his family. Church bells marked the body's passage to the Brown family home, where it was buried under a marker that connected the Harpers Ferry raid to the Revolutionary War. Sermons and speeches sang Brown's praises. Admirers collected money for his family. Even before John Brown's body was laid in the grave, his soul was marching on.

The body of Shields Green, on the other hand, resists such seamless translation. Green had made his way north after escaping from slavery. He first met Brown at the quarry in Chambersburg, Pennsylvania, when Brown was trying to persuade Frederick Douglass to join the raid on Harpers Ferry. Douglass famously refused the invitation, calling Harpers Ferry "a perfect steel trap." But Green decided to go with Brown. Of all the raiders taken prisoner, Green received the most derision. Proslavery accounts labeled him as impudent, and he attracted the particular fury of Andrew Hunter, the state's attorney in his trial. Even friendly accounts tended to depict Green as a noble savage. They called him "the Emperor" and compared him to "a very Turco in his hatred against the stealers of men." They described him as big, strong, and brave but also simple-minded and almost impossible to understand. It is telling that he is the only raider of whom no photograph survives. He is remembered through caricature and sketch (see Figure 6.1).[24]

After his execution the body of Shields Green was placed in a poplar casket. With the body of John A. Copeland Jr., another African American raider, it was moved to the jail. If their bodies were ever buried, they did not stay buried long. Students from Winchester Medical College stole the bodies for experiment, exploration, and willful desecration. The family of Copeland, based in Ohio, sent Oberlin professor and Congregationalist minister James Monroe to claim his body. Monroe traveled to Winchester, but the college refused to surrender Copeland's body. In a surreal parody of hospitality, a representative of the college did offer to take Monroe on a tour of the grounds on which the body they refused him was stored. While on that tour Monroe recognized the body of another man he knew from life in Oberlin: Shields Green. The sight was chilling. In a lecture years later, Monroe described seeing the "fine athletic figure" of Green lying on his back, "the unclosed, wistful eyes staring wildly upward, as if seeking, in a better world, for some solution of the dark problems of horror and oppression so hard to be explained in this."[25]

It can be tempting to interpret the body of Shields Green through the body of John Brown, burying Green with Brown and then raising Green to glory

FIGURE 6.1 Unsigned, undated sketch of Shields Green. Boyd B. Stutler Collection, West Virginia State Archives.

with the Old Man. Historians sometimes take this approach, letting Brown stand in for all the raiders. But the history played out differently. In 1899 the bodies of ten more raiders were delivered to North Elba to be buried with John Brown. The bodies of Osborne Anderson, John Copeland, and Shields Green—three of the African American raiders—were not among them. The location of these three bodies remains unknown. To tell the truth of these lost bodies, we cannot read the story of Shields Green through the story of John Brown. We should instead read the story of John Brown through that of Shields Green. Green's unclosed, wistful eyes see the deep wrong of narratives that treat centuries of slavery as the occasion for the heroism of one white man. They see the lie of stories in which heroes do not die but are translated into glory. They see the falseness of the promise that bodies can be incorporated into stories in which they die only on the way to victory. And they bear witness to the unfinished business of national redemption. The unclosed eyes of Shields Green look for something more.

Come Ye to the Waters

Fidelity to the body of Shields Green might lead us to reject any attempts to ascribe meaning to the dead of Harpers Ferry. But rejecting any kind of meaning for the bodies of Shields Green, John Brown, and the others killed in the last months of 1859 would not protect those bodies from being taken up into the workings of mythic violence. It would only expose them to the mythologies of a flat immanence that mistakes itself for the whole and denies the reality of anything beyond itself. And this vision of immanence-as-all has already demonstrated its own capacities to legitimate violence without limit. What we need is a vision of history that neither incorporates these bodies into smooth narratives of redemption nor refuses the very idea that they might have some significance beyond themselves.

W. E. B. Du Bois offered a vision like this when he told the story of John Brown's life and death. He described the violence done by and to Brown as having a significance that could not be captured within an immanent frame of causes and effects. He saw the ways the bodies of John Brown, Shields Green, and others pointed beyond themselves. But he denied the continuity of these deaths with any politics that might emerge in their wake. He refused to let the violence of the past offer mythological legitimation to the violence of the present.

Du Bois anchored his story in descriptions of Brown's love for African American people. That love came through, Du Bois wrote, over a long life of daily interactions that were rare for a white man of the era. It came through in the lack of condescension Brown showed his African American friends and neighbors. Above all, though, it came through in Brown's willingness to kill and die for African American people. The willingness to kill and be killed marked the limits of love. Sacrifice established the boundaries of community—and respect. Brown was not just willing to kill and die for African American people. He was also willing to stage a raid in order to arm them so that they could kill and die for themselves. Du Bois praised Brown not just for his love but also for his trust, respect, and recognition. One need not imagine Brown as completely free from racism—as David Reynolds wants to—in order to hear Du Bois's assessment that, of all white people, Brown had "come nearest to touching the real souls of black folk."[26]

Brown's life displayed the shape of a new social imaginary, a new America marked by equality and love between people of all races. He even wrote a constitution for this new America. The violence done to and by him played a crucial role in creating that community. Du Bois prized this vision of Brown's, but he refused to locate it in a narrative of sacramental redemption like Bushnell's or even a story of collateral damage on the way to glory, like Brown's version of the Samson story. In both of these narratives, Brown's violence is one step of many along the way to a just nation. But Du Bois, writing in 1909, saw history moving in a different direction. He noted the way an ethos of freedom and equality had been building across the globe through the Haitian, American, and French Revolutions. But, Du Bois wrote, all of that began to change in 1859, the very year Brown died. That year saw the publication of Darwin's *Origin of Species*. "Since that day tremendous scientific and economic advance has been accompanied by distinct signs of moral retrogression in social philosophy" (225). In place of the drive for equality that helped shape Brown's vision came a social Darwinism that argued for the evolutionary role of war, inequality, and even disease. Brown's violence may have incarnated a new community. But it was not a community in the flow of history. Brown was not, as David Reynolds put it, the man who "killed slavery, sparked the Civil War, and seeded human rights." He was not the beginning of something new, the first moment in a sequence that would roll to redemption. Brown was, Du Bois wrote, "belated," an "anachronism," a man out of time. His life emptied into a dry branch of the river of history.

Du Bois asked, "Has John Brown no message—no legacy, then, to the twentieth century? He has and it is this great word: the cost of liberty is less than the price of repression" (230). Brown's violence created no enduring earthly community. It launched no great tide of history. It redeemed nothing. But—exactly as a memory without a legacy, as a dream out of time—it "stands today as a mighty warning to his country" (231).

Du Bois ended the biography with an image of John Brown's body that looked more like the body of Shields Green than that of a mythical hero. Du Bois did not describe a body that had mouldered in the grave and risen to new freedom-fighting life. Instead, he described a body between life and death, a "white-haired old man" who lay "weltering in the blood which he spilled for broken and despised humanity" (237). This broken body neither purified the nation nor launched it on a new path to justice for all. It spoke instead a word of eschatological judgment. Du Bois quoted Brown at length to close the book:

> You had better—all you people of the South—prepare yourselves for a settlement of this question. It must come up for settlement sooner than you are prepared for it, and the sooner you commence that preparation, the better for you. You may dispose of me very easily—I am nearly disposed of now; but this question is still to be settled—this Negro question, I mean. The end of that is not yet. (238)

The end, Du Bois's Brown said, was not yet. Du Bois paired these last lines of judgment with an epigraph to the chapter that recalled another dimension to the eschatological promise: "Ho, every one that thirsteth, come ye to the waters" (219). Brown's legacy—the title of Du Bois's last chapter—was neither a redeemed nation nor a movement for justice. It was an eschatological sign, a portent, in history but out of it, a dialectical image of judgment and hope.

Lo, John Brown

Du Bois described a divine violence made manifest at Harpers Ferry that shattered the system of relations that legitimated the violence of the Commonwealth of Virginia and the United States as well as the moral obligations that bound their citizens. In breaking the death grip with which slavery and the nation held one another, it did not become a warrant for later action. It established nothing. It *did* open space for a new freedom in relation to that which had been destroyed. That freedom is not abstract and absolute. It is pointed and particular. And it invites responses that recognize its particularity.

Jürgen Habermas has worried that such a notion of divine violence would destroy the normative *as such*. But I have tried to describe the ways that divine violence can break the hold of some particular ethical system and then invite but not determine responses that include ethical deliberation. Divine violence cannot be reduced to ethics, for then it would lose the shattering power that saves ethics from idolatry—and the subjects of ethics from being bound to death. Divine violence is outside the limits of ethics. But it is not the end of the normative as such. It is the end of visions of the normative that take it to be complete in itself.

To insist on the need for theological deliberations about violence, and to argue for the need to keep them distinct from ethical considerations of violence, is not to argue that we should do away with ethical forms of reasoning about violence. It is instead to propose that we need to work in two registers, using the language of both divine and ethical violence. This involves a pluralism not just of values nor even of *kinds* of value but of modes of faithful discourse. The task of practical reason, then, would not be limited to ethics. It would involve negotiating between these two modes of discourse. And the conclusion of the practical syllogism would be not a systematic account of the relation between the two but a particular action in the face of concrete demands. In this instance, I would argue that free action in the wake of divine violence might begin with retrieving, burying, and honoring the body of Shields Green—and then working to undo that vast complex of powers that left his body not only dead but desecrated.

The divine violence made manifest in the execution of John Brown does not decide the question of whether just war, pacifism, or some other set of commitments offers the best ethics of violence. It does not even determine the form those options would take. But it changes the frame in which debates within and between them take place. The story of the disenchantment of violence argues that ethical deliberation about violence begins with elimination of the category of divine violence and survives only so long as this threat is kept at bay. But the opposite is true: the discernment of divine violence makes possible ethical deliberation that is worthy of the name.

Just so, the founding story of the modern state depends on the expulsion of any hint of divine violence. Religion and the state are separated, and the state holds a monopoly on the legitimate means of violence. But the very concept of "legitimacy" depends on what Benjamin called a "philosophico-historical" point of view. That is, the liberal state needs a theology of history in order to be a liberal state. That theology—that theological reasoning about divine violence—can be a disputed, contested category, argued over by people of many faiths and no faith at all. But some kind of deliberation about the meaning of history will be required.

Discerning the divine violence made manifest in John Brown does not just teach abstract lessons about the ethics of violence. Like any discernment of divine violence, it invites new understandings of our moment in time. It invites this of all the world, as commentators like Victor Hugo saw. But the portent of John Brown speaks with particular urgency to those of us who understand ourselves as Americans. By the indirect light of this hooded meteor we can see that John Brown was not a freedom fighter and that Americans are not the risen body of John Brown, marching on to complete his work. We can see that John Brown was not a fanatic and that America is not a besieged secular order needing to defend itself against religious extremists from far away and right next door. John Brown was neither Samson nor sacrament. He was a broken, bleeding body, more like Shields Green than any heroic history can acknowledge. And Americans are among the people set free to do politics under the sign of judgment revealed in his death.

NOTES

Introduction

1. Herman Melville, *The Battle-Pieces of Herman Melville*, ed. Hennig Cohen (New York: Thomas Yoseloff, 1963), 35 (italics in original).

2. Melville owned a set of Schiller's works and made reference to the Sais poem specifically in *Moby-Dick*. See Hennig Cohen, "Notes," in Melville, *Battle-Pieces of Herman Melville*, 205.

3. Kent Ljungquist, "'Meteor of the War': Melville, Thoreau, and Whitman Respond to John Brown," *American Literature* 61, no. 4 (1998): 674–80. J. Sella Martin, Henry David Thoreau, Henry Ward Beecher, and many others used images of meteors to describe the execution of John Brown.

4. In thinking about what it would mean to tell a "weird" history of John Brown, I have learned from Stephen Berry, ed., *Weirding the War: Stories from the Civil War's Ragged Edges* (Athens: University of Georgia Press, 2011). Berry's introduction describes "weirding" as "a way of alienating the past from its present purposes, releasing the past from its present work, and returning to the past a measure of its original 'foreignness'" (5). I hope to share in that work. I also hope to work with a measure of the three sisters' uncanny sense of history as something more than an immanent network of causes and effects.

5. Louisa May Alcott, "With a Rose, That Bloomed on the Day of John Brown's Martyrdom," in James Redpath, *Echoes of Harper's Ferry* (Boston: Thayer & Eldridge, 1860), 98.

6. Howells, "Old Brown," in ibid., 316.

7. In this section my thinking has been formed especially by Raymond Geuss, *Outside Ethics* (Princeton, N.J.: Princeton University Press, 2005).

8. All biblical quotations are from the New Revised Standard Version unless otherwise noted.

9. On the pervasiveness of this "immanent frame" for practical reasoning, see Charles Taylor, *A Secular Age* (Cambridge, Mass.: Belknap Press of Harvard University Press, 2007).

10. See, for instance, Eric Gregory, *Politics and the Order of Love: An Augustinian Ethic of Democratic Citizenship* (Chicago: University of Chicago Press, 2010).

11. Among the many excellent recent histories of John Brown's life and work, I have learned especially from David S. Reynolds, *John Brown, Abolitionist: The Man*

Who Killed Slavery, Sparked the Civil War, and Seeded Civil Rights (New York: Alfred A. Knopf, 2005); Tony Horwitz, *Midnight Rising: John Brown and the Raid That Sparked the Civil War* (New York: Henry Holt, 2011); John Stauffer, *The Black Hearts of Men: Radical Abolitionists and the Transformation of Race* (Cambridge, Mass.: Harvard University Press, 2002); and Stephen B. Oates, *To Purge This Land with Blood: A Biography of John Brown* (New York: Harper & Row, 1970).

12. Recent outstanding histories of the interpretation of John Brown include R. Blakeslee Gilpin, *John Brown Still Lives! America's Long Reckoning with Violence, Equality and Change* (Chapel Hill: University of North Carolina Press, 2011); Franny Nudelman, *John Brown's Body: Slavery, Violence, and the Culture of War* (Chapel Hill: University of North Carolina Press, 2004); Peggy A. Russo and Paul Finkelman, eds., *Terrible Swift Sword: The Legacy of John Brown* (Athens: Ohio University Press, 2005); Andrew Taylor and Eldrid Herrington, eds., *The Afterlife of John Brown* (New York: Palgrave Macmillan, 2005). Anthologies of responses to Brown were being collected before his body was cold in its Adirondack grave. James Redpath's *Echoes of Harper's Ferry* was one of the first collections and remains an important source. Benjamin Quarles's *Blacks on John Brown* (Urbana: University of Illinois Press, 1972) performed crucial work in gathering up responses of African Americans. The appearance during my research for this book of *The Tribunal: Responses to John Brown and the Harpers Ferry Raid* (Cambridge, Mass.: Belknap Press of Harvard University Press, 2012), an exhaustive collection edited by John Stauffer and Zoe Trodd, rendered much of my own digging redundant even as it opened up a new range of sources.

13. The counterfactual question of whether slavery might have ended without war has provoked long debate. For a good summary of the debate—and a strong argument that slavery could have gone on for a long time if it had not been ended by war—see David Brion Davis, "Should You Have Been an Abolitionist?," *New York Review of Books*, June 21, 2012.

14. Marilynne Robinson, *Gilead* (New York: Farrar, Straus & Giroux, 2004), 42.

15. Ibid., 42–43.

16. For a rich genealogy of this reduction, see Stanley Hauerwas, "On Keeping Theological Ethics Theological," in *The Hauerwas Reader*, ed. John Berkman and Michael Cartwright (Durham, N.C.: Duke University Press, 2001), 51–74.

17. For a concise, nuanced commentary on Benjamin's relations to religions, see Michael W. Jennings, "Walter Benjamin, Religion, and a Theological Politics, ca. 1922," in *The Weimar Moment: Liberalism, Political Theology and Law*, ed. Rudy Koshar and Leonard V. Kaplan (Lanham, Md.: Lexington Books, 2012), 109–22.

18. Søren Kierkegaard, *Fear and Trembling; Repetition, Kierkegaard's Writings*, ed. Howard V. Hong and Edna H. Hong (Princeton, N.J.: Princeton University Press, 1983).

19. Vincent W. Lloyd raises these concerns with particular power in his introduction to *Race and Political Theology*, ed. Vincent W. Lloyd (Stanford, Calif.: Stanford University Press, 2012).

20. Walter Benjamin, "Welt und Zeit," in *Gesammelte Schriften* [hereafter *G.S.*], ed. Theodor W. Adorno, Gershom Scholem, Rolf Tidemann, and Hermann Scwep-

penhaüser, 7 vols. (Frankfurt: Suhrkamp, 1972), 6:99. English translation (hereafter ET): Benjamin, "World and Time," in *Selected Writings* [hereafter *S. W.*], edited by Marcus Bullock and Michael W. Jennings, 4 vols. (Cambridge, Mass.: 1996–2003), 1:227.

Chapter 1

1. William Allinghame [*sic*], "The Touchstone," in Redpath, *Echoes of Harper's Ferry*, 10.

2. On Brown as an enigma, see W. A. Phillips, "Three Interviews with Old John Brown," in *A John Brown Reader: The Story of John Brown in His Own Words, in the Words of Those Who Knew Him, and in the Poetry and Prose of the Literary Heritage*, ed. Louis Ruchames (London: Abelard-Schuman, 1959), 210.

3. Frederick Douglass, "Did John Brown Fail?," in *The Frederick Douglass Papers, Series 1: Speeches, Debates, and Interviews*, ed. John W. Blassingame and John R. McKinigan (New Haven, Conn.: Yale University Press, 1992), 7–35; "John Brown Souvenir" available at the World's Columbian Exposition in Chicago in 1893, Boyd B. Stutler Collection, West Virginia State Archives, Charleston.

4. See W. E. B. Du Bois, *John Brown*, ed. David Roediger (1909; repr., New York: Modern Library, 2001); Eugene V. Debs, *Appeal to Reason* (1907), quoted in Julie Husband, "W. E. B. Du Bois's *John Brown*: Placing Racial Justice at the Center of Socialist Politics," in *The Afterlife of John Brown*, ed. Andrew Taylor and Eldrid Herrington (New York: Palgrave Macmillan, 2005), 168; Charles Sheldon, "God's Angry Man," *Independent* (New York) 69, no. 3216 (July 1910): 113; Countee Cullen, "A Negro Mother's Lullaby (After a Visit to the Grave of John Brown)," in *Allies for Freedom and Blacks on John Brown*, by Benjamin Quarles (New York: Da Capo Press, 2001); Michael Curtiz, director, *The Santa Fe Trail*, Warner Brothers, 1940; Comer Vann Woodward, "John Brown's Private War," in *The Burden of Southern History* (1960; repr., Baton Rouge: Louisiana State University Press, 2008), 41–68.

5. See Malcolm X, "Speech for Organization of Afro-American Unity" (July 5, 1964), in *By Any Means Necessary: Speeches, Interviews and a Letter*, ed. George Breitman (New York: Pathfinder, 1970), 81–82; Lerone Bennett Jr., "Tea and Sympathy: Liberals and Other White Hopes," in Quarles, *Blacks on John Brown*, 139–43. For examples of relatively positive considerations of Brown by white authors from this period, see Oates, *To Purge This Land with Blood*; Russell Banks, *Cloudsplitter* (New York: Harper Perennial, 1999); Louis DeCaro, *"Fire from the Midst of You": A Religious Life of John Brown* (New York: New York University Press, 2002). For examples of recent considerations of Brown that have foregrounded questions about terrorism, see Christopher Hitchens, "The Man Who Ended Slavery," *Atlantic*, May 2005; Barbara Ehrenreich, "*John Brown, Abolitionist*: A Soldier in the Army of the Lord," *New York Times*, April 17, 2005; John D. Carlson and Jonathan H. Ebel, "John Brown, Jeremiad, and Jihad: Introductory Reflections on Religion, Violence, and America," in *From Jeremiad to Jihad: Religion, Violence, and America*, ed. John D. Carlson and Jonathan H. Ebel (Berkeley: University of California Press, 2011); Edward Rothstein, "One Man's Crusade against Slavery, Seen from Two Angles," *New York Times*, October 28, 2009; Joel Olson, "The Politics of Protestant

Violence: Abolitionists and Anti-Abortionists," in *The Blackwell Companion to Religion and Violence*, ed. Andrew R. Murphy (Blackwell Reference Online, 2011). On McVeigh's citation of Brown, see Sean Wilentz, "Homegrown Terrorist," *New Republic*, October 24, 2005. Cornel West tweeted about Edward Snowden as John Brown @CornelWest at 1:21 p.m. on June 28, 2013.

6. Here and throughout this book I use "United States" to designate the formal state established in laws. I use "America" to designate what Benedict Anderson has called the "imagined community" of the nation. I do not mean to endorse the imperial ideals within this sense of "America," ideals that would ignore or subsume most of two continents. I do mean to use the term that participants in this imagined community most often use to describe that community. See Benedict Anderson, *Imagined Communities: Reflections on the Origin and Spread of Nationalism*, new ed. (London: Verso, 2006).

7. Ernst H. Kantorowicz, *The King's Two Bodies: A Study in Medieval Political Theology* (Princeton, N.J.: Princeton University Press, 1997), 8; Eric L. Santner, *The Royal Remains: The People's Two Bodies and the Endgames of Sovereignty* (Chicago: University of Chicago Press, 2011), xv.

8. See Paul W. Kahn, *Sacred Violence: Torture, Terror, and Sovereignty* (Ann Arbor: University of Michigan Press, 2008), esp. 33–34.

9. Henry David Thoreau, "A Plea for Captain John Brown," in Redpath, *Echoes of Harpers Ferry*, 30.

10. Hannah Arendt, *On Revolution* (New York: Viking, 1965), 152.

11. Talal Asad, *On Suicide Bombing*, Wellek Library Lectures (New York: Columbia University Press, 2007).

12. On the parallel between Brown and suicide bombers, see Michael Ziser, "Emersonian Terrorism: John Brown, Islam, and Postsecular Violence," *American Literature* 82, no. 2 (2010): 333–60.

13. Du Bois, *John Brown*, 202.

14. The summary of the raid relies on a public record drawn from many sources. I have learned especially from the comprehensiveness of Reynolds, *John Brown, Abolitionist*; the concision of Stauffer and Trodd's introduction to *The Tribunal*; the lively narrative of Horwitz, *Midnight Rising*; the thoughtful reading of Brown's religious life in Oates, *To Purge This Land with Blood*; and the moral passion of DeCaro, *"Fire from the Midst of You."* When some fact or insight appeared in only one source, or when I have borrowed from the distinctive point of view of a source, I have added a note with a reference to the relevant source.

15. Quarles, *Blacks on John Brown*, x–xi.

16. See Gary Alan Fine, "John Brown's Body: Elites, Heroic Embodiment, and the Legitimation of Political Violence," *Social Problems* 46, no. 2 (1999): 225–49, quote on 230.

17. "Letter to the Wife of John Brown," in *Weekly Anglo-African* (New York), December 17, 1859, in Quarles, *Blacks on John Brown*, 18.

18. Bill of J. M. Hopper, undertaker, for preparation of John Brown's body, Boyd B. Stutler Collection, West Virginia State Archives.

19. Paul Finkelman, introduction to *Terrible Swift Sword: The Legacy of John Brown*, ed. Paul Finkelman and Peggy A. Russo (Athens: Ohio University Press, 2005), xxiii.

20. David Blight, "John Brown's Holy War: Terrorist or Heroic Revolutionary?," Lecture in HIST-119: The Civil War and Reconstruction Era, 1845–1877, Yale University, February 12, 2008, http://oyc.yale.edu/transcript/550/hist-119.

21. Franklin County Historical Society, "John Brown in Chambersburg: Freedom Fighter or Fanatic?" (Chambersburg, Penn.: Franklin County Historical Society, 2011).

22. The *New York Independent* quote appears in Stauffer and Trodd, *The Tribunal*, xxxiv; Henry Ward Beecher, "The Nation's Duty to Slavery" (October 30, 1859), reprinted in Stauffer and Trodd, *The Tribunal*, 103–4; Greeley, quoted in Fine, "John Brown's Body," 241.

23. Horwitz, *Midnight Rising*, 229.

24. On the politics surrounding Wise's decision, see Robert E. McGlone, "John Brown, Henry Wise, and the Politics of Insanity," in *His Soul Goes Marching On: Responses to John Brown and the Harpers Ferry Raid*, ed. Paul Finkelman (Charlottesville: University of Virginia Press, 1995), 213–52.

25. H. A. Wise, speech in Richmond, October 21, 1859, quoted in Reynolds, *John Brown, Abolitionist*, 535.

26. Strother, quoted in Nudelman, *John Brown's Body*, 29.

27. Washington Gladden, *Recollections, by Washington Gladden* (Boston: Houghton Mifflin, 1909), 65. For Gladden's "evenhanded" argument that Brown was seen as a traitor in the South and a patriot in the North, see Washington Gladden, *Social Salvation* (Boston: Houghton Mifflin, 1902), 116.

28. Washington Gladden, "A Plea for Pacifism," *Nation*, supplement to vol. 103 (August 3, 1916): 2.

29. Wilentz, "Homegrown Terrorist."

30. Kenneth R. Carroll, "A Psychological Examination of John Brown," in *Terrible Swift Sword: The Legacy of John Brown*, ed. Peggy A. Russo and Paul Finkelman (Athens: Ohio University Press, 2005), 136.

31. James West Davidson and Mark Hamilton Lytle, *After the Fact: The Art of Historical Detection* (New York: McGraw Hill, 2010), 153.

32. John Brown, interview with Mason et al., in Ruchames, *Making of a Revolutionary*, 133.

33. Frederick Douglass, "Capt. John Brown Not Insane," *Douglass' Monthly*, November 1859, in Stauffer and Trodd, *The Tribunal*, 118–19.

34. Thoreau, "A Plea for Captain John Brown," 19.

35. E. B., "To John Brown," Newport, Rhode Island, October 27, 1859, in F. B. Sanborn, *The Life and Letters of John Brown, Liberator of Kansas, and Martyr of Virginia* (Boston: Roberts Brothers, 1885), 581–82.

36. Countless versions of the "John Brown Song" were printed. Many more were sung. The text here comes from the Library of Congress collection, http://www.google.com/url?sa=t&rct=j&q=&esrc=s&source=web&cd=2&ved=0CDIQFjAB&url=http%3A%2F%2Fwww.loc.gov%2Fteachers%2Flyrical%2Fsongs%2Fdocs%2Fjohn_brown_trans

.pdf&ei=3M9BT_bVFNGUtwf1nKTZBQ&usg=AFQjCNHT51CAripR_AohmvIRhthql
4N00A&sig2=FNGD16h30ECVf9W9jdRN8Q.

37. Thoreau, "A Plea for Captain John Brown," 24.

38. See Nudelman, *John Brown's Body*, 15.

39. Reverdy C. Ransom, "The Spirit of John Brown," in *Making the Gospel Plain: The Writings of Bishop Reverdy C. Ransom*, ed. Anthony B. Pinn, African American Religious Thought and Life (Harrisburg, Penn.: Trinity Press International, 1999), 92–102. Subsequent page references are cited parenthetically in the text.

40. See, for instance, DeCaro, *"Fire from the Midst of You"*; Reynolds, *John Brown, Abolitionist*.

41. David S. Reynolds, "Freedom's Martyr," *New York Times*, December 2, 2009.

42. T. Thomas Fortune, "John Brown and Nat Turner," in *New York Age*, January 12, 1889. Reprinted in Quarles, *Blacks on John Brown*, 75.

43. Theodor W. Adorno, *Gesammelte Schriften*, 20 vols. (Frankfurt: Suhrkamp, 1977); ET: Theodor W. Adorno, *Minima Moralia: Reflections from a Damaged Life*, trans. E. F. N. Jephcott (New York: Verso, 1978); Giorgio Agamben, *Means without Ends: Notes on Politics* (Minneapolis: University of Minnesota Press, 2000), 95.

The best example of the critique I try to do is Walter Benjamin, "Zur Kritik der Gewalt," in *G.S.*, 2.1:199; ET: Walter Benjamin, "Critique of Violence," in *S.W.*, 1:249. See also Gianni Vattimo, "Postmodern Criticism: Postmodern Critique," in *Writing the Future*, ed. David Wood, Warwick Studies in Philosophy and Literature (London: Routledge, 1990).

44. This understanding of political theology has been shaped especially by Claude Lefort, "The Permanence of the Theologico-Political?," in *Political Theologies: Public Religions in a Post-secular World*, ed. Hent de Vries and Lawrence Eugene Sullivan (New York: Fordham University Press, 2006), 148–87; and Carl Schmitt, *Politische Theologie: Vier Kapitel zur Lehre von der Souveränität* (Berlin: Duncker & Humboldt, 1990); ET: Carl Schmitt, *Political Theology: Four Chapters on the Concept of Sovereignty*, trans. George Schwab (Chicago: University of Chicago Press, 2005).

45. Frederick Douglass, "John Brown," in Ruchames, *A John Brown Reader*, 331–32.

Chapter 2

1. John Brown, note handed to one of his guards on the morning of his execution, Charlestown, Virginia, December 2, 1859, in Ruchames, *Making of a Revolutionary*, 157. Spelling, grammar, and capitalization in all quotes reproduce the original as closely as possible.

2. Max Weber outlined these features in canonical analyses that have both reflected and shaped realities on the ground. On the differentiation of spheres, see "Science as a Vocation," in *From Max Weber: Essays in Sociology*, ed. H. H. Geerth and C. Wright Mills (New York: Oxford University Press, 1946), 129–58. If many of Weber's claims about secularization have proven to be wrong, or at least limited, his claim about the differentiation of religious and political spheres remains, in José Casanova's words, "the valid core" of any secularization theory. See José Casanova, *Public Religions in the Modern World* (Chicago: University of Chicago Press, 1994), 212.

The renunciation of political power by religious institutions and movements proved to be essential for the consolidation of violence in the hands of the state. The modern state, Weber famously observed, "has been successful in seeking to monopolize the legitimate use of force [*Gewaltsamkeit*] as a means of domination within a territory." See Max Weber, "Politics as a Vocation," in Geerth and Mills, *From Max Weber*, 82–83.

Weber also saw the ways in which the state's monopoly on the legitimate means of violence depended on the rule of law. The rise of a democratic ethos, coupled with a view of the world as a regulated system, has led people to call for equal treatment before a system of law. These demands have been especially strong in relation to the state's coercive powers. Thus, what Weber called "a formal and rational 'objectivity' of administration"—a legal authority—has displaced "the personally free discretion flowing from the 'grace' of the old patrimonial domination." See Max Weber, "Bureaucracy," in Geerth and Mills, *From Max Weber*, 220–21.

3. Phillips and Hanway are quoted in Reynolds, *John Brown, Abolitionist*, 230.

4. John Brown, "Provisional Constitution and Ordinances for the People of the United States," National Archives, from records relating to John Brown's Raid at Harper's Ferry, Virginia (now West Virginia), in October 1859, http://research.archives.gov/description/300375.

5. I borrow this phrase from the description of Theodor Adorno's project in Lambert Zuidevaart, "Alienated Masterpiece: Adorno's Contribution to a Transformative Social Theory," in *After Modernity? Secularity, Globalization and the Re-enchantment of the World*, ed. James K. A. Smith (Waco, Tex.: Baylor University Press, 2008), 100.

6. Mark Lilla, *The Stillborn God: Religion, Politics, and the Modern West* (New York: Knopf, 2007), 57. Subsequent page references are cited parenthetically in the text.

7. On the wider threats to modern political formations—and especially to the state sovereignty that is at their center—see Saskia Sassen, *Losing Control? Sovereignty in an Age of Globalization* (New York: Columbia University Press, 1996); Wendy Brown, *Walled States, Waning Sovereignty* (New York: Zone Books, 2010).

8. See Charlie Savage and James Risen, "Federal Judge Finds N.S.A. Wiretaps Were Illegal," *New York Times*, March 31, 2010; "A Guide to the Memos on Torture," *New York Times*, 2005, http://www.nytimes.com/ref/international/24MEMO-GUIDE.html; Neil A. Lewis, "Memos Reveal Scope of Power Bush Sought in Fighting Terror," *New York Times*, March 2, 2009.

9. For a comprehensive account of these concerns, see Kevin Phillips, *American Theocracy: The Peril and Politics of Radical Religion, Oil, and Borrowed Money in the 21st Century* (New York: Penguin, 2007). For a more everyday manifestation of uneasiness about Bush's religiosity—all the more evident in moderation—see Robert Wright, "Faith, Hope and Charity," *New York Times*, October 28, 2004.

10. On the pervasiveness of this view in the Bush administration, see Seymour M. Hersh, "The Gray Zone: How a Secret Pentagon Program Came to Abu Ghraib," *New Yorker*, May 24, 2004, http://www.newyorker.com/archive/2004/05/24/040524fa_fact.

11. William T. Cavanaugh, *The Myth of Religious Violence: Secular Ideology and the Roots of Modern Conflict* (Oxford: Oxford University Press, 2009), 4.

12. Patrick Worship, "Bush Promotes Religious Freedom at UN Gathering," Reuters, November 13, 2008, http://www.reuters.com/article/2008/11/13/us-un-interfaith-id USTRE4AC75Y20081113.

13. On Obama's use of Niebuhr, see John D. Carlson, "A Moral Guide to Obama's Foreign Policy," *Religion and Politics*, December 10, 2012, http://religionandpolitics.org/ print/?pid= 4160.

14. David Johnston, "U.S. Says Renditions to Continue, but with More Oversight," *New York Times*, August 24, 2009.

15. Viki Divoll, "Who Says You Can Kill Americans, Mr. President?," *New York Times*, January 16, 2013. See also David Cole, "Killing Our Citizens without Trial," *New York Review*, November 24, 2011.

16. On the number of drone strikes, see Peter L. Bergen, "Warrior in Chief," *New York Times*, April 28, 2012. On the question of their relation to the rule of law, see Brian Bennett and David S. Cloud, "Obama's Counter-Terrorism Advisor Defends Drone Strikes," *Los Angeles Times*, April 30, 2012.

17. John O. Brennan, "Strengthening Our Security by Adhering to Our Values and Laws," remarks at the Program on Law and Security, Harvard Law School, Cambridge, Massachusetts, September 16, 2011, http://www.whitehouse.gov/the-press-office/2011/09/16/ remarks-john-o-brennan-strengthening-our-security-adhering-our-values-an.

18. Even if the Obama administration succeeds in rolling back or repealing the AUMF, one could not describe the general pattern as one in which the country "toggled" on to emergency laws and then toggled off. The vast majority of laws passed and institutions created would remain.

19. Kim Lane Scheppele, "The International State of Emergency: Challenges to Constitutionalism after September 11," in *Yale Legal Theory Workshop* (2006), 42, 49 (italics in original), http://digitalcommons.law.umaryland.edu/cgi/viewcontent.cgi?art icle=1048&context=schmooze_papers.

20. John Locke, *Two Treatises of Government*, ed. Peter Laslett, Cambridge Texts in the History of Political Thought, ed. Raymond Geuss and Quentin Skinner (Cambridge: Cambridge University Press, 1988), chap. 14, § 160.

21. Clement Fatovic, *Outside the Law: Emergency and Executive Power*, Johns Hopkins Series in Constitutional Thought (Baltimore: Johns Hopkins University Press, 2009), 255.

22. 65 S.Ct. 193 (1944), at 245–46. I am grateful to Chris Manzer for pointing me to this case.

23. Jack Goldsmith described the irony of this story in "The Great Legal Paradox of Our Time: How Civil Libertarians Strengthened the National Security State," *New Republic*, March 16, 2012. Goldsmith tells the story as a comedy in the classical sense, with the nation bumping its way through unexpected consequences to a happy result. I would tell the story as tragedy.

24. Taylor, *A Secular Age*, 509.

25. Pub. L. No. 107-40, § 2(a), 115 Stat. 224, 224 (2001).

26. Unsigned, "Lawfulness of a Lethal Operation Directed against a U.S. Citizen

Who Is a Senior Operational Leader of al-Qa'ida or an Associated Force," Department of Justice white paper, released February 4, 2013, http://www.cfr.org/terrorism-and-the-law/department-justice-memo-lawfulness-lethal-operation-directed-against-us-citizen-senior-operational-leader-al-qaida-associated-force/p29925, 3.

27. "Instructions for the Government of Armies of the United States in the Field," prepared by Francis Lieber, originally issued as General Orders No. 100, Adjutant General's Office, 1863, http://www.loc.gov/rr/frd/Military_Law/Lieber_Collection/pdf/Instructions-gov-armies.pdf.

On the Lieber Code's tendency to expand rather than limit violence, see Burrus M. Carnahan," Lincoln, Lieber and the Laws of War: The Origins and Limits of the Principle of Military Necessity," *American Journal of International Law* 92, no. 2 (April 1998): 213–31.

28. Benjamin, "Zur Kritik der Gewalt," in *G.S.*, 2.1:199; ET: Benjamin, "Critique of Violence," 249.

29. My reading of the logic of necessity has learned especially from Giorgio Agamben, *State of Exception*, trans. Kevin Atell (Chicago: University of Chicago Press, 2005), 29, passim.

30. Adorno, *Gesammelte Schriften*, 6:394; ET: Theodor W. Adorno, *Negative Dialectics*, trans. E. B. Ashton (New York: Continuum, 1973), 402. Translation altered.

31. Locke, *Second Treatise*, in *Two Treatises of Government*, ch. 14, section numbers cited parenthetically in the text.

32. Fatovic, *Outside the Law*, 276.

Chapter 3

1. Schmitt, *Politische Theologie*, 50; ET: Schmitt, *Political Theology*, 46. Subsequent references are cited parenthetically in the text, with the page numbers for the German edition listed first.

2. Here Schmitt is using a phrase from Gerhard Anschütz.

3. Agamben, *State of Exception*, 36–37.

4. In Paul Kahn's words, "Within a legal order, there is always a 'should.' About the exception there is only the decision in the concrete situation." Paul W. Kahn, *Political Theology: Four New Chapters on the Concept of Sovereignty* (New York: Columbia University Press, 2011), 41.

5. Agamben, *State of Exception*, 36. For a rich display of the potential of Schmitt's concept of sovereignty for cultural criticism, see Kahn, *Political Theology*.

6. For a brilliant analysis of the ways sovereign violence plays out in terrorism and in states' responses to terrorism, see Kahn, *Sacred Violence*.

7. Samuel Weber, "Taking Exception to Decision: Walter Benjamin and Carl Schmitt," *diacritics* 22, nos. 3–4 (1992): 11.

8. For an excellent history of the Benjamin-Schmitt exchange, see Weber, "Taking Exception to Decision." My purposes in this chapter are more constructive than historical. This purpose shapes the scope of the chapter. I take up only those texts that I think allow me to build my argument most clearly. The constructive purpose of the chapter

also shapes its form. Most histories of the exchange frame Benjamin as responding to Schmitt. Correspondence from Benjamin and direct references in *The Origin of German Tragic Drama* make clear that he was. But Giorgio Agamben, in his work as editor of the Italian translations of Benjamin's works, makes a strong case that Schmitt must have read Benjamin's "Critique of Violence" before writing *Political Theology* (*State of Exception*, 52–54). Thus, Agamben writes, Schmitt was responding to Benjamin before Benjamin was responding to Schmitt. I mean to remain agnostic in this dispute. I present the two thinkers in the order that I do not as any kind of claim about historical precedence but as the clearest way to develop the line of thought I am trying to offer here.

9. Jacques Derrida, "Force de loi: Le 'Fondement mystique de l'autorité' / Force of Law: The 'Mystical Foundation of Authority,'" *Cardozo Law Review* 11 (1989–90), 920–1045.

10. On the difference between Benjamin's vocabulary and Schmitt's, see Sigrid Weigel, *Walter Benjamin: Images, the Creaturely, and the Holy*, trans. Chadwick Truscott Smith (Stanford, Calif.: Stanford University Press, 2013), 60–61.

11. Walter Benjamin, "Welt und Zeit," in *G.S.*, 6:99; ET: Benjamin, "World and Time," *S.W.*, 1:227.

12. On Benjamin's wider project, see Uwe Steiner, "The True Politician: Walter Benjamin's Concept of the Political," *New German Critique* 83 (2001): 43–88.

13. On the relative significance of Scholem and Rang, see Jennings, "Walter Benjamin, Religion, and a Theological Politics," 109–22.

14. I owe the language of sublation as a description of Schmitt's view—and the contrast with Benjamin described in the next two paragraphs—to Weigel, *Walter Benjamin*, chap. 2, esp. 37, 42.

15. Carl Schmitt, *The Nomos of the Earth in the International Law of* Jus Publicum Europaeum (Candor, N.Y.: Telos Press, 2006), 121. Quoted in Weigel, *Walter Benjamin*, 39.

16. Walter Benjamin, "Über den Begriff der Geschichte," in *G.S.*, 1.2:691–704; ET: Benjamin, "On the Concept of History," in *S.W.*, 4:389–411.

17. The list of pairs comes from Weigel, *Walter Benjamin*, xxii. The dynamic of an incomplete secularization is perhaps clearest in Walter Benjamin, "Über Sprache überhaupt und über die Sprache des Menschen," in *G.S.*, 2.1:140–57; ET: Benjamin, "On Language as Such and the Language of Man," in *S.W.*, 1:62–74; and Benjamin, "Das Kunstwerk im Zeitalter seiner technischen Reproduzierbarkeit (dritte Fassung)," in *G.S.*, 1.2:471–508; ET: Benjamin, "The Work of Art in the Age of Its Technical Reproducibility (third version)," in *S.W.*, 4:251–83.

18. On wish-images, see Walter Benjamin, *Das Passagen-Werk*, in *G.S.*, 5.2:1224–25; ET: Walter Benjamin, *The Arcades Project*, trans. Howard Eiland and Kevin McLaughlin (Cambridge, Mass.: Belknap Press of Harvard University Press, 1999), 893–94. See also Susan Buck-Morss, *The Dialectics of Seeing: Walter Benjamin and the Arcades Project* (Cambridge, Mass.: MIT Press, 1989); Margaret Cohen, "Benjamin's Phantasmagoria: The Arcades Project," in *The Cambridge Companion to Walter Benjamin*, ed. David S. Ferris (Cambridge: Cambridge University Press, 2004); Michael William Jennings, *Dialectical Images: Walter Benjamin's Theory of Literary Criticism* (Ithaca, N.Y.: Cornell

University Press, 1987); and Ted A. Smith, *The New Measures: A Theological History of Democratic Practice* (New York: Cambridge University Press, 2007), 33–34.

19. Benjamin, *Das Passagen-Werk*, in *G.S.*, 5:609; ET: Benjamin, *Arcades*, 486.

20. Benjamin, "Zur Kritik der Gewalt," in *G.S.*, 2.1:199; ET: Benjamin, "Critique of Violence," *S.W.*, 1:249. Subsequent references are cited parenthetically in the text, with page numbers for the German edition listed first.

21. Walter Benjamin, "Welt und Zeit," in *G.S.*, 6:99; ET: Benjamin, "World and Time," in *S.W.*, 1:227.

22. Walter Benjamin, "Welt und Zeit," in *G.S.*, 6:99; ET: Benjamin, "World and Time," in *S.W.*, 1:227.

23. Judith Butler, "Critique, Coercion, and Sacred Life in Benjamin's 'Critique of Violence,'" in de Vries and Sullivan, *Political Theologies*, 210–11.

24. Giorgio Agamben, *Homo Sacer: Sovereign Power and Bare Life*, Meridian: Crossing Aesthetics (Stanford, Calif.: Stanford University Press, 1998).

25. The translation here is my own. In translating this crucial passage, I have learned especially from Weigel, who makes a convincing case for translating *in ungeheuren Fällen* as "in monstrous cases" rather than as "in exceptional cases," which is the translation in *S.W.* Using language of "monstrous" rather than "exceptional" cases helps retain the gap between Benjamin's thought and Schmitt's. I translate *abzusehen von* as "to abstain from" rather than "to disregard," as Weigel does, to emphasize the ongoing validity of the commandment. The commandment is still regarded, still recognized, even in a decision not to follow it.

26. Carl Schmitt, *Über die drei Arten des rechtswissenschaftlichen Denkens* (Berlin: Duncker & Humboldt, 1993), 23–24 (translation mine).

27. Gillian Rose, "Walter Benjamin: Out of the Sources of Modern Judaism," in *Judaism and Modernity: Philosophical Essays* (Oxford: B. Blackwell, 1993), 188–89.

28. Gillian Rose, "Introduction," in *Judaism and Modernity*, 9.

29. Gillian Rose, *Mourning Becomes the Law: Philosophy and Representation* (Cambridge: Cambridge University Press, 1996), 72.

30. Rowan Williams, "Between Politics and Metaphysics: Reflections in the Wake of Gillian Rose," *Modern Theology* 11, no. 1 (1995): 9.

31. The roots of Rose's project in a critique of neo-Kantianism are clearest in Gillian Rose, *Hegel contra Sociology* (London: Verso, 1995). If her arguments—and especially her constructive proposals—evolved over time, they continued to depend on this core critique.

32. Benjamin, "Theologico-Political Fragment," in *G.S.*, 2.1:305; ET: Walter Benjamin, "Theologico-Political Fragment," in *S.W.*, 3:305.

33. I argue for a notion of presence without identity in theological history in *The New Measures*, 1–42.

34. Jacob Taubes, *The Political Theology of Paul*, trans. Dana Hollander, Cultural Memory in the Present (Stanford, Calif.: Stanford University Press, 2004), 72.

35. Cf. Romans 8:19–23: "For the creation waits with eager longing for the revealing of the children of God; for the creation was subjected to futility, not of its own will but

by the will of the one who subjected it, in hope that the creation itself will be set free from its bondage to decay and will obtain the freedom of the glory of the children of God. We know that the whole creation has been groaning in labour pains until now; and not only the creation, but we ourselves, who have the first fruits of the Spirit, groan inwardly while we wait for adoption, the redemption of our bodies."

36. Christoph Menke, "Law and Violence," *Law & Literature* 22, no. 1 (2010): 13.

37. Agamben, *State of Exception*, 62.

38. Benjamin, "Theologisch-Politisches Fragment," in *G.S.*, 2.1:204; ET: "Theologico-Political Fragment," in *S.W.*, 3:305.

39. Benjamin, "Theologisch-Politisches Fragment," in *G.S.*, 2.1:204; ET: "Theologico-Political Fragment," in *S.W.*, 3:306.

40. James Martel also argues that Benjamin's notion of divine violence makes possible a secular politics. But Martel sees both sovereignty and eschatology as problems to be overcome. He pits Benjamin against the whole idea of sovereignty, missing, I think, the ways in which Benjamin tries to retain sovereignty for a Messiah that is not identical to any earthly power. Martel also describes Benjamin as resisting eschatological thinking. He therefore misses the complex participation-through-mortality that Benjamin describes. He misses the way that earthly goods return as earthly goods—goods to be sought "as if not"—on the other side of nihilism. Martel's version of Benjamin is therefore much closer to the neo-Kantian version of Benjamin that Rose describes—and much more vulnerable to her critique. See James R. Martel, *Divine Violence: Walter Benjamin and the Eschatology of Sovereignty* (New York: Routledge, 2012).

41. Benjamin, "Zur Kritik der Gewalt," in *G.S.*, 2.1:199; ET: Benjamin, "Critique of Violence," 249.

42. Slavoj Žižek, *Violence: Six Sideways Reflections*, Big Ideas (London: Profile, 2008). Subsequent page references are cited parenthetically in the text.

Chapter 4

1. John Steuart Curry, letter to Reverend A. Christensen, January 12, 1940, John Steuart Curry Papers, Archives of American Art, Smithsonian Institution, Washington, D.C. Quoted in Gilpin, *John Brown Still Lives!*, 154.

2. Ralph Waldo Emerson, "Courage," lecture at Tremont Temple, Boston, November 8, 1859, as quoted in the *Liberator* (Boston), no. 45, November 11, 1859, 178, column E.

3. Robert Penn Warren, *John Brown: The Making of a Martyr* (New York: Payson & Clarke, 1929); Avery Craven, *Edmund Ruffin, Southerner: A Study in Secession* (New York: D. Appleton, 1932); Curtiz, *The Santa Fe Trail*.

4. The mural frames the introduction to a recent and important collection of writings on religion and violence. See Carlson and Ebel, "John Brown, Jeremiad, and Jihad." For the "Tragic Prelude Mints," see http://store.kshs.org/SelectSKU.aspx?skuid=1001018.

5. For two depictions of Brown as a religious person on the fringe of society—with two different evaluations—see Wilentz, "Homegrown Terrorist"; and DeCaro, *"Fire from the Midst of You."*

6. On McVeigh's citation of Brown, see Wilentz, "Homegrown Terrorist." The

Weather Underground named their typescript journal *Osawatomie*, an early editorial said, to recall the battle at which "John Brown and 30 other abolitionists, using guerrilla tactics, beat back an armed attack by 250 slavery supporters, who were trying to make Kansas a slave state." Unsigned editorial, *Osawatomie*, no. 2 (1975): 2.

7. DeCaro, *"Fire from the Midst of You,"* 4.

8. Brown's language is not a direct quote of any English translation of Matthew 7:12 or Luke 6:31, the verses where the "Golden Rule" appears. Instead, he uses a paraphrase that was in circulation in and beyond abolitionist networks.

9. John Brown's last speech to the court, November 2, 1859, in Ruchames, *Making of a Revolutionary*, 139.

10. John Brown, letter to Reverend Luther Humphrey (Windham, Ohio), dated Charlestown, Virginia, November 19, 1859, in ibid., 148.

11. Fales Henry Newhall, *A Funeral Discourse Occasioned by the Death of John Brown of Ossawattomie* (Boston: J. M. Hewes, 1859), 5.

12. For a full text of the "Declaration," see Richard J. Hinton, *John Brown and His Men* (New York: Funk & Wagnalls, 1894), 637–43. Subsequent page references are cited parenthetically in the text.

13. On the details of the scroll, see the curator's note in H. W. Flournoy, ed., *Calendar of Virginia State Papers and Other Manuscripts from January 1, 1836 to April 15, 1869* (Richmond, 1893), 11:279. Unfortunately, the scroll has disappeared from the state archives.

14. Gilbert Haven, "The Higher Law," preached in Amenia, New York, in November 1850, in *National Sermons: Sermons, Speeches and Letters on Slavery and Its War: From the Passage of the Fugitive Slave Bill to the Election of President Grant* (Boston: Lee & Shepard, 1869), vi.

15. *The Minutes and Proceedings of the First Annual Meeting of the American Moral Reform Society: Held at Philadelphia, in the Presbyterian Church in Seventh Street, below Shippen, from the 14th to the 19th of August, 1837* (Philadelphia: Merrihew & Gunn, 1837), 3.

16. Henry Highland Garnet, "An Address to the Slaves of the United States of America" (1843), in Philip S. Foner and Robert Branham, eds., *Lift Every Voice: African American Oratory, 1787–1901* (Tuscaloosa: University of Alabama Press, 1997), 200–201.

17. Daniel Webster, "The Constitution and the Union," speech delivered in the United States Senate, March 7, 1850, http://www.senate.gov/artandhistory/history/resources/pdf/Webster7th.pdf.

18. Quoted in Frederic Bancroft, *The Life of William H. Seward* (1900; repr.,Whitefish, Mont.: Kessinger Publishing, 2006), 247.

19. Albert L. Brophy, "Fugitive Slave Act of 1850," in Leslie Alexander, *Encyclopedia of African American History* (Santa Barbara, Calif.: ABC-CLIO, 2010), 2:417.

20. Haven, "The Higher Law," 6. Subsequent page references are cited parenthetically in the text.

21. Jermain Wesley Loguen, "I Won't Obey the Fugitive Slave Law" (1850), in Foner and Branham, *Lift Every Voice*, 225.

22. Samuel Ringgold Ward, "The Fugitive Slave Bill" (1850), in Foner and Branham, *Lift Every Voice*, 220.

23. Frances Ellen Watkins, "Liberty for Slaves" (1858), in Foner and Branham, *Lift Every Voice*, 307.

24. Mary Ann Shadd, "Break Every Yoke and Let the Oppressed Go Free" (1858), in Foner and Branham, *Lift Every Voice*, 320.

25. John C. Lord, "'The Higher Law' in Its Application to the Fugitive Slave Bill: A Sermon on the Duties Men Owe to God and Governments," delivered at the Central Presbyterian Church (Buffalo, New York) on Thanksgiving Day, 1851 (New York: Published by order of the Union Safety Committee, 1851). I am grateful to Trent Frank for pointing me to this sermon.

26. See Orestes A. Brownson, "The Fugitive Slave Law" (1851), in Henry Francis Brownson, ed., *The Works of Orestes A. Brownson* (Detroit: Thorndike Nourse, 1884), 17:34.

27. Orestes A. Brownson, "The Higher Law" (1851), in Brownson, *The Works of Orestes A. Brownson*, 17:6.

28. George B. Cheever, "The Martyr's Death and the Martyr's Triumph" (preached December 4, 1859), in Redpath, *Echoes of Harper's Ferry*, 217.

29. Ibid., 227–28.

30. Henry David Thoreau, "The Last Days of John Brown," in Henry D. Thoreau, *The Higher Law: Thoreau on Civil Disobedience and Reform*, ed. Wendell Glick (Princeton, N.J.: Princeton University Press, 2004), 147.

31. The accuracy of Brown's claim to be descended from Peter Brown remains a matter of some dispute. What is clear, though, is that his ancestors included Puritans who were settled in New England by the middle of the seventeenth century. Reynolds, *John Brown, Abolitionist*, 19–20.

32. Wendell Phillips, "The Puritan Principle and John Brown," in *Speeches, Lectures, and Letters, 2nd Series* (Boston: Lee & Shepard, 1892), 298.

33. On this point I have learned especially from the argument in Cavanaugh, *The Myth of Religious Violence*.

34. Andrew Delbanco, *The Abolitionist Imagination* (Cambridge, Mass.: Harvard University Press, 2012), 36. Subsequent page references are cited parenthetically in the text.

35. Woodward, "John Brown's Private War"; Oates, *To Purge This Land with Blood*.

36. Delbanco, *The Abolitionist Imagination*, 41–42.

37. For Hill's statement, see Mireya Navarro, "Jury Recommends Death Penalty for Abortion Foe Convicted in 2 Killings in Florida," *New York Times*, November 4, 1994. In his own final statement to the court, Brown said, "Now if it is deemed necessary that I should forfeit my life for the furtherance of the ends of justice, and mingle my blood further with the blood of my children and with the blood of millions in this slave country whose rights are disregarded by wicked, cruel, and unjust enactments,—I submit; so let it be done!" Ruchames, *Making of a Revolutionary*, 134.

38. Paul Jennings Hill, "Mix My Blood with the Blood of the Unborn," August 2003, http://www.armyofgod.com/PHillBookForward.html.

39. Delbanco settles near something like this view, which he dubs the "Foner synthesis" (p. 21) after Eric Foner, *The Fiery Trial: Abraham Lincoln and American Slavery* (New York: Norton, 2010).

40. Gerrit Smith, "Bible Civil Government," in *Sermons and Speeches of Gerrit Smith* (New York: Ross & Tousey, 1861), 103–20; Manisha Sinha, *The Counterrevolution of Slavery: Politics and Ideology in Antebellum South Carolina* (Chapel Hill: University of North Carolina Press, 2000); Manisha Sinha, "Did the Abolitionists Cause the Civil War?," in Delbanco, *The Abolitionist Imagination*, 81–108. See also Lord, "'The Higher Law.'"

41. On whether Sherman's campaign reached the standards for "total war," see Mark Grimsley, *The Hard Hand of War: Union Military Policy toward Southern Civilians, 1861–1865* (Cambridge: Cambridge University Press, 1995). James McPherson argued that in the Union campaign in South Carolina "reality approached myth" of total war. James M. McPherson, *This Mighty Scourge: Perspectives on the Civil War* (New York: Oxford University Press, 2007), 128. Whether the Union prosecuted "total war" or not, my main line of argument holds: appeals to military necessity can justify transgressions of limits on violence just as surely as appeals to higher law. Grimsley's paradigmatic cases of total war include civilian bombings in World War II, which were driven more by nationalism and necessity than by any kind of higher law.

42. William T. Sherman, letter to James M. Calhoun et al., September 12, 1864, in William T. Sherman, *Memoirs of General William T. Sherman*, 2 vols. (New York: D. Appleton, 1876), 1:126–27.

For a larger history of the tendency of military necessity to end up justifying expansions of violence, see Carnahan, "Lincoln, Lieber and the Laws of War," 213–31. Carnahan wants to retrieve military necessity as a limit on violence. But he acknowledges that it has tended to function in just the opposite way. While Carnahan is surely right about the original intention of the military necessity clause, it is difficult to imagine—and Carnahan does not suggest—the institutional arrangements and individual characters that could let it function as a limit.

43. James M. McPherson, "Lincoln and the Strategy of Unconditional Surrender," in *Lincoln, the War President: The Gettysburg Lectures*, ed. Gabor S. Boritt (Oxford: Oxford University Press, 1992), 29–61.

44. It is worth noting that many nonresistant abolitionists gradually came to endorse the war. Their understanding of the significance of the government of God shifted from its negation of all earthly authority to its imposition of a positive obligation to resist slavery. In the language of this chapter, they shifted from a negative account of the higher law to a mythic one. See Lewis Perry, *Radical Abolitionism: Anarchy and the Government of God in Antislavery Thought* (1973; repr., Knoxville: University of Tennessee Press, 1995), 260.

45. For a succinct statement of Niebuhr's rejection of simple appeals to a higher law, see Reinhold Niebuhr, "Christian Faith and Social Action," in *Christian Faith and Social Action*, ed. John A. Hutchison (New York: Charles Scribner's Sons, 1953), 225–42.

46. Delbanco, *The Abolitionist Imagination*, 35.

47. C. C. J. Carpenter et al., "Statement by Alabama Clergymen [A Call to Unity],"

reprinted by the American Friends Service Committee, 1963. Archives of the Martin Luther King, Jr. Research and Education Institute, Stanford University, http://www.stan ford.edu/group/King/frequentdocs/clergy.pdf. For a comprehensive discussion of King's letter, and a full account of its context, see Rieder, *Gospel of Freedom*.

48. Martin Luther King Jr., "Letter from Birmingham Jail," reprinted in Rieder, *Gospel of Freedom*, 176. Subsequent page references are cited parenthetically in the text.

49. Delbanco, *The Abolitionist Imagination*, 23.

50. Carpenter et al., "Statement by Alabama Clergymen."

51. Charles Taylor, "The Perils of Moralism," in *Dilemmas and Connections: Selected Essays* (Cambridge, Mass.: Belknap Press of Harvard University Press, 2011), 351, 353. For a more compact version of Taylor's critique of code, see Charles Taylor, "Foreword," in *The Rivers North of the Future: The Testament of Ivan Illich, as Told to David Cayley*, by Ivan Illich (Toronto: Anansi Press, 2005).

52. Aleida Assman, "Exkarnation: Gedanken zur Grenze zwischen Körper und Schrift," in *Raum und Verfahren: Interventionen*, ed. Alois Martin Müller and Jörg Huber (Basel: Stroemfeld/Roter Stern, 1993), 133–55.

53. Taylor, *Dilemmas and Connections*, 361.

54. Wilfred M. McClay, "The Continuing Irony of American History," *First Things*, February 2002, 20–25.

55. Giorgio Agamben, "The Messiah and the Sovereign: The Problem of Law in Walter Benjamin," in *Potentialities: Collected Essays in Philosophy*, ed. Daniel Heller-Roazen (Stanford, Calif.: Stanford University Press, 2000), 164.

56. Ibid., 167. See also Giorgio Agamben, *The Time That Remains: A Commentary on the Letter to the Romans*, trans. Patricia Dailey, Meridian: Crossing Aesthetics (Stanford, Calif.: Stanford University Press, 2005).

57. Agamben, *State of Exception*, 64.

58. Here I read Agamben in ways that have learned from Randi Rashkover, *Freedom and Law: A Jewish-Christian Apologetics* (New York: Fordham University Press, 2011), 15–30. I share Rashkover's desire to construe Judaism and Christianity in ways that do not presume an original and insuperable enmity. And I share her sense that this will involve a sense that freedom and law "are not diametrically opposed but reciprocal concepts so far as they emerge first from an act of divine freedom and subsequently infuse the performance of human freedom" (188). But I do not read Agamben as antinomian in the same way that Rashkover does. I see him as describing not the negation of law but a transformation of its role and so its content. And I see that transformation not as an example of the state of exception—force without law—but as an inversion of that state—the law without force—that performs a valuable critique. The question is how to let go of the logic of force and continue to talk about justice.

59. Peter Fenves, *The Messianic Reduction: Walter Benjamin and the Shape of Time*, Meridian: Crossing Aesthetics (Stanford, Calif.: Stanford University Press, 2011), 199–200.

60. Ibid., 199.

61. To say that an indicative understanding of the higher law fits with Christian understandings of the world is not to say that it fits *only* with those understandings.

Philippe Nonet, for instance, uses Heidegger to pry *Antigone* loose from Hegel's grip and restore to it a sense of the higher law as an indicative *phusis*. See Philippe Nonet, "Antigone's Law," in *JSP/Center for the Study of Law and Society Faculty Working Papers* (Berkeley: Center for the Study of Law and Society Jurisprudence and Social Policy Program, University of California, Berkeley, 2005).

62. See Russell Jacoby, *Picture Imperfect: Utopian Thought for an Anti-utopian Age* (New York: Columbia University Press, 2005), 31–33.

63. Gershom Gerhard Scholem, *The Messianic Idea in Judaism and Other Essays on Jewish Spirituality* (New York: Schocken Books, 1971), 21.

64. Gabriel Marcel, *Homo Viator: Introduction to a Metaphysic of Hope* (London: Gollancz, 1951), 133–34.

65. Michel de Certeau, "How Is Christianity Thinkable Today?," *Theology Digest*, 19, no. 4 (Winter 1971): 334–45, quote on 336.

66. Ibid. For a more complete development of this account of presence and absence in the wake of the ascension, see Ted A. Smith, "Theological History, Practical Reason, and the Demands of Preaching Today," *Homiletic* 37, no. 2 (Fall 2012): 15–26.

67. William T. Vollmann, *Rising Up and Rising Down: Some Thoughts on Violence, Freedom and Urgent Means* (New York: Ecco, 2004), 2:355.

68. Quarles, *Blacks on John Brown*, x–xi.

69. Du Bois, *John Brown*, xxiv.

Chapter 5

1. James Redpath, *The Public Life of Capt. John Brown* (Boston: Thayer & Eldridge, 1860), 309.

2. Reynolds, "Freedom's Martyr."

3. William Blackstone, *Commentaries on the Laws of England*, 4 vols. (1765–69; repr., Buffalo, N.Y.: William S. Hein, 1992), 4:389–90.

4. Thomas Paine, *Common Sense: Addressed to the Inhabitants of America* (1776; repr., New York: Dover Publications, 1997), 31–32.

5. Locke, *Two Treatises of Government*, II.xiv.159. Subsequent citations are cited parenthetically by section numbers in the text.

6. Alexander Hamilton, "The Federalist No. 74: The Command of the Military and Naval Forces, and the Pardoning Power of the Executive," March 25, 1788, Library of Congress, http://thomas.loc.gov/home/histdox/fed_74.html.

7. Austin Sarat, "At the Boundaries of Law: Executive Clemency, Sovereign Prerogative, and the Dilemma of American Legality," *American Quarterly* 57, no. 3 (2005): 611–31, quote on 619.

8. 32 U.S. 150, 160 (1833).

9. On the history of pardons in US law, see Sarat, "At the Boundaries of Law"; David Gray Adler, "The President's Pardoning Power," in *Inventing the American Presidency*, ed. Thomas E. Cronin (Lawrence: University Press of Kansas, 1989), 209–35; and John Dinan, "The Pardon Power and the American State Constitutional Tradition," *Polity* 35, no. 3 (2003): 389–418.

10. For a sharp denunciation of the idea that Brown was above racism—and all claims to white antiracism—see Tamara K. Nopper, "The White Anti-racist Is an Oxymoron: An Open Letter to 'White Anti-Racists," *Race Traitor*, Fall 2003, http://racetraitor .org/nopper.html.

11. On Kara Walker's criticism of Brown—and, more, the enduring fascination with Brown—see Gilpin, *John Brown Still Lives!*, 181–95.

12. John Brown, "Sambo's Mistakes," reprinted in Oswald Garrison Villard, *John Brown, 1800–1859: A Biography Fifty Years After* (Boston: Houghton Mifflin, 1910), 659–61.

13. Stauffer, *Black Hearts of Men*, 173.

14. Tony Horwitz, "Why John Brown Still Scares Us," *American History* 46, no. 5 (2011): 38–45, quote on 45.

15. Schmitt, *Politische Theologie*, 21, 43; ET: Schmitt, *Political Theology*, 15, 36.

16. Blackstone, *Commentaries on the Laws of England*, 4:395.

17. On Adorno's distinction between "abstract" and "determinate" negation, see Adorno, *G.S.*, 3:40; ET: Max Horkheimer and Theodor W. Adorno, *Dialectic of Enlightenment*, trans. John Cumming (New York: Continuum, 2000). 23. See also Elizabeth Pritchard, "*Bilderverbot* Meets Body in Theodor W. Adorno's Inverse Theology," *Harvard Theological Review* 95, no. 3 (2002): 291–318.

This emphasis on the determinate quality of negation marks the most significant difference between the reading of "divine violence" that I am offering here and readings that see divine violence as more thoroughly anarchic, like the one offered in Martel, *Divine Violence*.

18. Taylor, *Dilemmas and Connections*, 350.

19. Reynolds, *John Brown, Abolitionist*, 337.

20. Naming the ongoing power of slavery in the United States as "mythic violence" or even "original sin" does not preclude the naming of other strands of enduring, systemic violence. One could argue, for example, that the mythic violence of the destruction of Native American lives and cultures continues to run through American laws, institutions, and forms of life. Such violence might be addressed by pardons of its own. Identifying the pardon of the Harpers Ferry raiders as a singularity means that it would neither justify those pardons as a precedent nor exclude them as a rival. The pardon of John Brown would not preclude the pardon of Crazy Horse.

21. Abraham Lincoln, speech at Leavenworth, Kansas, December 3, 1859, in *The Collected Works of Abraham Lincoln*, electronic edition, http://quod.lib.umich.edu/l/ lincoln/, 3:502.

22. There has been some dispute about exactly when Lee was pardoned. But any doubts were removed in 1975, when President Gerald Ford signed a joint resolution of Congress that addressed Lee's case in particular and restored him to full citizenship. On the earlier pardons, see Jonathan Truman Dorris, *Pardon and Amnesty under Lincoln and Johnson: The Restoration of the Confederates to Their Rights and Privileges* (Chapel Hill: University of North Carolina Press, 1953).

23. Immanuel Kant, "The Metaphysics of Morals," in *Practical Philosophy*, ed.

Mary J. Gregor, Cambridge Texts in the History of Philosophy (Cambridge: Cambridge University Press, 1998), 477–78.

24. *Collected Works of Abraham Lincoln*, 8:254.

25. For a full text of the December 1863 Proclamation of Amnesty and Reconstruction, see ibid., 7:53–56.

26. David W. Blight, *Race and Reunion: The Civil War in American Memory* (Cambridge, Mass.: Belknap Press of Harvard University Press, 2001), 44–45. My reading of Reconstruction is deeply indebted to Blight and to Eric Foner, *Reconstruction: America's Unfinished Revolution, 1863–1877* (New York: Perennial Classics, 2002).

27. Frederick Douglass, "The Color Question," in *The Frederick Douglass Papers* (1875), Library of Congress Digital Archive, http://www.loc .gov/item/mfd.23001/, 3–4.

28. In considering reparations, I have learned especially from Jennifer Harvey, "Which Way to Justice? Reconciliation, Reparations and the Problem of Whiteness in US Protestantism," *Journal of the Society of Christian Ethics* 31, no. 1 (Spring–Summer 2011): 57–77; Randall Robinson, *The Debt: What America Owes to Blacks* (New York: Plume, 2001); emilie m. townes, "Empire and Forgottenness: Abysmal Sylphs in the Reparations Debate for Black Folks in the United States," *Union Seminary Quarterly Review* 56, nos. 1–2 (2002): 99–115.

29. Jacques Derrida, "On Forgiveness," in *On Cosmopolitanism and Forgiveness*, Thinking in Action (London: Routledge, 2001), 48. Subsequent page references are cited parenthetically in the text.

30. Dietrich Bonhoeffer, *Nachfolge*, Dietrich Bonhoeffer Werke, Bd. 4 (Munich: Chr. Kaiser, 1989); ET: Bonhoeffer, *Discipleship*, ed. Geffrey D. Kelly and John D. Godsey, trans. Barbara Green and Reinhard Krauss, Dietrich Bonhoeffer Works, vol. 4 (Minneapolis: Fortress, 2003).

Chapter 6

1. On the disappearance of typology from American preaching, see T. Smith, *The New Measures*, chap. 6.

2. See Marcel Gauchet, *The Disenchantment of the World*, trans. Oscar Burge (Princeton, N.J.: Princeton University Press, 1999); and Taylor, *A Secular Age*.

3. Geuss, *Outside Ethics*, 40–46. Subsequent page references are cited parenthetically in the text.

4. Theodor W. Adorno, "Minima Moralia: Reflexionen aus dem beschädigten Leben," in *G.S.*, 4:43; ET: Adorno, *Minima Moralia*, 39.

5. Alasdair MacIntyre makes this point in a review of Geuss's *Outside Ethics* for Notre Dame Philosophical Reviews, March 5, 2006, http://ndpr.nd.edu/news/24977-out side-ethics/. Ironically, Jeffrey Stout made this same argument against MacIntyre's own account of modernity as a disaster. See Jeffrey Stout, *Democracy and Tradition* (Princeton, N.J.: Princeton University Press, 2004), chap. 5.

6. Francis Lieber, letter to Dr. Henry Drisler, December 4, 1859, in *The Life and Letters of Francis Lieber*, ed. Thomas Sergeant Perry (Boston: James R. Osgood, 1882), 307–8.

7. George W. Light, "John Brown's Final Victory," in Redpath, *Echoes of Harper's Ferry*, 332.

8. Thoreau, "The Last Days of John Brown," 152–53.

9. Douglass, "Captain John Brown Not Insane," 119.

10. Newhall, *A Funeral Discourse*, 22–23.

11. John Brown, Letter to the Rev. Heman Humphrey, November 25, 1859, in Ruchames, *Making of a Revolutionary*, 157–58.

12. John Brown, Letter to the Reverend H. L. Vaill, November 15, 1859, in Ruchames, *Making of a Revolutionary*, 144.

13. Reynolds, *John Brown, Abolitionist*, 42–43.

14. Stauffer, *Black Hearts of Men*, 13–14.

15. John Brown, letter to the Reverend Heman Humphrey, November 25, 1859, in Ruchames, *Making of a Revolutionary*, 157.

16. Henry C. Wright, letter to the Richmond *Enquirer*, quoted in Perry, *Radical Abolitionism*, 258.

17. Harriet Beecher Stowe, "The Chimney Corner I," *Atlantic Monthly* 15, January 1865, 115. Quoted in Blight, *Race and Reunion*, 38–39.

18. Horace Bushnell, "Our Obligation to the Dead," in *Building Eras in Religion* (New York: Charles Scribner's Sons, 1881), 319–55, quote on 322. Subsequent page references are cited parenthetically in the text.

19. Drew Gilpin Faust, "'We Should Grow Too Fond of It': Why We Love the Civil War," *Civil War History* 50, no. 4 (December 2004): 368–83, quote on 380–81.

20. Harry S. Stout, *Upon the Altar of the Nation: A Moral History of the Civil War* (New York: Penguin Books, 2007), xxi. Stout's book is one good model for the form a "Thucydides who philosophizes" might take. If it starts in historical studies and reaches to moral philosophy, I hope to meet it moving from the other side of the divide.

21. Chris Hedges, *War Is a Force That Gives Us Meaning* (New York: Anchor, 2003). For further works that bring this mechanism to consciousness without endorsing it, see Kahn, *Sacred Violence*; and Carolyn Marvin and David W. Ingle, *Blood Sacrifice and the Nation: Totem Rituals and the American Flag* (Cambridge: Cambridge University Press, 1999).

22. Reflecting on Harry Stout's *On the Altar of the Nation*, Stanley Hauerwas reaches a similar conclusion: "If the Civil War teaches us anything, it is that when Christians no longer believe that Christ's sacrifice is sufficient for the salvation of the world, we will find other forms of sacrificial behaviors that are as compelling as they are idolatrous. In the process, Christians confuse the sacrifice of war with the sacrifice of Christ." Stanley Hauerwas, *War and the American Difference: Theological Reflections on Violence and National Identity* (Grand Rapids, Mich.: Baker Academic, 2011), 34.

23. Jackson Lears, "Divinely Ordained," *London Review of Books* 33, no. 10 (2011): 3–6, quote on 3. I borrow language of "redeemer nation" from Ernest Lee Tuveson's classic *Redeemer Nation: The Idea of America's Millennial Role* (Chicago: University of Chicago Press, 1980).

24. Frederick Douglass, *The Life and Times of Frederick Douglass* (1881; repr., New

York: Pathway Press, 1941), 350–54; "The Trials at Charlestown," *New York Semi-Weekly Tribune*, November 18, 1859, http://www.wvculture.org/history/jbexhibit/tribunetrial. html; Osborn P. Anderson, *A Voice from Harper's Ferry: A Narrative of Events at Harper's Ferry* (Boston: Printed for the author, 1861), 45; Hinton, *John Brown and His Men*, 348, 376, 404, 488, 507–8.

25. James Monroe, *Oberlin Thursday Lectures, Addresses and Essays* (Oberlin, Ohio: Edward J. Goodrich, 1897), 175.

26. Du Bois, *John Brown*, xxv. Subsequent page references are cited parenthetically in the text.

INDEX

ENCOUNTERING TRADITIONS

David Decosimo, *Ethics as a Work of Charity: Thomas Aquinas and Pagan Virtue*

Francis X. Clooney, SJ, *His Hiding Place Is Darkness: A Hindu-Catholic Theopoetics of Divine Absence*

Muhammad Iqbal, *Reconstruction of Religious Thought in Islam*

CPSIA information can be obtained
at www.ICGtesting.com
Printed in the USA
LVHW091346100720
660342LV00002B/511

9 780804 793308